MEMORIA

zoom.us لا زال

\# 17741 7886
\# 601744

MEMORIA

BOOK II OF
THE WAY OF THE MARYS

From A COURSE OF LOVE's First Receiver

MARI PERRON

A Dialogue on Mary of Nazareth's Way of Mary

Course of Love Publications
432 Rehnberg Place
St. Paul, MN 55118
Library of Congress Cataloguing-in-Publishing Data
Perron, Mari.
Memoria: The Way of the Marys

ISBN: 978-0-9728668-1-1
Spirituality, The Feminine, Alchemy, Prophecy, Mysticism
Cover design by Terry Widner
Cover photograph: "Passion Heart," E. Katie Holm, Photographer
Editor: Michael Mark

All quotations are from *A Course of Love* (ACOL) unless otherwise
noted. A reference Guide to *A Course of Love* is provided at the end
of the book.

DEDICATION

To you, the reader . . .
May you cherish the sacred privacy in
which you read, and find there,
your own heart's wisdom.

M

$\mathscr{C}$ONTENTS

REVELATIONS

LETTERS

NVOCATION

Our Holy Ones do not often choose their messengers from among the . . . "fine." Jesus, and now Mary, take in the walking wounded, the hard cases, the troubled hearts. For the healing of the heart.

As we heal our hearts, we are healing the world.

Blessed Mary came . . . to me and to us.

She came "back" to us.

She is one of us.

She lived. She birthed. She hurt. She healed.

She went all the way down before she rose.

Then she came back to us, to be for us.

For us and our counterpart Mother Earth.

M

THE DECADE: 2020

We are close now, close to a time in which a new choice
can make true living available here and now.
This is the decade in which transformation proceeds,
and the time in which the mother's heart enters
to show the way to care of the living,
and the end of what does not need to be.

This is the time of Memoria: The Way of the Marys.

M

INTRODUCTION

Epiphany: The Breach

Just as I was drawn to begin assembly of this second book of *The Way of the Marys*, the world changed again. On the Feast of the Epiphany, January 6, 2021, it was said that "The Capitol has been breached." As with the image that began "Mirari," there was the feeling that wild dogs had been unleashed and the babes of The New needed protection. *

Holy Mary, I feel a link, here, to what you said in "Mirari," when you called time a "continuum," and said "this continuum is being breached."†

Yes, Mari. As sorrow and worry collide, let there come a sense that this act has opened the way for The New. ‡

Traitorous acts and the response to them "do" pierce the space-time continuum because space and time are intimately linked together. Visualize how many this event reached. All over the world people were shocked by what they saw. We speak not of a scientific breach, but of the miraculous and often ignored human capacity for, and continuum of, memory.

The "idea" of the United States of America is one that exists as historical "memory," a memory of freedom. People from across the globe were welcomed to make a home here. Many aspired to an

---

* "*The wild dogs are in position to take over the world. They have, in many ways, done so. They would devour the babe. Participate no more in feeding the dog that will ravish the newly born. Feed no more male egos, no matter how uncomfortable it is for you to withdraw this support.*" Mirari: The Way of the Marys, p. 15

† *Ibid p. 271*

‡ Throughout this book, Mary of Nazareth's voice is presented in italics, and Mari Perron's in plain text.

ideal of unity, even despite the treatment of the Native American people.

But now your country is being seen as what it has always been—a dichotomy, a to and fro of arrogance and benevolence taking place in a universe far more multidimensional than was realized.

Such revealing incidents call you to see what is untrue and disloyal, to see faithlessness. In those enduring the experience, as well as those witnessing it, an opening occurs. Ruptures ensue, not through the occurrence itself, but through the event of memory. This Epiphany event will be remembered, as all other violations that come of betrayal are remembered.

Insurrection is a consequence of the division that makes corrupted power obvious in its weakness. Experience and witness tell you that "what you are a part of you must love and protect." Such profound violations of love and protection affect you. They find you realizing that your pulse is not the pulse of your heart alone, but of your connection to time, to space, to your esteemed and symbolic places, to ideas made manifest, and to humanity's own fall from its ideals.

In absentia from protection, your body itself remembers your union with Source, your relationship to the ocean and the sky, to your Earth Mother, and to the Mother of Heaven. The heavens and the earth are personified. And as your body responds to its own recollection, your eyes peer deeply into the thrall of trickery so that all—ocean and sky, earth and heaven, Source and Mother Liberty—all that appears to be disrespected, is shown at the same time to be treasured. While you act, on occasion, as if one thing is not connected to another, memory connects all events. It reveals patterns. In memory you see the terrain behind you, and also the shoreline ahead.

No one's memories are "all good." Unhealed memories are often subdued, set aside, and suffered in a silence that eventually becomes a shriek. Your world is shrieking. And world leaders continue to posture. It is heartbreaking. History is heartbreaking. What makes you go on? What makes you remember love and believe in creation of The New?

And I tell you, it is your longing, your longing—like the whale—to know a different kind of breach. In freedom, a leap can be made from the ocean to the sky, and the foundational elements can be distinguished from the ethereal. Through "Memoria," you know of the need to protect the intangibles, and that in their protection is your freedom.

Even those born to slavery could remember freedom. Memory, and love's longing, go together.*

To recognize your longing for all that is held in Memoria for the unique selves that you are is your most blessed Act of The New.

$\mathcal{M}$

---

* "Love was [never] lost, but shadowed over by longing... Longing is your proof of love's existence, for even here you would not long for what is not remembered.... [I]n your longing for love, you recognize as well, your longing for your Self." ACOL C:4.3-4

HOW IT ALL STARTED: DISCOVERING FEMINISM

Today, I find my memory scanning my life in a way like my eyes scan the view, or these pages of writing. It is almost unbelievable how true this is.

And my scanning has finally revealed what I was doing when we began with the scene of the fire in 2013. I still can't find an exact date for the writing, but I know that during that year I was exploring feminism! This led me to write a manuscript I never published, "Discovering Feminism in the Canning Room."

It was after Christmas 2012, that having taken down the decorations, I decided I needed to re-organize the room from which they'd come. As I worked on the project, I unearthed books on feminism from my college days. One by one I took them upstairs to read. Then I bought new ones. I signed up to be a presenter at the "Women and Spirituality Conference" at Mankato University so that I could get responses to a questionnaire about how the overwhelmingly female attendees saw feminism at that time. I was talking to Akila t'Zuberi, and to Starhawk who wrote decades ago that "Patriarchy has created us in its image."[*]

How could I have forgotten that? . . . Was it trauma?

It was only months after the conference that my daughter Angela had to almost die before either of us could admit she was an alcoholic. Mad as hell at first (both of us), we had our feet to the fire. Due to "enforced help," Angela got started on recovery, and Henry

---

[*] Starhawk. *Truth or Dare: Encounters with Power, Authority, and Mystery.* Harper & Row, 1987, p. 67.

came to live with Donny and me. Those first months were fraught with all we're talking about. The need to be fierce for the babe. The support and protection needed.

A year later, Henry still with me, *A Course of Love* was republished. With my focus there, I forgot about feminism and never realized, until these memories came forward today, that even if I'd forgotten "about it," I was living it. I was, then, one of those women before the fire, protecting my own babes.

The strain must have been greater than I realized for me to entirely blank it out. How could I not have seen it? How could I have written a whole book, started by that vision, and another with you, before memories of this chain of events returned? Before I made the connection? Even while I was literally the protector of Henry and felt myself to be the protector of his mother, our family, and the future too. It's not that I forgot that those things occurred, but that I didn't, until now, relate them to what you were offering with that vision.

I was too overwhelmed by it all. There were court appearances, and counseling, and getting Henry to school. My whole life was turned upside down in a way both physically difficult and emotionally draining. I had to have my feet on the ground of life as it was, and as it was unfolding.

I've never regretted it, Mary, and Angie is seven years sober. Still, I don't know if anything reveals the toll it took more than this "not seeing" of what now seems so obvious.

Mary, you said, "We are in solidarity, in the new 'feminism' as [I] put it," and went on to say:

"There are many loving others 'protecting their own' but this is

not enough in itself. It cannot be done without, but it needs to extend. This extension is what you are beginning simply by being who you are, and the more you are who you are in your own life, in your own microcosm of biting dogs and as protector of the lovely Henry, the more you will be ready to extend beyond your current borders."*

How much clearer could it be?

You announced a time to end the distraction and diversion. And yet I felt terribly distracted from my life's vocation. At the same time, and perhaps as a result, the sense of victimhood I'd briefly abandoned returned to me.

$\mathcal{M}$

You were still in need of support, my erstwhile companion. To endure the last vestiges of the old—without support—is too much. Rather than being supported, you were providing the support. It will begin in this way for many. Such life situations are what call up your courage for the new and let you claim your power.

But here, now, it is the "feeling" of finally being supported in your own life, inner and outer, that will allow you, and all those of the awakening feminine, to emerge into The New. Feeling supported will allow many memories of life situations to return when the time is right.

Do not worry. Do not doubt. And consider this. Could it be, my Mari, that beyond what your conscious mind could take in,

---

* "Mirari," p. 16

it was that image and those words, lodging in you unconsciously, as unknown knowing, that supported you to do all that you did?

Could it be that what you were experiencing was the beginning of the end of your victimhood? Is it possible that the visual message I presented to you was what initiated your own breach, your leaving behind of the disempowered woman you had been? Can you imagine the power that made this so?

I am so stunned by this that I have sat looking out the window a long while, trying to take it in, even though, as I listened to you speak, I felt an absolute certainty that it is exactly what happened. I had to wait for words to form beyond those that immediately ran through my mind, which were "Oh my God, Oh my God, Oh my God."

My words from all those years ago, began your new life.

How could I not have seen it, my Mary?

You did not see it because you were enacting it. This often happens in times of trauma. Few realize they are being brave as they perform courageous acts. Few realize that they are embarking on something new at the moment of its inception. It is only afterwards, often by years, that realization comes.

Hasn't the same thing happened with your Course of Love? Haven't you looked back, only recently, and seen your courage?

This is precisely what we are enacting, Mari. All who take in our words, who share in this dialogue, will look back newly to go forward newly. Many will have already begun without realizing, as you did not realize, the nature of what is initiated through rejection of victimization and the New Acts that follow.

Here, you view, and are given to regard, that breach of the past. Others will have their own experiences of such events. For you, that time was an initiation. You took up your new life. And only now do you understand the power of that image and where it has taken you. Here you will see that Acts that end the old, are as well, Acts that begin The New. And you will see that New Acts are always both personal and universal. Always.

Memoria:
The way of the marys
In four heart treatises

The Treatises of Mary

"These words are fashioned for the future yet to be created."

"Memoria," the revelation of memory, along with the wonder of "Mirari," invite your desire, imagination, and orientation to be guided by the heart.

Acts

Memoir is the feminine form of memory. It is autobiographical. Memoir is true to life, to its movements, and to the feelings that propel its movements. . . Memories of what could be, are memories of what is alive within you, calling you to what is before you in time and beyond time. Divine memory is of a time you but think you know not.

Revelations

The new knowing will come out of hiding. It will be "revealed" by each of you who has held your knowing in waiting; held it in hope of a world that would welcome its revelation. You are the hope of the world. Revelation is really a form of dialogue drawn near and abiding with you and within you.

LETTERS

We are walking away from the definitive of time and space. We are walking away from the elevated and the not elevated. We are shedding the tether. We are doing this together by accepting the lack of divisions that have appeared to exist. We are doing this by seeing in wholeness the nature of the divine duad of Heaven and Earth. In relationship, we are attesting to the divinely human duad by being a duad that is equally human and divine.

TESTAMENT

The Testament of the New is your witness to the new covenant that opens the realm of creation to you. The imaginal is what is here, and forever on its way into Being. The imaginal is the fruit of our joining and the gift of all time. It is a way that the power of evolution cannot touch or halt.

The Treatises of Mary

First Heart Treatise

Acts

To Make Sacred Through Acts

From *Mirari: The Way of the Marys*

"I return the word 'sacrifice' to its original meaning: to make sacred through acts. I add it to the lexicon of spiritual virtues where it has fallen into disrepute and no longer is acknowledged.

"To make sacred through acts always blesses in the way needed. It is always a liberation, and never, ever, a debt owed or paid, given, or received with expectancy."

~ Mary of Nazareth

To Gain Refuge

I can feel myself growing distant to anyone and anything outside of this rugged cove in which I have found myself. Yet it is no longer the cave in which I once was hidden and voiceless.* It is an inlet, an anchorage, a natural harbor in which I have obtained refuge. I am here to eulogize the old and hail The New.

~ Mari Perron

---

* The reference is to a vision of a past life, shared in "Mirari," p. 30 in which I experienced myself in a cave.

$\mathcal{A}$CT OF PASSAGE

As you enter the time of Memoria, what you feel will be akin to memory's prayer, the prayer of longing. Her way is that of remembrance, tinged with grief's yearning for the end of what need not be.

Memoria breathes herself forward and backward as an Act of Passage that carries you through and beyond what was. She sends out a call that thirsts for the response of love in which you participate. Memoria's wonder comes of an awareness within you, within your being, of your Being. As remembrance lifts unity to communion—to union with—Memoria is personified and made flesh.

I can feel each word you speak to me, Mary. I can feel in Memoria.

Yes, Mari. You, who have called out so often when you are in pain . . . have been comforted. In your call's response, you have begun to feel accepted, identified, distinguished, at times forgiven. You are recognized. In Memoria you are comprehended: known.

To be recognized in one's pain is a supreme acknowledgment that Yeshua knew of and found honoring. After having given his all for The New—not only his words but his life—it was not only my witness but my remembrance, and that of many, that grew the in-common compassion distinguished by the breach that occurred.

In Memoria you feel anger, compassion, and attentiveness in *a necessary response to what need not be. Memory is the language of the heart.**

M

---

* ACOL C:30.31

Memoir

Memoir is the feminine form of memory. It is autobiographical. Memoir is true to life, to its movements, and to the feelings that propel its movements. This is a major reason why, in our account, your presence isn't being removed. This inward, subjective, personal way of knowing is the very memory that the training of the dominant males have dismissed. Those so trained call this way of knowing "irrelevant," and pertinent only to certain private situations . . . if any.

But the richness of memory, and thus all that is held in Memoria, cannot be denied.

Mari, you, and all women and men who embrace the feminine within, and all recovering from the training,* and those who are just beginning to revolt against it, will realize that knowing includes unconscious memories, as well as one's dreams and hopes. Memory also includes what has not yet occurred but is palpable and present within, and imaginal memories of what could be.

Memories of what could be, are memories of what is alive within you, calling you to what is before you in time and beyond time. Divine memory is of a time you but think you know not.

---

* "You can dismantle the ego and build another in its place, and this has at times been done in the individual with great training, as in military training, or in cases of great abuse when a second ego personality is developed to save the first. The ego has also been dismantled and rebuilt over time and been seen as the rise and fall of civilizations. But as we have said before, the only replacement that will work is the replacement of illusion with the truth. The very purpose of this Treatise is to prevent the replacement of illusion with illusion, or one ego-self with another. The training of this Course, while gentle in nature, has been great, as great as that of any military training, as great as any emotional trauma that has left one in a state of emptiness. This is, in effect, the state in which you currently find yourself." ACOL T3:4.7

Memory also holds situations unresolved and situations unanticipated. It dwells within relationships. It lodges in hearts.

Memory's prayer, a way of communion with your Holy Ones, is a call and a response.

*T*HE BEGINNING OF VISUALIZATION AND THE END OF VICTIMIZATION

What words and manner am I to have now, my Mary? My Jesus? Loving? Radical? I feel weak with what I've received, and at the same time as if new life has been breathed into me. Still, I do not in any way feel released from the claims of my humanity. In truth, it is as if I am being newly claimed.

But am I bold enough? Am I a bold person at all? Really? When it comes right down to it? Am I brave enough to stand in my humanity *and* enter the imaginal realm of Memoria?

*My Mari, remember what I said to you as we began "Mirari." "There is 'energy' that comes of no longer being a victim. There are new resources." You are not escaping life but giving a human face to love.**

Love not only accepts but rejects.

Now it is time to reject being victimized. The majority of women, feminine leaning men, minorities of color and of sexual persuasion, as well as all of those who live in poverty today, have been oppressed by the primarily male egos that have dominated.

You have been victimized. But you need not "feel" like victims any longer. You are not victims. You are the ones. You are the new

---

* "Mirari," p.15

future. You are the many who have not forgotten how to tend the fire.*

ℳ

The blaze of the fire has grown. The swell of women around the fire has multiplied. Many new babes have been born.

In this time of the breach, many desperate, victimized ones have lashed out. They have harmed themselves as they harm others. They are prisoners to a world that has not cared about them. Many will bring their pain to the inferno. Each new hurt brought to love intensifies the fire that is the cause of The New.

This is not a gentle time coming.

Yet, to be consumed by the flame of The New will release these, too. All are to be freed from the prison that comes of feelings ruled by the anger of unseen victimization. Feelings of deep sadness, longing, and heartbreak.

The women who murmur around the fire tend the underworld of feelings.

Our image of the women will remain until the time passes when egoic men would assume to take charge of the rescue. This they have done throughout time. They have taken up their flags,

---

* "My son spoke of anchoring The New, and I want you to imagine now the women around the campfire, squatting while they tend the fire, squatting as they birth new life. This is the posture of the anchor, solid as an anvil, feet planted, balance fine and deliberate, poised. Poised for what will be needed next. Poised and ready for the invasion of The New and the old's lingering encroachment, as mesmerizing as the flames of the fire that signals The New. The invasion is an intrusion of The New into the old, a force meant to quicken the passing of all that lingers of death in the living. To end living death and welcome living life. To end division and become one with what is being birthed. To mother The New into existence." Ibid, p.18

and with their bows and arrows, their bayonets, their guns or bombs or poison, taken over in order to keep the old order. As long as they assume that they know best, they will seek to lead, and see great risk in those who will no longer be silent victims of their leadership.

This time, those egoic men who cannot see themselves as wild dogs will see the real threat as the women. They will sense that the risk comes from victimized ones who no longer choose to be victims.

Yet the true culprit is unconscious pain. Unconscious pain has always been the problem. It has been used as an excuse for far too long.

Here, we bring pain to consciousness.

What you viewed in your mind's eye as you listened to me, Mari, was an archetypal scene, timeless and haunting and obscure . . . for a reason.

What did you imagine, then? What do you see now?

Truly, I saw as you described but I felt more than I saw. The scene was potent and touching and somehow empowering. The women weren't going anywhere. That was the strongest feeling I had. They had conceived of a new time and were going to see it through. They sat on their haunches and I could feel the strength of that anchoring posture. Also, the way they appeared cloaked reminded me of the mantle spoken of in *A Course of Love* (ACOL): "You must take on the mantle of your new identity, your new Self."*

You spoke of it, Mary, as the mantle of "love's nature," as well as of our true Self, saying that . . . "This mantle does not reveal but

---

* ACOL T2:3-4

conceals. It protects the living Holy Ones until the moment for which they have prepared arises. It is given those who gather in [anticipation] of The New."*

My memory reminded me of all these things. The image did feel ancient, but it felt current as well. I imagined actual dogs in a near distance, but knew they were representative. What I most knew, was that the women were together because, together, they could help each other, and endure birthing in a time of danger. The scene was so intense! So evocative! Yet it scared me too.

I knew they protected both the new life they carried, and the time of The New. The babes, as I believe you said, were symbolic of The New, and yet they were actual as well. There was a birth about to happen. That's how it felt. I could feel, more so than see, the women's fierce resolve.

And when you felt and saw it in them, you felt and saw it in you.

Yes. That is true. But only momentarily.

A moment is enough, my Mari, enough that it lingered in you and resurfaced when the time was right. It will be so for all who feel into the scene. It will arise when they are ready, as it has in you.

Most essential was that you saw, and knew, that the women were "already" aware of the threat. They saw the threat to new Life as actual, even when the danger was hidden in darkness, and they chose not to be victims.

Women are ready. We are not excluding men, but the readiness that has come of the foresight of the women needs to be seen.

---

* "Mirari," p. 27-28

It is the women who must sound the call and be the heralds of this new time.

This awareness is one that won't let women be victimized any longer. The threat is now sensed, but it is far too widespread to be specific. You are together as the Marys, to be vigilant, as Jesus once called you to be.* And with vigilance, you will not fall victim to carnage again. You will rather, together, and singly, each according to your own nature, usher in the new time. Women are sounding the call, and they call to all equally. They know that the true masculine creative energy is essential, and it is welcomed.

With this new alertness to feelings, men, as well as women, will overcome their propensity to think about how they feel. As you see newly every day, what you think about how you feel does not end your confusion or give you the peace to usher in The New. Vigilance, in seeing and releasing these thoughts, will awaken the reflective feminine in you, in men, and in women.

ℳ

"Man" is a word whose original meaning was to think. It also referred to the use of the thumbs. These features distinguished "mankind" from the animals. Thinking was the distinction that began all such discrimination by characteristics, and commenced to operate in a way that disallowed intuitive knowing, even though countless hunches and flashes of insight were the true inception of brilliant notions, from medicine to democracy to physics. This distinction also came to disallow, in many, the wonder of the natural

---

* "I will keep your vigil. Now keep mine. Keep your candle lit for me." Perron, Mari. "The Jesus Chronicles." *Mari Perron*, www.mariperron.com/the-jesus-chronicles.

world, the felt knowing of women, and nearly obliterated from their consciousness the imaginal realm.

As this ancient memory is recognized, more and more men, and women too, will feel their grief and be moved by it. You will feel sorrow for all that has fallen from love and, from your heartache, discover all that has descended into the unconscious realm. You will seek, rather than block, its return to you. This will instill faith in the promise of The New. You will let "all" true feelings guide you as you create your own new lives.

Your own new lives are what you are birthing. You are pregnant with the coming of your own birth. You are coming to life, and your new lives will create The New.

M

$\mathcal{T}$HE CHAIN OF EVENTS

Mary, at the end of this long blessing that was also the trial of manifesting "Mirari," our country and the world are in a different place. The manifesting needed to be done, but it came at a cost. I am weary, and my "symptoms" of The New growing daily. I almost asked, "How do I get back to where we were?" but realize there will be no getting back. Even with the introduction you have given, you did not "introduce," but brought forward The New.

Looking out the cabin window, the trees are finally emerging out of the depth of the darkness of morning that is leaving. Still, I hear nothing.

Feeling my own distraction lingering in the silence I look up the word "distract" in all its variations. I find, from my old dictionary, whose front cover has finally given up its last tether, that to distract is to draw apart! To draw the mind, or attention, in another direction— to divert it, or to draw in "conflicting" directions, create conflict and confusion, great mental disturbance, distress; mental "intrusion!" *

I suppose that's what we mean when we say something "drives us to distraction!" I'm not quite in that place, Mary, but boy, I can feel how near I am, and that my distraction with events needs to give way, again, to devotion! I am not to be diverted. We women are not to be diverted. That is the message. With your help and assurance, I will find my way . . . forward.

$\mathcal{M}$

---

* *Webster's New World Dictionary, Third College Edition.* Simon and Schuster, Inc., 1988.

CRUST

Holy Mother,

I love it that you have announced how we will proceed with this second book of our way of Mary. I am enamored by the naming of the treatises and especially by this wonderful declaration of the feminine way as that of memoir.

Yet I must admit to you that I am unsure of these Acts that we wrote together almost two years ago. So much has changed that they don't feel current.

Here is where you discover that your real act of trust is trusting yourself. Do you trust in what you received in Acts?

I do, but in addition to all that has happened since, it includes the time of my daughter returning home for a while as she and her husband divorced, and the meeting with Kate and Rick.*

Some of it seems ill equipped to convey the new acts.

Really? When you chose not to let your daughter move home permanently? When you chose to speak up about your needs with your friends?

Well, "my piece" of this writing feels stuck in time. Your words never do, even when you speak of the past. I find that so comforting.

As you review what we shared together last year, you will see. This must proceed as it is.

Holy words removed from human events reach you, at their best, at one half of their potential. Words removed from story,

---

* Kate Macnamera, an author and therapist, and Rick Mercer, who maintains the "Teachings of Christ Mind" library on-line.

and thus your personal protection, are those most easily co-opted. When it is not seen that they emerge from within one person's life, from its context and its time, they may feel more universal, but are also more available for depersonalization. With the common spiritual avoidance of the personal, this delicate, subjective way of knowing is lost. It now must be returned.

How will objective, neutral language soothe our people in a seething world? With depersonalization, they wind up lost, when what they long for is to be found. The personal and the universal are not separate! They belong together.

What we share will lead, quite surprisingly, to each reader delving into her or his own memories, own heart, soul, and spirit . . . naturally. It occurs naturally. This is what you do when you read memoirs, is it not? You see your own life newly? In all its opulent fullness?

That is so true and so varied! From Thomas Merton's diaries to the writings of Emily Carr, and really all the feminist writers I have read: Betty Friedan, Gloria Steinem, or Meridel Lesuer. Simone De'Beauvoir, Clarissa Pinkola Estes. . . they all combine the personal with the vocational.

But Merton and Carr were the first with whom, as an emerging woman, I felt the grandeur of being "let in" so strongly because they were immersed in the conflict of being creators: Merton with writing, Carr with painting. I can't honestly think of other books that propelled me the way these two did. I needed to see their inner conflict. I needed their examples, their personal expression. They included great faith and beside it, their wrestling with the demands of expressing it individually, as it lived within them.

Of course, there were others who nudged me along, and a new

form of feminist writing such as that by Elizabeth Lesser. But I have been most inspired by Toni Morrison's non-fiction writing, which I also consider feminist writing, yet broader. This paragraph in particular, from which she draws the title of her book of essays, has stayed with me since I first read it:

"Tell us what the world has been to you in the dark places and the light. … Tell us what it is to be a woman so that we may know what it is to be a man. What moves at the margin. What it is to have no home in this place. To be set adrift from the one you know. What it is to live at the edge of a town that cannot bear your company." *

Only a few days ago I was thinking of getting away from the thoughts that such ideas inspire. Every deep thought seems to lead to a contemplation of what spirituality is not, the against-ness of my thinking of it, my hope of coming at a new view more purely and boldly. Either way, it is clear there can be no standing in the same spot. We are now on the edge of something new.

Morrison wrote from the depths of memory, and memory is precisely what will anchor this sea-tossed time. Memory possesses you.

You long to repossess yourself to finish this work we have begun. You will see. You will be internally reframing these events as you return to them so that you view them as being about trusting in yourself. In that way, you will reveal how personal Acts include a trust you do not yet recognize. Everyone wavers. But this too, is

---

* Morrison, Toni. "The Nobel Lecture in Literature." *What Moves at the Margin*, edited by Carolyn C. Denard, University Press of Mississippi, 2008, p. 206.

trust. Nothing is static. Everything moves into being. As it does, you waver.

You must waver. You tremble, you hesitate . . . but you believe, you imagine, and you move forward. You quiver with a trust that is far greater than any you envisage, or feel that you can actually carry, or will enact. Yet in this way, you entrust your very self to the coming of The New. You commit to it.

I think maybe you encouraged me to ask about this, for having brought to my awareness, earlier, that trust would be one of the New Acts.

Have you considered that what I came to tell you is to trust in You? In what you do? In your Acts? We are together as a duad, two as one, and you are in no need of permission to act. The only thing I will remind you of, is that there is a "then" and a "now" and a "here."

"Here," your trust in yourself has increased exponentially as a result of publishing our first book. This was tantamount to accepting that you can trust yourself . . . completely.

The New Acts relate to your, and each one's, source of power, which is exactly this: trust in your Self.

M

THE POWER TO CHOOSE AND THE ACT OF MOVEMENT

The power to choose is an Act, an act of trust that gives you the authority to make your own way. It is a huge part of your power to reject the old and create The New.

Your Self has an inability now to take comfort in the old. It will come to be so with many.

It was the old that gave you the opportunity to realize your need to stand in your power. It will continue to give you many opportunities as the new time moves into being. This movement is the Act that we are in.

Here is where you discover that your real act of trust, is trusting yourself. Trusting your Being.

I know that trust is calling to you here, not only due to the circumstances of the past, but the circumstances that are here and ahead. You are called to see that the New Acts and trust both go together and direct the moving, being, expressing energy of The New. Yes, this is so in every part of life: between partners, between friends, between family members, between citizens and governments.

Remember that in Yeshua's life, he was prone to saying, "Begone hypocrite." The word "hypocrite" refers to a person who is not being her or his Self, who is not being who she or he is. Not being true. He, your Jesus, called you to be true from his own longing and hope that you will Be Who You Are.

I have as well.

M

SELF-REGARD AND DISREGARD

New Acts are also about equity, fair play, and justice. But what comes before these acts of trust?

It is often the recognition of "dis"-regard.

What you have experienced has finally given you cause to see yourself with radical "self"-regard. The word "regard" has been coming to you lately for a reason.

Yes, I looked it up recently and "regard" is everything—everything I've yearned for: respectful attention, affection, appreciation, good wishes. One description is to regard one's friends highly. To have "relation" to. I like that. My friends and I do offer such regard in relation to each other.*

This is the way you each are now to live: with radical self-regard. Such regard will extend from those who embrace it, to all who are hungering for it—all who are starving for lack of it. The upside-down thinking of the world would reverse what I have said. But it is from "radical" rather than "complacent" self-regard, that such hunger will be sated.

M

---

* *Webster's New World Dictionary*, 1988.

DIVINE MEMORY

When you first brought me the word "memoria," I thought of a postcard that I once displayed on my bookshelf for years. This glass fronted antique shelf was once in my sunroom and now is in my living room. I was thinking that it was on this postcard where I first saw the word "memoria," and wished I knew where it had gone. Then it just "showed up" one day in my bedroom. I hadn't seen it in years!

The picture is from an old monument in a cemetery, and the word was not memoria but a phrase: memento mori. Still, having it turn up in a way that was all but impossible, feels to be of consequence. I learned the phrase means "Remember you must die." Some took it as a way of preventing hubris. Others as cause to focus, not on this life, but an afterlife. Maybe in our context it means we must die to the old.

M

You know I love cemeteries, Mary, especially the one here in Minnesota, where my father's people are buried (and Mom now, too). St. Peter's is the oldest Catholic Church in Minnesota and so its cemetery is likely one of the oldest as well. It is lovely.

On Father's Day, a few months after Dad died, I found a belt buckle on his stone while visiting his grave. He was a Veteran of WWII and it is Vets that the buckle depicts with the words, "Stand Up Speak Out." I don't know who left it, but I was so taken by it, I not only brought it home with me, but brought it with me to the first Miracles in the Mountains Conference in Colorado. It was my first big one, and I gave the best presentation I've ever given.*

You know too, Mary, that I have collected records of family history: oral, written, and recorded. I believe so much in preserving memories, and feel so sincere about my own. I can view something that reminds me of my grandmother, or my childhood, a cousin, or an outing, and be taken right back there.

I was telling someone the other day about how, when my mom died, I wanted the set of china that her daddy had given her. There was nothing like a full set left, and the cups were so small they probably didn't hold six ounces. In other words, the set was totally impractical—but it reminded me of my granddaddy and my mother's love for him. Mom called him† "Daddy" until the day she died.

My mother changed in her forties after divorcing my own dad. I was a teen. She was no longer the sweet person she'd been when younger, except with babies, and with each thought of her daddy. I could hear it in her voice. I could imagine that, from her exile in a bad marriage in Minnesota, each contact from her family in Georgia gave her the strength to go on, just as she may have sensed how Granddaddy missed his home in Sicily, and likely got sweetly nostalgic, the same way she did, in remembering the home he left.

Remembering the home we left... I surely did that in "Mirari."

I know that what we will speak of will be bigger than this kind of memory, and yet it is so like this in its longing. And I believe

---

this kind of memory is honoring, and being honoring, greater than people imagine. I know this in my bones as well as my being.

This is why we add "Memoria" to "Mirari" and speak of memoir. With me, you know that memory is not "only" linear. There is also a lineage of divine memory. As Jesus said in ACOL,

"This memory lies within your heart and has the ability to turn the image you have made into a reflection of the love that abides with it in holiness."*

To call upon memory is an Act of The New.

Your divinity lives within you, right within your humanity. To call upon divine memory is the supreme Act that we are about. It is to pray in a manner that brings divine memory forward. It is a means of revelation. The prayer of memory is not rote or mechanical but an interactive catalyst for movement to The New. †

You knew, from your time of Jesus (ACOL), and know now, in the time of the Marys, that your own desire is to call people to what stands before them, without leaving behind what has shaped them. You want no one to disregard their humanity or their story. You have realized that for a future not predicated on the past, you must Act by moving from within the life you have lived, to what is propelling your love and longing to new life. This new horizon encompasses all of your memories and calls you to be accepting of them, or to be propelled by them. As your brother phrased it:

---

* ACOL T3:2.11

† See divine memory, ACOL T1:6.2 and 6.6

"A tiny glimmering of memory has returned to you and will not leave you to the chaos you seem to prefer. It will keep calling you to acknowledge it and let it grow. It will tug at your heart in the most gentle of ways. Its whisper will be heard within your thoughts. Its melody will play within your mind. 'Come back, come back,' it will say to you. 'Come home, come home,' it will sing. You will know there is a place within yourself where you are missed and longed for and safe and loved. A little peace has been made room for in the house of your insanity."*

Your longing can be toward fond memories of the past, as your mother remembered her daddy, or as you remember your dad. Some memories are not as pleasant. But memories arise because they have something to say. This is intimate and highly appropriate knowing. We do not discount the past, nor memories of the past.

Yet there is more. Memories that extend your view beyond what you know of this life are crucial to your life here. What is remembered in this extension of memory is remembered "for" the life you are living now. We do not speak of memories of past lives, but of your life, here, and yet to come. It is "this life" in all its circumstances, that remains essential to The New. This is true for all.

Memory exists only in its relationship to you.

M

---

* ACOL C:10.32

FAITH

Have you ever thought, you daughters and sons of the Most High, that your faith—that all faith—is an inner knowing? Acts that make a difference in the world of time and space come of this "faithful" way of knowing. Faithful knowing is "fateful" knowing, the knowing from which New Acts arise. Faithful knowing engenders the very Acts that change the fate of the world.

$\mathcal{T}$HE RETURN: ACTS OF TRUST

Now that I have reassured you, we return. Here we can go back to your recent memories—those that feel so long ago, memories that came before this time of COVID-19, and before your Capitol was breached, not only by protestors, but by your posturing leaders. Here, we also move beyond those memories to the time we spent together, and to the new future.

Remember the Act of Trust, for this is needed here. Trust— not in externals but in your internal and eternal memory. You do not need to explain anything. In this non-explanatory way, your response to memory grows to become an Act that is all-embracing. It also may starve those looking for explanation into self-reflection and eventually self-regard.

As a whole, you may see this period as part of your movement out of the past and into The New. In the same way, those reading may see their own first movements into The New. You will each meet these ways of movement, being, and expression and see how they "become" one, and becoming one, become The New.

When you first published The Dialogues of A Course of Love,* you separated the chapters into three sections: Acceptance, Discovery, and Becoming.

I want to remind you of "becoming." The chapter on "Becoming" began in this way:

---

* Published as a single volume in 2002 and again, along with single volumes of the Course and Treatises, in 2005.

"Before creation of the new can begin, you must come to know the way of creation as it is. It has not always been the same, and it will not be the same in the future as it is now. But there are certain principles that govern creation. These principles are like unto the patterns that were created for your time of learning and that will be applied anew to the creation of new patterns for the new time that is upon us."*

As you immediately recall, this is where movement, being, and expression were first introduced† as a single profound Act of The New. The principle of movement was revealed as "life as itself." We spoke of this in a new way in Mirari, as life as it is.‡

Your creation of who you are and your creation of The New are happening in unison as you proceed through the year 2019 into the all-important decade of the 2020s. Creation in unison is the new pattern.

M

---

* ACOL D:15.1

† ACOL D:15.11

‡ "Mirari," p. 114

2019
REFLECTION AND REMEMBRANCE

JUNE 2019

The way of Mary, foretold by your brother, is speaking of a truth that counters what, in A Course in Miracles, he called the projection of your fears. The way of reflection is not that of projection. Projecting is a defense that misplaces your feelings and stymies your acts. It gives your inner feelings to others or takes on their way of thinking. Reflection, as of a mirror, throws back the projection.

Reflection also shows, or expresses, what is "before" you. In a mirror you see "your" image. With reflection, your image, the image of your true Self, and of your Soul, is before you and reflected in your eyes and the eyes of those who know along with you.

Right now, you are caught in remembrances. This you are feeling as a remembering of your past.

Yes.

What you need to see of the past, since we began talking, has been landing nearer and nearer. What you are seeing is not sailing over your head. It is at your feet. This is what your tears are about on this day, as you review. It is why I have interrupted your review—to follow the call you just had with Kate, and your earlier talk with Christie*—by opening this space to you: to show you that your past has landed at your feet.

This is hard for you to share, and yet is very much in need of being shared. I've been waiting for you to join this dialogue. You

---

* Kate Macnamara and Christie Lord are among my companions in The New.

have held yourself back. You have been reserved, as if it is not your place.

Yes.

But it is your place.

Yes. I know. I see it now. I think of Henri Nouwen and his expression of the "wounded healer." That might capture a bit of what I'm feeling about myself. Something has been sneaking up on me, and I've been feeling it, but not knowing what I feel.

Now we pause for you to know what you feel.

M

$\mathcal{C}$OMING TO VOICE

Dear One,

The end of being a victim is the finding of your voice.

The word "victim" is derived from ancient times when it was used as a description of the sacrificial animals that were slaughtered as offerings to God. Let this be a warning to you. God needs no such sacrifice. No one needs to offer themselves in the stance of the victim. Here we heal the victim and, in this healing, save and revive your energy for The New.

I am not here to share information for the world through you. I am here "for you." We are here, one-on-one. We are so very near, and you have remained so far from "here." Not in "feelings," I know this, my daughter. Your feelings are present and palpable. But you have not shared them. You have remained concealed. Why?

I wish I could answer that.

You will. You are so sad that you are not "here." This is what you have been feeling. This low drone of sadness that has brought up memories of the sadness you have masked for many years. The sadness of "stepping aside . . ." because it was expected of you to do this.

But with you and Jesus, as with you and me, you could not do this—you did not step aside. You could only join with us.

Yes. I do open to you completely, join with you, even when I don't talk a lot, or at all, as was the way in *A Course of Love*.

This joining was hard for you to deny, but you did do it for a while. You did it for the same reason you have always denied yourself: because it was expected of you. This is true for so many, Mari, especially women.

It is why we begin immediately with coming to voice.

But, Mary, it is as if I cannot find my "own" words, the words that would convey how I feel. My feelings come—but my words do not. And when my words do come, it is as if they are just words, worth less than nothing.

It takes a lot out of you to receive from us. This I know. But it is due to feeling the words, and the words are less than the feelings. And this is why "your words" have felt so silent within you.

This happened in the only way it could.

Now . . . we go back before we go forward. Now . . . you respond. You will see. You will see that going back, and going forward, are not opposites.

This will allow you your voice. "Being in voice" is at the heart of Acts of The New. This is why you are feeling so compelled to be done with your busy life and to make time for "this" life. Now it is time for your response, and your words.

I will wait. I will listen. Here we begin again. We begin tomorrow when you are fresh. You have cried tears with your friends today as you began to see your voicelessness. But you have already begun. Tomorrow, you will step out of exile. You will step out of the shadows.

M

THE HOLY OF IT ALL

For a minute, as I found myself rocking, your image, in the statue before me, felt as if it moved with me, my Mary. Thank you for asking about me.

There's this idea I have, an idea that I want people to know things I haven't told them, and also that I've said everything—over and over—and likely not said the thing at the heart of the matter. And if I did really get to it, would anyone even care? Would it matter to them, or only to me?

I just have hated how people separated me and Jesus, and how they will want to do the same with you and I. They want me to be like channelers or scribes of the past. Yet, I would guess many others also pretended that they didn't share the experience, that they weren't part of it, didn't feel it, weren't moved by it. If I'm right, many have done this—denied themselves and you—because it appears to be what people want, and then also, for the humility of it all, but that is always present in this joining. The "not me" feelings are so true, at least in the beginning. But it changes. As you continue, you realize you've entered relationship, and that the flow of love is an energy, moving like a mobius strip between the two of you.

I did "truly" see myself as "needing to get out of the way" when I began. But it ended for me in the first year of *A Course of Love*. Everything changed after I was halted in my reception to receive, and to feel, "The Embrace."*

I step out the door for air but don't have my glasses on. In the range of my raw eyes, one star is all that is visible. It is enough.

---

* ACOL C:20

I sit back down and turn the light on for a minute. When I do that, my face looks back at me from the window. The world outside becomes uniformly dark as the inside of the cabin is reflected in the window's glass panes: the cabin's pitch and walls, windows, ceiling fan. The inside and the outside, right here, right now. Surrounding me.

What do I care how I am seen, other than for the desire to express something of it and me, together. To express the holy of it all. It's only a little about me, and a lot about the need for one's own view of the holy and how you come to feel consecrated to it. And how everything I do, and we do, is as it is . . . and more too. That's one thing.

Then there is the world. This world has our hearts. Unless it is ignored. Or we are convinced it—the world—is not real. But even then, the world still holds our hearts. Even in those who have felt that love is elsewhere.

Oh, Mary, I am so privileged to get to love where I am.

$\mathcal{M}$

Writer and poet William Stafford said, "Be sure you are fighting the right enemy." He was a passivist, a conscientious objector during World War II who nonetheless lived in a world where such as "enemies" were seen, and I think I do too. There are enemies of liberty "out there," and "inside" as well, enemies of one's own liberty. Overarching atmospheres of judgment, inside and outside.

And the Earth's benevolence and godliness keep hanging out with us—neutral it seems.

Maybe neutral is the biggest judgment of all. Yes. I think that's it. Neutrality seems to be the goal. The *surprise* is that of being affected by what is not neutral. By what is passionate!

Jesus was passionate. You are passionate. Yes, I think I've hit on it. Passion is what is lacking. And this is a passion. I am a passionate woman. And maybe nobody knows that I am! Maybe nobody knows what such ardor looks like. I am not showy with my fervency, but it's there in my tears, and my rocking. And now, a whisper at a time, maybe my voice.

Quiet passion, maybe like yours, Mary.

You are passionate about this experience.

How could I not be? If I weren't, these words would not be. I am certain of it.

So you add passion to the mix, my daughter? You go beyond devotion to passion? And you see it as a necessity? Even when passion brings suffering?

Does it? Maybe then, what is called "suffering" can't be done without. The poignant, the affecting, and that which brings change, that which is so compelling you can't shield your heart or your eyes. You can't not look. You can't not see. You can't turn a blind eye. Passion overcomes our reason, our reluctance, our idea that what we're doing makes no sense, or needs to make sense. Passion overrides our idea that the world makes no sense. It builds a narrative.

I want to build a narrative around love, affection, longing, our stories, and our quest for a life of meaning. Significance. Sense. Not the trifling but the intense. The restless kindling within, not only the restful.

I can't vote for peace at any price. I refuse to be callous.

Oh yes, my Mari, you are a sister of my heart. The heart is never neutral. It is the heart that holds passion.

M

THE SOUL'S EPIPHANY

All is in flux at the moment and it doesn't matter. I am in my space before the day has begun, listening to tire "flaps." For a moment, walking the neighborhood before coming here, I heard that quiet, early morning sound of childhood, a time when the frail white curtains of my bedroom blew inward like the wings of the birds whose calls they carried.

I rise and put on my noise-blocking earmuffs. It is a little better, but the traffic noises still come through and the earth sounds lessen.

Still, I accept this mild relief by watching the bobbing heads of the nasturtiums. There is a low wind, jiggling everything close to the ground, swaying the middle branches, and leaving the tree tops serene. What a wonder it all is.

M

Somewhere in life it seems our dreams get away from us. The derailing of "the dream" begins, and with it, the decline of our potential. Who would we be if we were doing what we love? How many know what that is?

Here I am, in the last quarter of life, finding myself at my poised point, and my greatest desire is to live a quiet writer's life, which might have been the underlying desire all along.

Of course, I once thought writing books would be of my own composition. But I love sharing writing with you. And doing what you love, is doing what you love. There is a power in it. My current theory is that, while writing rarely lets us make a living, there is a "benefit" as well, in not having money: It keeps you humble.

Humility is good much of the time. But not always. Sometimes, humility blocks recognition of your power.

The greatest power of all is the power of joining. This we have done. We have joined heart-to-heart. This is where we are, and where your passion lies. You are rich with it, with that which is the power of life. To be humble with this power is perfectly appropriate . . . but not to be so humble you fail to recognize it.

Joining is the Act of Uniting one-to-one, of forming the duad. This is the embrace that reveals who you are. There is no reason to see that as anything other than a "passionate" embrace, and for you, it is an embrace of your writing life as well.

This passionate embrace can be as happens here with me, or with soul, or art, or spouse or friend. And you are passionate about joining, my Mari. You are passionate about any instance of joining where knowing and being known arises; passionate about writing (a way of knowing); passionate about dialogue (another way of knowing); passionate about the return of love . . . the greatest way of knowing of all.

Are you content to know your passion is needed, my Mari?

Yes, I am, Mary.

Good. Then we will continue.

𝓜

While the body is neutral, it is also the canvas on which, and with which, you paint your life—your life being the opus, the composition of your heart. There is a circle of exchange between it and you, a conveying of sensation and your response to sensation, just as your eyes see beauty and your heart and soul respond with awe and wonder. The seat of your passion and compassion are the same. You have responded with passion.

Passion and compassion feel like vastly different energies, I know, but you sense, as I speak this, that in truth they arise from the same source. You know the truth when you hear it, and you know that the difference between passion and compassion comes by way of impassioned Acts.

Yes, I do.

Then we stay with the joining, the relationship that occurs between the heart and soul of being, the epiphany of the supernatural that shines forth at the moment of intuitive understanding. The supernatural is the natural, glimmering with its full creative and sensory power. The epiphany is to the soul what the quickening is to the womb.

You think of the quickening, during pregnancy, as the moment when first movement is felt. It is also often when the woman first begins to "show," when she begins to appear to be pregnant, and often when she begins to share "the news."

Every creative epiphany shows forth in its manifestation. And so, the two Acts are analogous to each other. The Act of Epiphany is the birth of an idea, a revelation, an internal process of the soul that inspires greater understanding and vision.

The womb of the soul inhabits each one who holds, envelopes, and generates. And yes, Mari, we could add those who retain their passion for life: for a life of truth or beauty, for connection, or for "new life." The womb of the soul is the holder of new life that includes imagining far beyond the life you have thought yourself to be living. It is the particular place where a new image of life begins to quicken—to show itself. The womb of the soul is masculine as well as feminine. It is the embracer of the life-giving power it has been given, in the way it has been given.

The soul's epiphany is the soul's awakening to The New. Each soul passionately embraces its sacred charge, which is New Life.

You are held passionately, as you too are to hold: closely enough to create, loosely enough to share, and boldly enough to love in the same fashion. To love in the same fashion is to Love.

Love is not neutral. It is the page on which you write. It is the canvas to which you apply your attributes of being. Love is the source from which, and on which, your creative nature comes to be expressed and made real in the world. This is what creates a new reality: revealed attributes of Love's Being and Expression.

Loving in such a wholehearted and creative way is a continual movement "into" Being—a continual coming to know without division of the knower and the known. Expression is the culmination of the movement of Being.

The experience you had with your Jesus revealed this way to you and it is continued here in its feminine form.

Our way chases the money changers from the temple body. It is not about "getting" anything. The way of the Marys is about the Act of Living and creating New Life.

M

LIFE AS ITSELF

The power of the way of Mary is life as itself.

You have chosen a new kind of experience. In the divine One's own evolution (which is also our evolution), a desire to experience in relationship was born.

This choice, for us, is one of living in awareness of relationship and union with the divine One, in whom we all have our being.

As you remember, Mari, in the dream that told you, "You can no longer sell your mind for money, your mind now belongs to God," it was God to Whom you were consecrated. God to Whom you were asked to be dedicated—to the All of All. This idea, and the reality of being "One in Being," was passed on through many Holy Books.

You each see this most clearly, first, in the beholding of your beloved Ones, those with whom your own knowing and being known occurs. What is "first" is Source, Origin, Significance. Life as Itself.

Life is the first Coming. Life as Its Self is the second coming. This second coming is what God the Mother and Mother Earth facilitate. Here, on this Earth, you are held in the womb of the Great Mother.

It is this living union that the feminine ones hold as their sacred seal of the Divine: the power to birth new life into being and to let it grow into what it will be. Yet assuring the continuation of the coming of Christ is not by way of populating the planet, but by living life as Life It-Self: manifesting true Life in form and time.

Remember, Christ-consciousness is your will to know, to be, and to express, and that all are held within this consciousness.*

The secret lies in our own way of being. Yes, "ours." Mine and yours. Yours and mine. The nonduality of the duad is "one in being and different in relationship." It is two "together." The duad allows the ability to relate, without which, life would not be. The duad enables the essence of living to be as one, and to create as one . . . the two. Birth is the demonstration as well as the manifestation.

Birth is the mirror in which rebirth, what is here and yet to come, shows your Self to you.

M

Do know

Do be

Do express

---

* "You have been told Christ-consciousness is neither God nor man but the relationship that allows the awareness that God is everything. You have been told Christ-consciousness has also been known as wisdom, Sophia, spirit. Christ-consciousness thus obviously predates the man Jesus, and creation itself. It is both the feminine and masculine, the 'identity' of God, or in other words, the All of All given an identity." ACOL D:Day17.2

$\mathcal{T}$HE UNDOING

Good morning, Mary.

Today, my daughter's situation fills my mind the way every un-tenable situation of my life has done. I must be inviting this "fight-ing for my life." It's much like what this vulnerable youngest daugh-ter is doing—fighting instead of living.

Donny is accommodating to her, and the food he makes could, alone, ruin my days. Food, and dishes, and the smell of frying or baking, smashing up garlic, slicing things for salad. Him trying so hard to be the Papa Bear to his young, liking having someone to care for . . . I think. I'm not sure, to tell you the truth.

I found myself back here because I didn't open my mouth at the right moment. He sat her in front of us to tell of her impending divorce and became a problem solver. "I'll move you back here," he said.

I said nothing.

Lord and Mother, when will I ever learn?

Kate and Rick are arriving, and I feel stalled, not only for my house being occupied in this way, but for the oddity of hearing some kind of pronouncement in last night's dream. I heard, "It's not about the future but the past."

Then, as I went out to walk, just after I awoke, a rainbow hung over the house. It made me attend the dream message more than I might have otherwise. All I can think of is that maybe it is about an undoing of the past in the present.

$$\mathcal{M}$$

JUNE 18, 2019

Today is the birthday of my first born and only son, James Ian. Blessings to him ... and me.

Just yesterday, I drove by the house on Bradley—the rental in which his dad and I were living when he was born. What an odd coincidence. He was born in 1973 and the neighborhood, over forty years later, looks much the same.

Each of St. Paul's neighborhoods has always had its own vibe, even amid change. I was from the West Side. Charlie, Ian's dad, grew up on the East Side. One on one side of the Mississippi River, one on the other.[*]

Both of our areas were working class, but his was perhaps a rung lower on the social ladder, and more of what we might have called "redneck" whites. The West Side had a flavor. We, many of us, sat on the high ground of the river's banks rather than the low. These neighborhoods sitting far above the river held classic homes. Other neighborhoods were rather hip. Plus, along our low ground, there was an area of immigrants. Donny's Lebanese parents had once lived there. Then came the Mexican Americans who were, for

---

[*] The East Side and West Side, were, I learned from a St. Paul Pioneer Press columnist with the wonderful pen name of Oliver Towne, actually the north and south sides. But they were named by river boat captains to whom there were only two directions—the west bank and east bank of the river, in this case, the Mississippi. *St Paul is my beat*, (Gareth Hiebert aka Oliver Towne)

the most part (at least to those my age), considered a bit cooler and tougher than the white kids.

On my street, the fathers in our "headed by the father, stay-at-home mother" households were well-paid union workers: Dad a truckdriver, Mr. Bultman a plumber, Mr. Schewiler a fireman. Mr. Meehan worked for the railroad.

I was seventeen when I got pregnant. Charlie's plan, as we married, was to go into the Air Force. Days after we were wed, my long-haired, guitar playing boyfriend-now-husband had his head shaved. He departed, while I remained at my mother's. It was on his return, a month or so later with an honorable discharge, the circumstances of which were never fully disclosed, that we began to seek our own place.

That's how we came to be renting the upper floor of a duplex. Neither of us were working, and it was a strange thing for me. I had always worked. I started babysitting at 11, then before I was 16 worked in a bakery and a movie theater and at Bridgeman's, and after 16 at a well-paying grocery store. I was still working there when I met Charlie. I suppose I left to get married, and because I was pregnant, as well as the expectation of being a "military family." It's funny how vague memories can become. I know I imagined myself moving somewhere to be with my new husband.

The apartment in which we landed had two bedrooms and our rent was ninety-five dollars a month. The house was crammed right up to the house next to it, as was common, but it was a unique property with a turret.

I was eighteen and Charlie twenty when our son was born. We didn't have a phone, and hadn't had a car either, but I think someone must have paid the insurance on my old one, because as my time drew near, the red Ford Fairlane that I loved was back. My clearest image is of Charlie dropping me off at the bottom of the pyramid-like stairs that led to the doors of Miller Hospital. The dome of the St. Paul Cathedral loomed beyond it. I wore a flower-patterned dress and couldn't see my shoes.

ℳ

After my trip down memory's aisle, I continued on to check out the duplex that Kate and Rick had rented for their stay, only to find that the area didn't appear safe. This made for an upsetting day all in all. I went home and got on-line to see if I could find them something better, and after a scene with my daughter in the evening, looked for one for myself too. Nothing came of either search, but it altered my mood.

This morning, I'm all tight across my womb, but I won't speculate. Having woken before the alarm once again, and taking my time for meditation before my cat Simmy knew I was up, I...

And the thought trailed off and I can't pick it back up.

Oh, I know! The thought that came to me (and I admit that it came because I was wondering what ails me) was a remnant of, "It's not about the future but the past." I went through ACOL and all of our writing, Mary, looking for "the past." So, I've been thinking about that, and thinking about my current dilemma at home, and then Kate and Rick became a dilemma too and I thought . . . what will save me?

That's when I realized that being creative would be my salvation. There you have it. And so, I went to the writer's journal of

Joyce Carol Oates* and opened at random, to a day in August of 1979, when Joyce is speaking of the exquisite pleasure of contemplating a new novel.

I find myself holding my breath between breaths. Wondering... can't I at least "contemplate" The New?

M

---

* Oates, Joyce Carol. *The Journal of Joyce Carol Oates 1973–1982*, edited by Greg Johnson, Ecco, 1988.

*T*HE NEW ACTS

This feels like an auspicious date. Its auspiciousness may be in the meeting between Kate and myself . . . Kate and Rick, but mainly Kate and myself. She and Rick have traveled to meet me due to *A Course of Love* and a burgeoning friendship between Kate and me. We have an idea that is no idea. Just the meeting. Meeting with nothing in between. No plan, no theme, no agenda . . . just us. And it's so hard! Can I, my mother, go back and look at what has come of Kate and me so far?

I apologize for asking you, as I need to trust myself—which I feel I would have done if not for the events of the past weeks. Just when I want to be at my best, to have my life humming along smoothly and my home to myself, current events are challenging me. My peace, as well as my home, are not what I would have them be for this much awaited visit.

Still, Mary, it arises again just how perfect it is that we are speaking of Acts as new acts are coming into my life due to this meeting.

Yes, my daughter, and you have seen how your every attempt to prepare for this time has been thwarted until now. Having tried and failed, you begin to see that the preparations, other than those necessary to shelter the physical, are for naught, and even these have escaped your control. You do not know what will happen, do you?

No. And I will admit, I am excited for the non-physical "revelations," even as I remain a bit concerned over the physical unknowns.

Do not fault yourself! I cannot say this enough! Life "on the ground" includes both!

The example you have in your life, at this exact time, is one that coincides with this issue, as you relate to an innocent one who truly doesn't understand the necessity—the reality—of the needs of physical life in all its form and complexity. One way alone is never the way!

We had many who were not realistic about the physical in my time as well. These were the "wanderers," present throughout time. Many were moved by faith in God alone. This is not the time that is now. *What, and who, is this "God alone" who stood apart, and acted through signs and wonders, as well as man? This "mighty" God? A God blighted by the ideas of those men who insisted on being led through the desert, not for being called, but for following in the way of others.*

The men of this time were incomparably holy "in the way of their time," but that time has passed. The women of this same time were also incomparably holy, both in the way of their time, and in ways that were not understood, or even noticed, and so were barely recorded! Then, as now, what was "taken in" that felt most akin to the ways of the world of the time, was what was promulgated. Do you see this, my daughter? Do you see how closely this time in which I lived has been duplicating endlessly, as it has with A Course in Miracles, *and as you have tried to prevent occurring with regard to* A Course of Love?

Your brilliance is in your acceptance of unknown knowing, which is not an easy acceptance to hold, to express, or even to acknowledge. The way that is passing is the way of "known knowing." This way attempts to make the unknown known, through the known, which is the way it has always been. Once a period of "making known" is begun, it proceeds by way of organization, education, and helpfulness. While the intent of this way was often true, what was "known" was less than what truly was, and as you have seen, closer to "the knowable" than the "unknowable" knowing of which we speak.

Our way of knowing is unknowable except by way of union and relationship.

In my time, even relationship was organized. It was "arranged." And although it is rarely seen, this still happens. Both relationship and knowing are still battened down. They are given four corners in books, enshrined in hallowed halls of wisdom, in churches, temples and academies. These became, and still become, the holders of wisdom or truth.

Such "wisdom" is then promulgated, then, as now, with the notion of spreading the Good News. Over time, even what good that could come of it was sanitized, altered into what would benefit both the one seeking benefit and those providing the benefit, all in the order of things "as they were," (and are).

Almost all of it is, and was, wiped clean of the relationships that would reveal the truly real, the true "reality" of the way The New comes into being. In its place came the truth as fact and custom, as well as those who led and those who followed, those who assigned meaning, and those who learned the meaning assigned.

While this worked for some, many others were left on the "outside" and, even when gaining entrance to the sacred halls of knowledge, were most often mandated to stay within walls where no "new" knowing was allowed, where a "personal" knowing of God or truth was suspect, and where the very notion of a knowing of "one's own" became antithetical to the Truth that had been established.

For every woman now designated as a Saint, there were thousands upon thousands of women who lived saintly lives they did not dare call attention to, or for which they spoke and were silenced, or even killed.

Barely adequate self-love and self-knowing were seen as blasphemy. And has this changed? Perhaps the God of Love has been changed to a god of intellect! In this dry and lifeless god, change can still be held at bay and not allowed to topple any structures of thought or form.

Still, this toppling at times comes about . . . temporarily. Few hear of these.

Acts that bless are carried out daily by millions of unknown women and men, circumstance by circumstance. While salvific, these acts do not change the trajectory of the past which, as you are seeing, endlessly creates a future like unto itself—much as many parents, without intent, repeat the patterns with which they are familiar, no matter how horrific.

Despite how different each era appears to be, regardless of how much physical change comes, without "actual" change to the nature of being, both of form and time, there will be no change that is not, in essence, a continuation of what has been.

Yeshua's life opened the door to recognition of the true nature of being, but it will take the feminine counterpart to this opening thrust to push life through the birth canal and into the new time.

Our call to The New is not callous. It does not in any way negate the actions of those called by any ministry to life on the ground. No. Those who protect the babes from the wild dogs are *more needed than ever. But the call of our way of Mary proclaims that such acts alone will not bring us to the real and lasting change that is the wonder, the Mirari of The New, that is our focus.*

As the form of The New will be new, the Acts of The New will be new. This you "know" even while you await knowing "something." Although I am following the past as revealed in our tradition, it is a tradition based largely on factual accounts of the progress of those men who were given to reveal The New. By their very nature, such "factual" accounts say almost nothing that is truly of The New. This is why I have stated that the two Courses given by Jesus could not have come before the discoveries at Nag Hamadi, and that this new time is helped along by all those traditions that, no matter how obliquely, include "non-interpretable," or "sacred" wisdom.

Now go make yourself ready for the New Acts that will occur this day.

M

$\mathcal{V}$ISITORS

Evening of an opulent day with Kate and Rick, started late and ended right on time. I'm home at 8:55 p.m. after a delightful dinner at Yarruso Brothers, a glass of wine, and plenty of F'ing-A talk. Oh, my loving Holy Ones, what companions you have brought me! Thank you, thank you, thank you.

I can't say I remember much of what was said in the Sims Avenue Victorian where they rented the lower floor. It wasn't as bad as I had feared. My real fear, that my new friends wouldn't "get real," is behind me.

What a loving demonstration, Lord and Mother! How amazing to have been "destination Mari," to know these two authentic people, and to receive the affirmation that there is "something happening" here. Here. With "us." US.

I am so delighted and amazed and in wonder, and somewhat expectant, even while I remain perfectly content in simply being real. What comes of being anything less? I am so happy! Who knows what tomorrow will bring? And what an exciting place this is to be!

If there is anywhere you would have us go, consciousness-wise, I know we are willing and that we invite it. I will take them to the Mississippi River and possibly Como Park.

No matter what happens, this is going to be, and already is, perfect. What a gift. It makes me really believe that *the way is open*, and that I can do this . . . whatever it is . . . that I'm going to do. And Mary, Holy One, you have inspired Kate and I to the writing we've

both dreamt of doing. We are worthy of your trust. How fabulous
to know that so quickly and surely.

$$\mathcal{M}$$

JUNE 23, 2019

It's morning and I am in the cabin. A duck couple occupies the roof
across the street, and the sky looks of rain. Kate and Rick are likely
sleeping. They got up at 3 a.m. on the other side of the world yesterday and traveled all day. It's six a.m. now with no visible sunrise,
a perfectly gloomy morning.

Squirrel babies are out on the freeway fence playing. Wrestling.
A lushness is already here that feels more like July. Ms. Maple has
so many fine limbs that she's peeking into the cabin now. I don't
know how this new growth happened, but I hope she lasts. It
would be a fine miracle for this old glory of a tree to come "back" to
life after I so mourned her need, due to a cracked trunk, to be taken
down to her stump.

And now a black squirrel, also a young one. He's clinging to the
side of the fence. I hope that's not what the wrestling was about, the
different color of the squirrel. So many cruelties that don't have to
be and yet are there in nature too!

A hymn has been going through my mind since I woke up. The
lyrics are "Dance, dance, wherever you may be, I am the Lord of the
Dance said He."* I'm just now realizing it was Dad's funeral song.
He so loved to dance.

With this reminder, I recall again the belt buckle I found on

---

* "I Danced in the Morning" by Sydney Carter

Dad's grave. Now it stays here in the cabin and reminds me that we all dream of standing up and speaking out.

M

JUNE 24, 2019

Monday. Another gloomy day, and noisy, as if the gloom is holding sound close to the earth. I'm hoping it will be a good day, or a good few days in terms of sound, for my visitors. Some days just aren't so bad as others, but I couldn't say why.

I believe Rick and Kate will come here today. I'm envisioning Rick taking a walk while Kate and I sit and write. That's honestly what I'm thinking as sirens go by, and trucks, and Monday morning traffic. I'm aware that I'm sitting here to let resentment go.

I became so distracted by my hunger yesterday! All day, I felt like I was just starving! I mentioned it several times to no avail. I took a pack of crackers and peanut butter out of their welcome basket and nibbled on the bowl of dried fruit and nuts that Kate got out, but that was all.

We were on fire as we talked, though!

I made fresh bread last night and used the old to make five peanut butter and honey folds. I've decided to go to Mary Love's house for a few nights. She and her husband John have gone camping and she offered it to me. I have waited so long for this visit, and I want and need to stay quiet and centered, as I can't at home these days. I have only come back for "cabin time" now that the others are off into their day.

Here, I've turned the heat on for a little release of the chill. Earlier when I was walking, a robin serenaded me and seemed to follow me, alighting across the street on the Morehouse's roof. Her landing was close, but not too close to the female mallard who, yesterday, was there with her male companion, and the day before, was in the little field of daisies that borders our yard.

It is blustery now, and I'm disturbed for being whiny, complaining about, of all things . . . food! Even so, we had this marvelous, revelatory day, and I know I wouldn't be remembering the lack of food if I could remember anything at all that we were speaking of! What would I remember of what you reveal to me, if each day I wasn't sitting here, recording as it comes? I really believe it would be the same . . . just gone! Even with writing, it is most often gone from memory (at least my conscious memory), a day later.

Despite our inspiring daylong dialogue, the only thing I recall is talking of "the field." This is Kate's language, not mine, but I love it, and am beginning to "know" it . . . the existence of this field. I even encouraged Kate's more prominent use of it in her writing. I had thought to before but hadn't, and "knew," while I was in the bathroom, (peeing a long pee) . . . that rather than call what she was writing a "handbook," it was to be a "field guide." That's just how it came to me—declaratory: not "handbook" but "Field Guide." She was so happy when I told her it "came to me!"

Writing is a bond we share. To have someone who knows what it is like to both write in an inspired way and to do the work (which she is doing now) of bringing it forward, is a solace.

M

JUNE 25, 2019

My mother, I feel better this morning for having reread our message of yesterday, the one received in the cabin (while Kate received as well). Mine was about being natural. This is it:

Dear Ones,

I'm sitting here this hour with my Australian friend Kate, who has come to visit. She is sending behind me. (I know that word "sending" is odd, but I feel to leave it.) Rick, her companion, has just fetched her cape (scarf) from the car. Leaves are falling and dancing outside. There is a sound that is halfway between chirping and a mechanical whine. I am in joy for being here, sharing my sacred space with these friends. The sense of a larger purpose looms, present and imminent, in the mix of time past, present, and future. There is no feel of pressure, but one of wanting to be available, in this brief period of togetherness, for anything that there is desire to share.

Yes, my daughter, it is still me with you. You have entered "our time" and our companionship is primary for this time, just as your companionship with Jesus was and remained for "your own" time in the way of Jesus. This does not mean your friendship with Jesus is behind you. No, quite the contrary. There is a "working together" that will not be far off but will be different as the many swirls of this time create new configurations.

Your own particular way is one that rests almost totally on "not trying," and so you feel a little strange today to "try" to communicate while you have this opportunity to share with Kate. It makes it a little different, doesn't it? You have felt this "trying" before and know that this you cannot do. Some do invoke us with intention. But intention will not work for you and me. The dif-

ference is minimal, but it is absolute. Many others do not find the effort you do in "the purposeful."

And so, as you let go of trying, which your dear woods help you each day to do, you become ready and feel the weight in your womb once again, that is the presence of new life.

Mary, there is some sort of odd insect, a big-winged fellow, doing circles outside. I comment on this because everything is so seemingly peculiar. The goofy yelling of a bird, the dashing about of the insect and the cars. It all sounds different when I am here without purpose.

Yes! But this darting and leaping and chirping and yelling is your way—not that of the purposeful. Here, ultimate purpose can present itself to you in such a light manner that you do not even see it coming. Yes, we know how to work with you! Happy tears fill your eyes as you feel deeply how true this is and how you are not called to labor.

And so, if there is that which is meant to come between you and Kate it will not be labored. It will be so natural you won't even know that it has come. And then later you will say, "Oh. What was that?" and the mystery will keep unfolding. There will be an act of undoing that alerts you of what is to come. Rather than the way of old with which you were once familiar (before the days of what is now your life), you will see that this "undoing" has become part of your continuum. What I speak of is the dynamic and powerful time that has arisen. Not only the unfolding but the "undoing."

The time of doing is the time that has come to pass. "Undoing" is a New Act, an Act of this time that you are in. It just is.

There is nothing to be done but to let the undoing do what it does without labor.

I remember ". . . An undoing accompanied by a new means of doing."*

Yes, this is what is to be, but I do not want you to think of this at all. There is nothing to be done but to let yourself be. Let yourself glory in the fanfare of your trees and feel the inspiration of the clouds that fill in the picture of the sky. This is your place, your time.

Your reception has become natural, and this is key. That's all you need to know. You are where you need to be. The undoing is what you were once so impacted by in the Course chapter on Oneness and Duality.† But now the "possibility" of light is the "presence" of light. This light joins in the swirl of energy that continues to unravel the threads of time. This is happening very gently. And then . . . then dear one . . . the weavers will come to create the new time.

I will tell you one thing. You and Kate will both grow younger in the undoing. You will grow young of heart.

Will we be among them, the weavers?

My dear one, the time of prophecy, regarding your life, is over. Remember, we know how to work with you. If you are a weaver, you will instinctively, and effortlessly, know you are a weaver. Now, there is nothing to do but what you are doing with me, and we will continue, as gently as the breeze moves through your window.

---

* ACOL C:23.28

† ACOL Chapter 19

Thank you, my Mother, for the "lack of labor" particularly, which helps as well in my "personal" life.

M

Now I realize . . . it was the subtle "trying" that made yesterday different. It was trying to be careful as I stayed at Mary Love's home, and then trying to have a plan in which eating played a part. I am sad that the trying and the planning got to me, and distanced me. Little as it was, I need to acknowledge it, and note that "in spite of it," true and "new" knowing occurred. I hate not remembering most of what we shared but know this must be as it is meant to be.

In the context of the way of Jesus and the way of Mary, Jesus spoke of weavers:

"[A]vailability is what is meant by the anchoring of the new. Those who, in relationship with the unknown, through unity and imagination, create the new by means other than doing, open a way previously unknown, and as all forerunners do, anchor that way within consciousness by holding open this door to creation. They, in truth, create a new pattern and begin to weave it into the web of reality, anchoring it for discovery by their brothers and sisters." *

M

---

* ACOL D:Day19.13

$\mathcal{I}$NTEGRATION AND INTUITION

In A Course of Love, *your brother spoke of a merger of integra-*
tion and intuition* that leads to "no escape." He spoke of what is
"expelled" and needs to be re-integrated for the wholeness of the
self.

You think of the physical. You see the scenes in which the feel-
ings that you carry arose, often without honoring the feelings that
were occurring within the scenes. You hold these memories and
think about them, remember them, play them in your mind and,
as you have recognized, they but shield your feelings. You, even
now, cannot quite get in touch with those feelings that have arisen
from your new circumstances. I am not asking you to name your
feelings or to investigate their source, but just to feel the heaviness
in your chest that comes as we speak of this.

It is your feelings that you actually "feel" within your body.
Do you see this? You do not "feel" your thoughts directly. You
"feel" your emotion . . . directly. You can locate a feeling's place
within your body. This one rests right near your heart. It is there.
Acknowledge that it is there, please.

Yes, I am feeling it.

My daughter, this link is so important! This is a feeling within
the body! It is a physical feeling of what is not of the physical, but
the emotional body. This is the integration that is no escape, the
integration that is the embrace, the integration that is so simple
it is missed.

You "feel" your "feelings."

---

* ACOL D:Day16.6

You, in your body, feel your emotions. They "become" physical. What your heart can feel becomes physical. What your heart cannot feel, stays mental. Painful or not, this way of bringing feelings that are not physical, into the physical, is creating wholeness of being. Recognize this, and you recognize so much more than you realize. In the New Acts, we acknowledge the feelings of the physical.

Your brother spoke of this as seeing that it is your feelings, rather than your thoughts about your feelings, that reflect who you are, and that by acting on your feelings, you will act in accord with who you are and thus in accord with the universe. He spoke of "reintegration" then, as the process through which you discover this proof—proof of the benevolence of your feelings and of the benevolence of the universe itself.*

No matter what caused your feelings, the feelings were real because you felt them. They are a response to what usually is an action, or even the action of an "inaction," a disregard of some kind.

Recognize what is there in you—the feeling. Respond with self-love. Embrace your Self. Embrace your tender body. Embrace how you feel. Then you remain whole and in a constant state of coming to know. You cannot "decide" what has happened, can you? No. You can only remain in a constant state of coming to know . . . even of what you do not want to know!

"To embrace is the opposite of to escape."†

Your intuition‡ is always available and will alert you to what is not yet known—and to what is coming into being—as is your

---

* ACOL D:Day16.7

† ACOL D:Day16.10

‡ See more on intuition in ACOL D:Day10.7-11

knowing of these new friends. Do not predetermine. Let knowing be revealed. You know this. You merely, in your tenderness, and eagerness, forgot briefly. What you bring here, you bring to help you remember, and this we have done together.

This is one of the important touchstones of dialogue.

Hold your friends, now, in the wholeness of the embrace, in your naturalness, and let yourself continue to come to know them. I am with you and within you.

I am absolutely ready to embrace this, and them, Mary.

You know, in the early spiritual work of so many of us, there was a rejection of feeling . . . well, anything but feelings of love. It happened with ACIM* and it happened in the early part of ACOL, and it happened for Kate and Rick in the Way of Mastery community, where "story" was particularly frowned upon.

Jesus speaks of the way emotion changes as we release the ego and become wholehearted. This is among the reasons I once published *A Course of Love* in separate volumes. As "one book," the sense of movement sometimes feels lessened. The "whole" is kept, rather than the sense of, "Oh yes, that was then, this is now."

I'm so glad we are exploring feelings further here. In this same Day of "The Dialogues," it is said, "Confidence in your *feelings* will lead to confidence in your Self,"† and for me, it is one of this work's truest statements. Confidence is so akin to trust in self. And as you can see, I am hampered a great deal when I "doubt" my feelings.

---

* *A Course in Miracles*

† ACOL D:Day10.6

When I betray my feelings, I hurt myself, and I have been hindered by this more than anything else.

M

Trust in your feelings is completely appropriate here.

In what manner will you come to trust how you feel, other than by seeing that feelings are relevant? How else will you come to trust your Self? If you did not trust your feelings, you would not be capable of this receiving, as it is a "felt knowing."

Yes, but it is different than what I feel in life situations.

Is it really, my Mari? Or do you only need reflection, as you have needed with these words, to come to your "own" knowing of what is being said, and even to trust in feelings some would call "untrusting."

Anything you feel can be used against you, by yourself or others, until you have confidence. Exploring your feelings here "is" bringing you to the confidence you seek, the self-confidence that is necessary to the New Acts. This is especially true with feelings that are, let's say, self-protective. At times, such as in your current family situation, they are feelings that are for your own human self, or one of your children or a grandchild. Even an idea—such as being the maker and matriarch of your own home—carries feelings.

I know I am overly sensitive, Mary. I know this. It seems in part to be caused from what we do here, as if I am so "open" that ordinary things of life are able to enter me and to do so with a ferocity that makes me feel battered. And, since I am so often alone (by choice and inclination) my interactions with people leave me almost . . . weak. I think that sometimes I shut down to protect myself.

I want you to see that self-protection is not defense. People in common life embrace protection and protecting in ways that many spiritual people do not, for feeling that protection is only defensive. But protection is also like offering shelter from the storm. Your concern for your friends to have housing was real and appropriate. Protection is a "looking after," a way people know that they are cared for. Protection saves from harm. To categorically claim that no defense or protection are needed is a remnant of the patriarchy. Your brother's voice, when he speaks of this, is directed exclusively at the ego.

Many actions are defensible and justified, rather than "defensive." Defensiveness, I agree, is resistant. But even resistance is, at times, necessary. Be wary of those who assure you there is never any cause for it.

Most often, when you, Mari, feel self-protective, you are, at the same time, feeling protective of the revolutionary change that began to land in you with "A Treatise on the New." Don't forget that your Jesus asked you to remove yourself from all else to receive this treatise, or that you, yourself, knew to take yourself away for "The Dialogues." The ending of the book can be truly read as contradicting the beginning in many instances. Those stuck in the beginning cannot see the end they are called to.

The end of A Course of Love "is" a contradiction of the ego, and of one's former ideas about oneself—those that were a negation of the truth. Yet these ideas have to be worked through before the "former" can be relegated forever to the "former," and the "here" of the present knowing, rise to ascendance. It may happen many times. Maybe many times in one day. But it will happen.

M

VULNERABILITY

It's 7 a.m. exactly on Wyoming Street in St. Paul. I am still at Mary Love's. It grew warmer in here yesterday and I just opened the back door to let in the breeze and fresh air. Lovely.

Yesterday, while Kate and Rick were with me in the cabin, Christie came and was her marvelous self as she shared with us.

Later, I went back to the East Side to see Kate and Rick off. We had already said our goodbyes through the windows of my old Buick, and they were walking away, when, with my hands on the steering wheel, my phone, which was sitting in the front pocket of my purse on the passenger seat, started blasting the song "Stranded" by Van Morrison (a favorite of mine). I rolled down the window and bid them to come over because I was so startled. But the words didn't really fit our mood and I soon departed. Then the next song was Eric Clapton's "Running on Faith," with the lyrics "Love comes over you." I thought it could be that we "were" stranded . . . and then, running on sheer faith, "Love came over us." The lyrics of both were more than the titles . . . and simply perfect.

I wouldn't have thought much of it if it hadn't been for the way the phone came on of its own.

Tonight, I will go home, and tomorrow Henry will graduate from middle school, and it will be a total family day, I am sure, and I'll be present and get updated on what's occurred since I left, and the influx of regular life will begin and maybe feel good, and maybe not.

Family life is somewhat natural out of habit, but this is no longer the norm and I can hardly wait for the "natural" of my quieter life to return. If that is selfish—then it is. (There's another thing we could speak of, Mary. The idea so many of us women have that taking care of ourselves is selfish!) I simply desire the return of what is natural to "me" and my time of life: living alone with my husband, not having too much family drama or too many expectations. This has to be "my" time, to be "our" time, doesn't it?

All of your feelings are tied here—as they've been for a long while.

For two decades you felt acute feelings concerning A Course of Love, *and for many years' acute feelings with your daughters and their children, especially Henry. You felt such feelings in a small way with Kate and Rick. You knew Kate was vulnerable and hoped to provide a safe place for her. Yet, sometimes you want to say, "What about me?"*

And sometimes you want to say, "Let me be," as if the power is in the hands of another rather than yourself.

Yes.

This is your "others" orientation. You know this, don't you?

Yes.

And you want to let it go.

Yes.

And you see that you have, but you haven't yet conveyed this to your whole being. Wholeness is about the whole Being. In your colloquialism, wholeness means your "whole being" is "on the same page." Your whole being is not yet on the same page, my daughter, and it is so for many.

Those whose Being is fully "whole" are comfortable within themselves. These are most often "ordinary" people you know to trust completely, and you felt this with Kate. She didn't have to be perfect or have the circumstances be smooth because she has this quality. Christina has it too. And because they do, both of these women find it difficult that they are not "seen" as also being vulnerable. Kate loved that you acknowledged her vulnerability. Christina often grieves that you do not acknowledge hers. And yet, here you are, feeling bad for showing your vulnerability, while those who do not show it, wish nothing more than for it to be seen.

And so, let me remind you how often you totally hid your own. Being unable to keep it hidden now is a step forward. We are done with looking at vulnerability as weakness or straightforwardness as strength. We feel each situation as it is. Your inability to keep your vulnerability hidden emerged from a time when you were confounded by your own and your daughter's conflicting needs. It is so for many mothers and daughters.

But, Mari, there is a completion that you have lacked, one that is still coming into being and that, when it does, will prevent you from the self-betrayal that it is to "go-along." You, in your kindness (at times) and muteness (at other times) get caught in going along, and in the repercussions (at times major repercussions), of having done so.

As your Jesus has told you, all these times of "going along" cause, is delay. They are not the end of the world. They are not lethal failings. But they do cause delay, and with the urgency of the time and your own true desires, it would be best that this not continue, correct?

Yes.

M

WHAT IF IT IS COMPLETE?

JUNE 29, 2019

Saturday. Henry is done with school. He and Ang and his friend Caleb spent a whole day at a water park hotel yesterday. I was alone all day. I spent the morning writing mostly dribble. I felt exhausted and still feel exhausted.

But Christina and I talked briefly. She said these words:

"What if it is complete?"

She was speaking of *A Course of Love*. She was also the one who asked, at the last conference, the question that spread and changed things: *Do we need to be here?* She is being a forerunner of the new. Thank you so much for her, Lord and Mother.

M

LISTENING

How quickly it has become seven o'clock, and it is 7:00 straight up. I have already experienced the way the sky becomes hazier as day comes, for it being neither night nor day. The hovering in between. That's me. That's the feeling: between realms.

Doesn't the sky seem so to you, as well, my Mari? A standing between heaven and earth, itself a plentitude with its sunlight and its delivery of the dark and the rain.

Yes! The dark and the light, the togetherness of them. We raise our eyes to the sky and call it the heavens. But it's the dual nature of dark and light that hold me. It seems the way everything might naturally be . . . like noise and quiet. Talking and listening. There don't seem to be very many good listeners, and I've wondered, sometimes, if I am one. Most of the time—yes.

I thought of the word "heed" in regard to what Christina said. That is still with me.

But I also think of listening with writing. When I get something from my writer friend Michael Mark,* it has to be listened to. That is so precious. And it can escape you at first. When we write each other, we both usually combine some kind of background about work or family or even information, as of a meeting, but his writing almost always comes with this glorious sort of speaking that must be "listened" to as well as read. It's all mixed up—which is part of its beauty.

But I know there are some who will not be able to listen to our

---

* Michael Mark, author of the blog *Embracing Forever.*

writing or see its beauty because it holds so much of this mix of things.

I got to thinking of it because of an old "friend" who thought he was in love with me but couldn't for a minute "*listen*" to me . . . and so couldn't hear. He wanted to "join" with me on another level of consciousness without knowing me at all—without all my human mess.

Such people would not have made good disciples, would they, Mary?

They may have enjoyed Yeshua's preaching. . . but still held it apart from the manner in which he lived his life, and the way they lived their own lives, and thus missed what his "life" asked of his companions—of those who loved him. Love was central, but not separate from its demands.

Many, hanging around the edges, had breakthroughs in which they heard what he was saying, but still did not listen. To listen is to heed what is heard.   ✴ ✴ ✴

There are many ways of coming to know. Listening is one. When you listen, you are held within an experience of value: something of significance is given and received. That is true listening. With listening, what you hear lives in you, and begins to unveil another to you and you to yourself. With listening, you are not separate from what you hear. There is a disclosure, one to another that speaks with you of truth, and you begin to relate to what is heard internally as well as in dialogue.

But many hear without listening. Your spiritual and religious communities often do this, by ignoring or dismissing unethical behavior in their leaders. Unethical behavior doesn't mean a person isn't hearing, but it does mean they are not listening.

Listening is an Act of Love that attends to the one being

heard. It is to heed another's words and all that is conveyed within them. Listening with care keeps and protects what is revealed, and allows it to grow within your singularity, and together in what you once called "twoness."* It is felt knowing that expands and connects you intimately.

You worry about your memory of words spoken, but when you listen and attend to what is being said, you have taken in what may not be readily retrieved. What you have heeded travels deep within you, interacting with you in a profound manner, like food being processed internally by each, even as you share of the same bread. Within you is where a "shared" knowing becomes part of you through the alchemy of its interaction with you. It is not yours alone, but it is also yours. It is the same but different. It bears your mark. Each one bears the mark of their own knowing.

How many of your dialogues with Mary Love have you wished you had captured? You wish you had every word recorded because what came of you—together—was spectacular. It feels as if, in the totality of your words, something miraculous was conveyed one to another. But you do not remember. Later, what you shared may come forth from each of you in your own ways.

This is the way of Memoria.

"We speak the way we do not to form new thoughts but to paint

---

* "Twoness" is a term I used in *Creation of the New*

new pictures, not to plot new maps but to stimulate vision—the vision of the heart. We join the listening ear to the seeing eye."*

M

---

* "Mirari," p. 87

JULY 1, 2019

I walked outside under an umbrella. I'm so thankful to be here in a light rain under somber skies and a kaleidoscope of turning leaves and limbs creating ever new scenes. They are there, even against the fence, especially with my glasses off.

I want to bring my own self into some greater clarity. I'm thinking about it because of attending the conference. What "I" want to say. What matters to "me." And I feel mute.

What if it really is complete? Over? Behind me?

M

JULY 4, 2019

Dear Holy One,

At 6:45 a.m. on this day of "Independence" in the United States, I have been reviewing my notes for the upcoming presentation for over an hour, and I do not feel natural, unless my natural state is one of desire, always, for more inspiration than I feel! I feel just overbearingly affected by this desire, especially when I'm expecting myself to have things to say in my "Course" life. The pressure drives "it"—my "naturalness" I suppose you would say—away.

I felt it affect Mary Love yesterday, too. As we "just talked," all was a flow. As soon as we began to batten down our upcoming presentation, to speak of how and when we would manifest, the pressure began. In a way, it is comforting to see it affect her. I am not feeling as judgmental of how I've felt these years, simply because one other person now knows what it is like, and I can see how it affects her with my own eyes. It is the fall from passion to pressure. How, oh Holy One, can this be prevented?

What have you seen, my daughter?

Other than that I do not want a pressured life?

No. That is enough. I would say that all you do not want has an element of this pressure in it. Is that correct?

Yes.

You feel that, as I begin to speak of Acts, there will only be more pressure.

I know! I dread more pressure.

What if the New Acts are not to be an added pressure?

That would be great.

You need no pressure to shape your diamond?

I almost don't care if I remain in the rough! I do not want to live out my life under the duress of "things that need doing," even if they are important. I thought having Mary Love join me would rid me of this pressurized feeling. That we would enjoy it. But the feeling is still there, and now, it is with both of us.

What a wonderful bonus that you have expressed this into the beginning of our time on this crucial subject of Acts. You are all so tired of your planned and scheduled lives, but are convinced that without plans and schedules, you will not have a place in the world. Yet this world into which you schedule yourself is the world of time as it has been, time that boxes you in rather than frees you.

Do you want to free yourself?

Oh, so much!

You could do this, but you don't. Why is that?

I feel, in one way, it is for not having fully found my voice, not having brought what I've come to know into my whole being (as you say). In another, it is for my difficulty with decisions. When asked, I must choose. Once I agree to do things, they become obligations. And there are requirements.

What if I tell you that the new way of Acts are choiceless ways of inaction?

Oh, Mary, that sounds so good!

I know we spoke earlier of the power of choice, but once you embrace the Act of Choice, you will often find that choice melts away. It becomes immaterial. You will know.

We are speaking of New Acts, and these are not acts of evangelizing or structuring. How could such actions be new? No. These are the very inner acts that you consider inactive. These are the unscheduled, unscripted acts of The New, the creative inspiration of The New. The very Acts you have so desired and denied yourself—as have many. You desire the private while you yield to the public, seeing the private in a non-productive way, as if you are here to produce. Are you brave enough, my daughter, to deny the public?

I had to pause after that question, as you surely know. I went in and made brownies for later, and, after cleanup, will return in mere minutes to get them out of the oven. My answer felt as if it would be automatic, but it was not. I think it will be hard to decline the upcoming 2020 conference, even while the very sound of "2020" makes me pause.

Holy One, it seems that when it comes time to choose, I suddenly become uncertain of what, before, I was certain.

Yes! As you sit quietly with our work, you have no need to choose, do you?

No.

It is blessedly liberating, is it not?

Yes, it is.

You've been raised to believe that freedom is about choice: the freedom to choose. I know your perplexity about this, and that you look for its cause. Here, I must speak to you about this, and ask you to consider choice newly.

Why do you cherish your quiet life at home and keep it one in which the choices are minimal? Because choices easily become tyrannical in your "thinking" of them, which is the pressure. If you knew for sure, it would not be so. And yet you remain unsure. Correct?

Yes.

At times you fault yourself terribly for this indecision. Even when you do not, you carry the pressure, sometimes for months. This is a great unkindness to yourself and a disservice to The New, of which, at this time, you are being made aware. When choices arise, all you wish for is time to be rolled back to when there was no decision before you. This is the depth of your antipathy for decision-making.

If you "knew," it would be easy, wouldn't it?

Most of the time? Yes. And the only reason I say "most of the time" is that feelings of friendship or gratitude cause me to feel, in a way that also feels "right," that the request is a return giving that is not to be denied. A completion of a giving and receiving loop.

But you might admit that the "giving" you most often respond to, as if you need to "return the favor," is for the most part a giving you have already done! Must you feel indebted forever to those who gave you a start, who helped you, when you and A Course of Love were unknown, to increase awareness of it?

I do feel forever indebted. That's how important it was at the time.

Does it have the same importance now?

Increasing awareness does, yes, but I will admit that the means of increasing awareness feel different than these ways that were first offered and have been offered again.

There you go! The true way will suit "you." And what suits you, will suit the work, and the "time" of the work coming into being newly, freely, and vibrantly. Time is changing very quickly now, and with it, the means of knowing and making known. And so, what must change with it, is your response, which at present is one that you label "uncertain" although it is not.

What is this hesitancy to say no, no matter the problems this has caused you in the past? How will you, and your sisters and brothers who are like you, fare in a new time in which "no" must be said to the old that a "yes" to The New may arise? You have your own struggles, and you have watched many more struggle in ways you have not, with this "no" to the old.

Yet I know your heart, and your wishes and dreams . . . and so do you. What you desire has nothing to do with anything you can calculate, and never did. What are often called "choices" are really calculations that would weigh and measure cause and effect. But you do not "naturally" calculate. No one does this "naturally." Such calculations are not natural to your innate ability to know. Everything you look at in this limited way is limiting you.

If you no longer want to live in the tyranny of choice, you need simply keep yourself available to The New, and live, rather, for the opposite . . . for your liberation.

M

The Whole and the Parts

What a great dialogue that was for "Independence Day." It was the same last year, I believe. I was doing the audio of "The Dialogues," and the next to be recorded was Chapter 4, the one in which Jesus spoke of how prison-like our lives have become. It was a reading for which I was exceptionally grateful.

Yet I am not out of my prison. I'm sorry, Mary, but I do not understand why this is so hard for me. I have a few things that I need to set right, one of which is saying no to the event we spoke of earlier, and the other is speaking with a person I feel is misleading readers of *A Course of Love*.

The question is particularly stinging as we are in the midst of an election in which women* are raising their voices in a way that I am so appreciative of! But when I think of tackling these two situations, and the time and energy it will likely take, I am anything but eager. A "part" of me wants to let it go. Another part of me feels bound to bring the situations to completion, knowing that they won't let go of me until I let go of them.

Since you feel bound to continue your struggle with this, let me call you to see that your recognition of "parts" is a recognition of the culprit. Instead of considering parts, let's speak of your "whole being."

Thank you. If we could clear this up it would be the greatest thing ever. It is exactly what "detains" me, over and over again.

It is the same for many. Let me posit that it is a matter of

---

* Those running for president.

self-protection that goes along with your feeling of being oppressed by busyness. You can address these "problems" one-by-one, you can let go, or you can step up your efforts to express the new way. These appear to be your options, correct?

Yes. That's about right. That or do nothing.

Oh, so the option to do nothing, exists?

It exists—yes. But it feels wrong somehow.

So you feel a sense of responsibility. Is it possible that this writing that we are doing may correct some of these false assumptions about the way to proceed?

I am not sure, Holy One. The old way feels so entrenched, even in me.

How, as the carrier of a new vision, which I say by way of it being an uncomfortable truth at the moment, can you release yourself and your beloved Course readers from being "handled" in the way that some would encourage? How do you prevent "yourself" from being handled? How do you "discourage" those whom you see as undermining the new way?

You do not know, and so you feel yourself to be caught in a double bind.

What if you were to just respond in the moment as you see fit and then release it. What you've said will be heard or it will not. What would that feel like?

Hard. Ineffectual. Tiring. Irritating. With a small chance of being liberating.

Can anyone, earthly or human, release you of these ideas until you are ready? Are you still not ready?

I am still uncertain.

You but "think" you are uncertain.

Oh, my mother, if this were hypothetical, I would agree with you in a heartbeat. But it is not. It is real. Real people have been hurt and, maybe incorrectly, I offered to make it right.

Your concern is for people in relationship to each other and your Course of Love?

Yes.

Then I bring you your brother's words: You "were created through union and relationship. Can you now turn your reproductive instincts toward the production and reproduction of relationship and union?"*

M

JULY 8, 2019

I keep feeling that my time with Kate represented an ending and am wondering if I am to vacate the family premises for this problematic time, or if it is my "Course life" that is moving toward an ending of some kind.

What is ending, my dear Jesus and Mary?

The "old" my sister, and your time of not remembering that you are in The New and a voice for The New. A time of your lack of remembrance that you are a herald to, and of, this new time that you have now "entered." A time that will draw forth New Acts.

I feel you missing me, as I miss you. Your exchange with Lee† yesterday was a dear one that reminded you of how we used to be when it was you and I, rather than you and

---

* ACOL T4:2.5-6

† Lee Flynn, friend and ACIM scholar

my Mother, working together. It is a beautiful way, though, for you to see and be totally certain of, the distinct voices of those of us who are guiding the way into The New.

I welcome all of creation and time outside of time, Jesus.

You are not a wanderer, Mari. You are not bred for it. You can walk new paths from time to time, make little side-trips as are needed or warranted. You can let yourself be as embraced by other places as you are by the cabin, but you are not a wanderer.

You have work that feels like a job, and creative work that is a vocation, and creative work that is your lifeline to yourself—your self-expression. You are embraced by essential relationships that further your movement and our way into The New. Nothing is accidental to your coming to voice.

I know it still feels like a long and harrowing road, but only because you have not realized what you have found! My sister, you *are* In Voice! And your experiences of being in voice are joyous. Where do you need to be to realize that this is so? For you do need to realize that this is so. I will help you. Do not worry. Do not worry my sister!

M

If You Want Something Enough

JULY 13, 2019

Well, Mary, there was a "spot" of wonder in a different area of my life. It happened in a place called West Side Flats, where I could envision Angela happy, and I knew she could vision herself so too. It is a new "smart" building, with a view of downtown and a coffee shop below. There was something elegantly simple about it. It was a place for which she could possibly get assistance, but it would take time. She would be on a list.

Then we went to see a place she could afford, and it was like hell. Dirty and smelly and common. Angie is a poor woman with refined tastes. And a woman who needs order.

The hellish apartment was near Henry's new school, but a beastly drive from my home. To think of making it every day! To make it in the winter! To spend hours each day fighting traffic. If something went wrong and we couldn't get to them . . .

The thing about the beauty of West Side Flats isn't that it is doable, but that it could be. If she wanted it enough, she might get a job and do everything in her power to keep it. Sometimes you just have to want something enough . . . as I want my own quiet life back enough that I may be able to see the way for me.

Imagining a quiet life "on the ground" makes me happy. And I can feel the ways in which I am like Angela that are not a sickness in either of us. They are natural longings for grace and order, and for life not to be so hard. Even a sense that it could be in our power to make it so is potent.

This "sense of it" is the quickening. Without a "sense of it," the imagining that would bring it into being is not enlivened. I am in joy along with you, that we, together, have come upon a way to express this feeling of hope that can be sensed, as a hope that can be manifested. This, too, is the beginning of new life.

$\mathcal{M}$

JULY 16, 2019

I was reading, today, in "Mirari," and taking in the way it was before my life became this dance of co-dependence or whatever it is. This dance of change. Our writing was more poetic than it is now. I pray, my mother and brother, to hear your poetry in the New Acts too, the poetry that moves us from where we were to where we are.

I declined the invite to the conference today. I knew, as I did it, that I was ending the way things have been. I was honest in my decline. I needed to be honest and state my feelings for "myself," because it is then Me, along with You, choosing THE WAY THAT IS OPEN BEFORE ME.

The way is open! Yet I can't "hear" from you much as I'm preparing for this other conference I committed to long ago. It's just not in me to split myself in that way.

But I know now. I can't give up "this" for "that." And the very air has opened itself to me!

If you want something enough . . . you do see, and you do protect the space it needs to come to be!

$\mathcal{M}$

JULY 18, 2019

This morning . . . a storm and a shiny full moon. Woken by a buzz that didn't feel right, I got up at 4:30 to investigate. I discovered quickly that it was loudest toward the back side of the house. Then that the sound wasn't coming from downstairs. I came back upstairs. Somewhat satisfied that the noise was external, and the house wasn't about to blow up, and with the storm calmed while I readied myself, I took a walk in her (the storm's) absence. It was beautiful to hear the morning birds.

To hear the songbirds sing.

I missed most of the dark in this way and it is light, even on the ground at 5:37 in the cabin, but still with the hint of the storm, the full moon, the weight of plentitude, moist and seeping into the ground.

Like me. I'm here with plentitude seeping in.

Christie came by and we talked of the dark night of the soul. I believe it is a new incarnation of who we are.

Mary came too, for a little while, home early from camping. She brought me rocks.

When she left, I read from "Mirari," finding it's ending very full.

"*Tread, my dear one, gently with these words that have been spoken one heart to one heart. If you let them be such to you, you will begin to allow for the natural once again, and to be in joy with what will flow forth as you rise to your true nature. You will begin to see that which effortlessly extends from your newly placed devotion 'to' your nature.*" *

Notice that, in A Course of Love, *Jesus asked this feminine receiving of all and said that those of the way of Mary are called*

---

* "Mirari," p. 275

to "*being what they are asked to become.*" *He called this an act of incarnation and revealed it as the new pattern.**

Later, I could smell something good from the kitchen and, finding tomato sauce and meatballs on the stove, got out the thin spaghetti and we sat down and ate as a family and all felt righted.

The way is open.

$\mathcal{M}$

---

* ACOL D:Day19.10

Acts of Creation:
WHAT YOU CREATE YOU KNOW

JULY 27, 2019

Morning. Another of the same! Gloom, a word I love!

Gloom, gloom, gloom. An hour of jumbled bird calls, five at least, in sporadic unison. A crescent moon seen on my walk. I feel a lessening, somehow, of some . . . thing: heavy, unnamable, unseen. A lightening, a hope.

I read from Joyce Carol Oates's journal:

"There is art only for its own sake. What is done for the sake of something else may be skillful, professional, extremely interesting . . . but it isn't art. And it won't satisfy, in the creator, the hunger for art's creation."*

This is so like what we've been talking about. Creating isn't a choice of this or that, it's a feast.

And then a sharing from Lee, Lesson 186 from ACIM:† "His gentle Voice is calling from the known to the unknowing."

Good morning, Mary...

Good morning, my writer friend, Mari. Now we create that which will unite the masculine and feminine in our passionate push to give birth to The New. It will take all your creative passion and that of many. It will be a movement.

Creation of The New will be a movement to all that is created

---

* *The Journal of Joyce Carol Oates 1973-1982*, p. 288.

† "Salvation of the world depends on me." *A Course in Miracles* WI-186.13:1

being life giving, and none of what is created being life annihilating. This is the Act of Incarnation, the "giving" of new life.

There will come now, "a knowing," that what you create is not separate from you. What you create you know, and what you know, you live. It is the way of creation. Each one's own creation expands the life of the living Holy One, whose way of creating is knowing, and whose way of knowing is creating. In the new time, the time that is both here and coming, there will no longer be anyone who wants to live with what they create to destroy.

"It is extremely important for you to realize that God's work takes place outside of time, as do all acts of true service or creation."*

"The very word 'remember,' as well as the concept of memory, implies mindfulness and the ability to reproduce or recall both what has been learned and what has been previously experienced. This reproducing and recollecting are acts of creation."†

"Those of the way of Mary 'become who they are to be through their acts of creation.'"‡

"Now is the time to truly begin to 'hear' my voice in every aspect of creation and to respond with your own voice in all of your own acts of creation. It is time to realize that you are a creator."§

$$\mathcal{M}$$

---

* ACOL C:29.12

† ACOL T1:1.4

‡ ACOL D:Day19.4

§ ACOL A:38

ACTS OF LOVE

You might see the Bible much as you would a history book if not for the places where love and its Acts are revealed, if not for the places where the names and the words recorded what occurred in relationship—in story. There are, in tales of history, war, rebellion, movements, those who take them beyond the facts. These are not the recorders of fact alone, but those who share personal accounts, who delve into the possible, who imagine what might have been felt, or uncover what was revealed in personal ways— as of letters or journals. There are also those who dare say what is not recorded as factual or "revealed" truth, who extrapolate, who weave and connect. Those who employ metaphor and poetry. These dear souls are due much honor, especially those who reveal the inner lives of those carrying out the acts.

What was not allowed in the time in which I lived, even despite its miraculous nature and Yeshua's presence, was the voice of the inner world that created the outer circumstance. Where was the inner "feeling" of the life of the person given voice? Only in a few words here and there was inner revelation of the person given outward expression. How many do not cling to these?

"Jesus wept."

We write in this way for the "inner" revelation of one person . . . you, and in this way, we invite each to their own revealing. This Act is exceptionally important now. It is how each person who reads our words will come to their own "inner" revelation. This is how people will "relate" in The New. They will relate and create in relationship with what is "personally" revealed. This is how we show the connection, the sympathetic understanding between the human and divine.

Yeshua cared about people, and had particular love relationships, as do you—love relationships that were distinct, person-to-person.

Love is "in" relationship, and that relationship has about it a quality of movement. It is that which moves the "action" along. Love is that which is at one with being and expression. Movement is what causes being and expression to manifest, to become visible and observable in the world as Acts.

Your "expression" is paramount within the New Acts. And this means... feeling. "Being," when opening to deep impressions, "reveals" feelings, even those that seem of little consequence.

Many, now as then, go through life with such barriers to deep feelings that they do not allow passion to arise. Passions are fought, and Jesus fought them as well. Much of my own inner life was comprised of an interior dialogue of prayer and reflection on "in what way" I could share the deep feelings that coursed through me. I understand you, Mari, in this way.

And, like any mother, I worried (as do you). Like any mother, I wanted to spare my son suffering. But unlike many other mothers I knew there was a divine orchestration going on. Oh, the confusion of it all. What I knew and what I felt, were confounding by nature.

As still happens in current time, we of deep sensitivity hold these feelings close while we go about tending to the things required in life, including those things required of these same deep feelings that we can't express, and yet that demand to be expressed lest they strangle us. You have felt this, and still do at times. Each one *will feel this way from time to time unless they have deadened depth entirely.*

Deadened depth is life lived on the surface and the source of all such acts of "going along" as have brought the world near to destruction, decimated populations and forests, plundered the earth, caused great migrations, created martyrs and mad men, and influenced evolution into your very time—for time is a continuum.

The way we bring forth here is a means to disconnect from this continuum, and to begin the movement, being, and expression of The New. This is done not by returning to old ways of reaction, but by going ever deeper into true feeling—expanded feelings—and giving our response to them.

My mother, I, who do not express my feelings well, feel saddened by the way that I first turn to all else, even with all the encouragement I have had. I seem to have a time-delay with feelings, as if they only occur . . . later, when it is too late to speak. And I feel as if I may have less compassion than I once did.

I wonder sometimes if it is age. I remember my dad less and less, yet I grieved him for three years. My mother not so much.

I do not expect you to answer this for me, but I am unsure of myself in this area. While I feel passionately about *A Course of Love* and our work together, I am not sure I know love in the selfless way I once did. I want, now, to love myself, and to hold myself in high regard. Yes, it seems to fly in the face of love for others. It makes me want to cry, as if I have grown callous for no reason, especially when the work does not call me to enthusiasm for spreading its message. I just want to stand in the background, hearing you in your Act of Speaking, ensuring the integrity of all Jesus spoke to me, waiting for the world to find it in as pure a state as it can be. I do not want to stay busy with things that have no ultimate value. This busyness feels like shortchanging myself. And it seems as if it is because this "receiving" is "all" I want to do, unless you count living, also, a peaceful and creative life.

In other words, I continue to feel such a great desire to escape the mess of complex feelings and situations that call for "needed actions" and must wonder if this is an escape also from the deep feelings that are almost too hidden to find the light of day. Because these feelings, of which the desire for peace is the greatest, along with freedom, seem to be the great desire of escape. It seems that, due to my time-delay with both feeling and expression, I stay with the complexity and don't reach either (peace or freedom). I continue to "feel" that I have no freedom of choice, even when I know this is not true. And so, I see patterns endlessly repeating.

I am a nice person. I do see that. It is gratifying to have others see that, and to have them love our work together. I just want . . . more.

As you should, my daughter—first from your Self!

There is a balance in what is needed to reveal what you reveal, and to tend to matters that often feel "lesser" and, in this time, confusing. You ask yourself so often what is "right" to do. It is in this way that you bypass feelings. Do you see this?

Yes. At least a little. It's not that the feelings go away though. It's that they remain muddled. This is what concerns me. I keep awaiting the kind of knowing that will let me feel "certain," and it doesn't come, particularly for myself.

Yet, I have had a revelation, odd in its way of coming (or coming back), which has to do with my time owning the coffee shop and working in it while in the midst of receiving much of *A Course of Love*. I was kept busy, I have come to believe, so that I wouldn't think too much. I feel this sometimes as I go about the "need to do" things of life, such as cleaning, released from thought. Especially those thoughts of the type I've had today, of which I feel a bit embarrassed. But when you couple this with my mind's new "incapacity," with the doing that requires more than cleaning, the tedium of certain mental tasks, and the sense that these things are no longer mine to do, then the sense that life ought to be easier is strong.

And what happens next, is I remember you, and your hard life, and realize mine is a cakewalk in comparison and feel as if I am just complaining.

Yes, your odd revelation is that you "think too much" and the busyness of your time with the coffee shop helped to prevent you from over-thinking. Now it is dialogue more than "work" that relocates you. Dialogue takes you from brooding mind into wholehearted sharing, which is creative. And in this, I want to remind you of the way that, as you shared your history with your new friends, you have seen "in retrospect" what you could not see in the time in which it occurred: what you call your time-delay. While this made your life far harder than it needed to be in the time of its unfolding, seeing it now is a marvel of this time and of your connection to Kate.

What you remembered as you spoke nonchalantly, just speaking of the course of your life with Jesus, was the courage you displayed . . . if belatedly. Do you know why your response was late in coming?

Because I thought too much? Trying to figure out what to do— while still being considerate of others?

Ah, there you have come upon the culprit, which is once again the "others orientation," often expressed as your gratitude (or over-gratitude) for assistance, or encouragement, and your fear of acting on what "you" know, but about which there is not "agreement." Oh, how courageous you were to move beyond this—even if you see it as belated, and not totally in the past. You are perfect in all these ways, for many, women especially, face these same issues, including the issue of self-regard.

This relates to your desire, to your knowing, that you must now regard yourself highly, even "first," where and whenever this regard can be given without direct consequence to an innocent other, such as Henry. This does not yet feel natural, but it is to become so. You do not have to worry about a single adult. I mean this. The worry is not necessary and so is a waste of time that keeps you from the very self-regard you truly are in need of possessing. I am affirming you so that you can affirm yourself.

Hold your head high and your heart higher!

M

$\mathcal{A}$CTS FROM A COURSE OF LOVE

Creation

" 'Listen and you will hear.' But to what are you listening? Entering the dialogue is akin to residing in the present moment and to hearing all that is being spoken in all the ways it is being spoken. Now is the time to truly begin to 'hear' my voice in every aspect of creation and to respond with your own voice in all of your own acts of creation. It is time to realize that you are a creator."*

Acceptance

"[O]ne of your first acts of acceptance is the acceptance of the end of the conditions of learning."†

Cooperation

"Miracles are expressions of love. You might think of them as acts of cooperation. Holiness cannot be contained, and it is not within your power to limit it. To feel the holiness of the embrace is to release its power."‡

Prayer

"We have spoken already of memory here and have presented the acts of reproducing and recollecting that are involved with memory as acts of creation. Prayer is but reproducing and recollecting a di-

---

* ACOL A:38

† ACOL D:3.6

‡ ACOL C:20.29

vine memory and divine memory cannot help but produce a divine outcome."*

M

---

* ACOL T2:6.2

$\mathcal{A}$CT OF TURNING TO THE HEART

More revelations and welling tears, and tears shed in bed last night after Angie made the case that moving out isn't a good idea. If she goes and can't pay the rent two months later, what then? It was a realistic question. But it made my heart stop . . . for her and for me.

Later, reviewing the archives for a point I'm clearing-up within myself, I see this message from Jesus. I print it out and bring it to bed with me. It is from twenty years ago!

$\mathcal{M}$

AUGUST 21, 2000

The need for response is yours. Now . . . how do you respond newly . . . both to needs and to things that you feel are part of who you are, and necessary to who you are, and to what you would achieve?

You bring them to your heart where truth and illusion are separated in relationship with me. This return to your heart, this ACT of consciously turning to your heart, to me, to the self joined in unity rather than the self in separation, is the new way. This is where you are taken care of and your needs immediately met.

I AM the relationship where your needs are met. I AM the relationship in which you are never alone. I AM the relationship in which you are never alone because I exist within you and you are never alone, never without me, never without the all-encompassing relationship that is both within and without, binding you to all living things and to your own Self and our Father. We are one in that relationship and so are all others with whom you would hope to give and receive love.

I AM in you and them and between you and them, the connecting lines of the web, and the center of the web, and the web itself. So are you. You are not the spider who sets the web to get your dinner. The ego would but tell you that you are. That you sit at the center of the web and draw to you what fulfills your hunger. This is what this contemplation of needs is doing to you. ...

You are not alone, and you know this. You have been looking for this writing and yet you carry this writing in your heart.

(I had a vision, while still working at the university, of standing before a crowd saying, "You are not alone, and you know this." I later wrote a long recitation that had "You are not alone, and you know this," following each of my other observations, but I have been unable to find it.)

M

"You are not alone, and you know this."

℘ERSONAL AND UNIVERSAL

I've just come to sit on the couch. It is July. I wonder if the light that drives me from the window is why I can only see myself sitting on this cabin couch writing *Creation of the New*.* It was about this time of year. Angie was pregnant and living in the basement.

Thirteen years ago.

I can't imagine how I would have felt then, if I could have seen myself in this place, thirteen years in the future. I have already lived with children or grandchildren for forty years of my life.

But here I am. And I turn to you, my Mother. I am giving what I can to offer temporary refuge, and this I am content to do. But more would not be right. This time, I know that, and will do my best to act on what I know. Still, I must bring my heart's condition to you as I view this situation.

We are to go on a summer outing—just three hours from now.

Dust motes float in the air, the very air that Kate, Rick, and Christie so recently graced with love and optimism.

I feel a little dejected due to Jesus' nearly twenty-year-old message.

My daughter, I'm glad you have come to me. It was a beautiful message, but men are "big picture" thinkers, especially those with a mission. And it is a good counterpart—the masculine way—to the feminine, as is the feminine to the masculine. Which isn't what you want to hear right now, and I apologize for beginning in this way.

No. It helps. Thank you. I know Donny doesn't understand the

---

* Published in 2011 by Course of Love Publications.

feeling of being "the woman of the house," the setter of its tone, of having my own space in which I can find my way, and in which I have the right to invite or not invite others "in." He's off each day now, and I get so overwhelmed by the presence of people, the talk of divorce, the noise, as filled the house yesterday. It exhausts me.

All the great truths that prevail in quiet get jumbled in the noise of activity and dramatic utterances. It was so for me and many in my time too. Then, we put one foot in front of the other, which was the way of our migration. We had to carry on to live. We had to carry on to survive. We had to carry on to protect and feed the children who Yeshua so loved to see being carefree and happy.

You must feel as if we have come a long way from that picture of wonder we were painting before life took this turn for you.

Yet we have come a long way, and our new migration is proceeding. There is no "expectation" in me as you see it and was never any in Yeshua. You, and those of your time, foresee with expectation, which comes of the mainly peaceful, routine lives you live in stability. In other parts of the world, such expectations are no more usual than they were in my time, and expectations are an impediment to Mirari and the New Acts.

There are those, many of whom you hold dear and admire greatly, who would rally the forces to attend to each situation, dispatching them with efficiency. They are the doers of the actions that are passing, and that you will come to miss . . . for a while. You will miss them until you realize efficiency is a replacement for wonder. Until you invite the New Acts.

Last night your heart not only saw in practicality, but was a mother's heart, and a grandmother's heart, and a personal, self-protective heart. You saw with a weary heart and one that yet carries a mission and a vision of The New. Personal and universal. Particular and all-encompassing. All of it was there in you. And with this you can see no way "out." This is what stops you. You look for a way "out" rather than in—into the heart of the matter at rest. At rest in you. Gestating.

The self-protective heart is not new to you, but Acts of Self-Protection are. You have inquired about feeling "selfish" when you look out for yourself, as you imagine that many women have, based upon the conversations and confidences you have heard throughout your life. You see selfishness as being overly concerned for your own life. Yet you cannot think of one woman who, having a choice between harm coming to them and someone dear to them, wouldn't sacrifice themselves. In the crises that present as emergencies, most men are the same.

But in this instance, you blame yourself a bit for the emergence of this situation with your daughter. You feel you sheltered her overly long and have a role to play in her dependency. Angela was the baby you almost lost and she grew in a manner that you considered frail, and in this way, you favored her, and you fear your favor hampered her in becoming independent.

But you want this for her now, so much! It is a sign that "you" are no longer co-dependent and, as with many other changes that occur within, this is one of those that many will be slow to recognize. Inner recognition is going to come faster and faster now. Remember, your mother heart is now called to be wise. It is not only wanting your daughter to be independent of you, but to be independent for the sake of herself and her child.

Let it be. Go about your day now without your "figuring it out" mind. What a gift this is. Some things are not yours to figure out. Go with wonder and invite the New Act. Invite the New Realm. Invite The New Way. Do not dismiss the indwelling of your Christ-self. Carry yourself in the way of the compassionate mother who is also fierce. She leads from the womb that will birth The New.

This is the way you will go out today, through my grace, and you will see, tomorrow, that you return to me with more vision and strength.

I am willing to imagine this will be so. Thank you, Holy One.

Acts of Kindness

Leading from the womb that births and births anew, is leading with kindness.

Becoming who you are is the greatest part of your journey here, and it rests on kindness, a kindness to yourself and all that is in your line of sight at this moment and every moment. In one moment, you notice your children and grandchildren, in another, as it is here, you regard the limbs of your trees and the delicate flight of the birds.

Kindness, one to one another, is the same "natural" Act of Regard, the Act true to your nature.

Kindness to each new babe birthed into The New will be your heart's way of movement.

While kindness will take in the outer world via observance of its beauty, it will be seen in relation to your own beauty. Your eyes will behold and become the conduit of that beauty, for such is the way that beauty actually is. "Beauty is in the eyes of the beholder." This beauty is of your inner sight, and it is through this inner embrace of kindness that the way of "becoming new" will reach its time of beauty. Being kind to yourself is the beginning, and oh, how hard it can be!

You, my Mari, and each one who is as embraced and cherished as are you, have seen how hard it can be to be kind to yourselves, and to find your own loving kindness—such loving compassion as greets the new babe—when it is you!

M

To become is "to come to be." To come into existence. To become who you desire, and are meant, to be. Because you do not desire, no, not any longer do you desire to be anything other than who you are naturally, in your creation, by your Creator. And you were created "in kind" to "be" kind.

Being kind is an agreement with one's own nature. Your kindness is a designation of meaning.

And to be kind, you must also know sorrow. You must also know depth. You must be aware of the kindness of the womb that brings life into being—life that knows sorrow at the sense of loss it is to depart from the womb's soft nest and that senses, yes, from the beginning, life's impending challenges. These challenges are part of life's embrace, and of life's own feminine nature. We are speaking of kindness toward the nature of generation and re-generation of being.*

Kind-heartedness is not separate from beholding, as well, the challenge it is to become, and to witness, the beauty of The New. For a move from "here" to another place that will become the new realm of "here," relies on kindness.

Kindness is becoming.

True becoming is the giving over of oneself to the desire to be one's self, which is the taking on of the breath at birth and the taking on of the mantle of the truth of who you are upon rebirth.

In A Course of Love, your Jesus said, "Becoming the elevated Self of form is becoming whole and will be the way in which source and cause transform body and mind, form and time."†

---

* "Love replaces fear and is life-generating rather than life de-generating. Your bodies will thus regenerate rather than degenerate." ACOL D:Day7.6

† ACOL D:14.17

Transformation becomes transfiguration in the eyes of the Be-holder of the Beloved One. You are called to realize your relation-ship with the Beloved One by beholding your conception from the womb of all Being.

The womb of All Being holds you in the arms of the embrace as you metamorphose, never separating from you.

In the feminine way of Mary, you are held in kindness as the wonder of the birth leads the way. Mirari is the wonder of the birth. The Birth is the New Act. The transformation to new life that is happening. It is a phenomenon that must be beheld, that must be seen.

It is happening and cannot remain unnoticed.

And so now you understand, or begin to understand, the New Acts. The first beholding is of your Self and your own changed state, for it is such transformed eyes that will see The New. And it is from these beholding eyes that the birth will proceed. As wit-nesses of The New behold The New, The New comes into being and is mirrored, one to another.

M

THE TENDER HEARTED AND THE COURAGE OF THE TENDER HEARTED

Yes, my daughter, we will speak of a life situation that has drawn you forward in a way in which you are not comfortable, but that you can find comfort in addressing, even while it does not seem so. No one is comfortable when they consider "confrontation" or "negotiation." There is no need to go there. Stay in relationship.

The situation is one that has arisen between two women in relationship, one of whom you fear has verged upon what you call bullying. And you wonder: is one a victim and one a perpetrator?

Your memory went to your brother's introduction to A Course of Love, *one in which he spoke of the tender-hearted and how the logic of the mind wounds the heart of the most tender. You sit in the cabin in this very moment, listening to the sound of thunder, the first heard on this gloomy day that didn't, until moments ago, begin to present itself as stormy. You just saw a deer move tentatively beneath your arbor . . . a young one, the picture of gentleness. And so, right outside your window, you have had a picture of the gentleness, and of the "logic" of the practical that storms the world with its sound and fury, and wounds the gentlest souls most grievously.**

"This is just the way it is!" they say.

Oh, what a cry of insane logic that is! "This is the way it is! This is the way it will ever be!" This "convenience" as an assertion of truth! This is the truth of the tried and true that saves office

---

* ACOL I:1.3

workers time and that keeps slaves enslaved. It is no different when it is the assertion of truth of one's spiritual thought.

"This is the way it is!"

You listen while the thunder remains distant. You listen for the rain, for the wind, for the tires flapping on the pavement. You listen for me and for your heart and for all hearts. And after all these years you do not "know what to make of it," and are heartened each time you share our work, and another sees and feels with wonder at the words. Mirari.

Your entire life is coming to know "what to make" of what is revealed. What to manifest. What to bring into form and time, and in what way, and by what expression you can live it.

Ah, my dear ones, there is so much in your words you do not see, words such as "knowing what to make of it." To approach this knowing as an "it" that has arrived, as if for your consideration, even when it stands in wholeness as what it is and what it is "to" you, and "in" you, is one-part denial and one-part acceptance. This is the counterpart, the partnership of knowing, the movement of knowing that, with faulty thinking, can make of what "is" a movement of denial.

The truth that you will live . . . is you. You will live your truth, or you will deny your truth. You will live your life as "your" truth, or you will deny truth. All that is, has to be "yours," before you can live it or deny it! Do you see?

And yet it is not a choice, because Truth "arrives" as an Act, an event that takes up residence within. You are in relationship with it because it is there, as it always was, and in your new awareness of it, you are present to it. You do not need to figure *out the truth, or to choose it or reject it. This is Truth's power. It is what is.*

The logical one gets panicked with this and denies the awareness. There is still disorder, there are still unknowns. She feels so vulnerable, and in one who has become familiar with what she sees as the danger of vulnerability, in her panic she lashes out, and the way of lashing out is to "do something." This lessens the panic momentarily but the panic, nor its cause, have been recognized. The mind is held prisoner.

I know this so well that my heart feels heavy with this knowing.

Yes, my Mari, you all experience this. You "all" experience this. You recognize that this is true as I speak of it. Sometimes you recognize it as it happens. Most times, now, if not right away, with only a short delay.

A dog barks down the way, uneasy in the storm that was long in its coming but has now burst into being. There *is* something natural about it all, isn't there? The uneasiness with The New, as for me with the knowing I hold but do not exactly "know" that I know.

You know it as you live it. And this you have often delayed with the instinct to do something about it—about the unease of it.

We speak now of a way of the female of the species and we speak of it alongside the feminine who would recognize cause: love held prisoner to old or new rules, laws, or actions. There is no "should" to come and rule the heart. There is no new prison. There is only an uncomfortable freedom, a freedom more uncomfortable to those who have been considered the "weaker" of the species: the protected, or the used. Those who see that their sweetness has been a liability. Those who feel wrong, or "not smart" to feel the way they do. Those who cover over their tender hearts with protection.

While that which needs release is that which is being protected, the way of Mary will not come to be.

Thus, it is crucial that those with tender hearts be encouraged to see that their tender hearts can lead the way and release other tender hearts from their concealment. It is the revelation, rather than the concealment of tender hearts, that is being enacted by the New Acts.

It is the "protection," the concealment of tender hearts and their wounds, that leaves the way open for the bullies to have their way. The bully and the victim are tied together in a way that makes some believe they are two sides of the same dilemma.

They "become" two sides of the same dilemma, yes. But one begins the act that causes the two to unite in this painful way, and the one whom this behavior is acted out upon is the one whose feet are trampled in the dance, often in ways that distort one's self-image or even physical form.

This is not a dance of correspondence.* Yes, it is said that until "she" chooses not to participate, this dance will continue. Oh, what a response! A response that denies the danger and imagines that, if it did not exist—if there were safety in refusal—this painful dance would still come to be!

Smaller dangers that do not cause lasting damage still affect the psyche. It is often a lifetime of small dangers that form the circumstances from which the bully and the victim are born, each as wounded as the other. The bully's hurt leads to abrupt actions,

---

* In relationship, every need is met by a corresponding need. It is a dance of correspondence. ACOL T2:9.6

lashing out, an unconscious arousal of anger and meanness that work against all honor and reason. The victim's hurt leads to stalled responses, timidity, self-doubt, and guilt that defies reason. But this is not all. There are the daily occurrences of "power over" that, while "small," are nearly as damaging and in equal need of being undone.

And so, regardless of station, courage is needed.

There is not one human being who has not stood on both sides of this way of acting that is in need of being undone. Only those human beings joined in unity have provided examples, some even amidst torture, as Yeshua did. By overcoming cause and effect, even unto death, Yeshua began this turn that we of the way of Mary must complete to put an end to the torture of both abuser and abused.

We overcome cause and effect by calling on the love of life to prevail over the love of death. By calling on life, rather than death, as the way to peace. When we are wholehearted enough to stand in wholeness and to refuse division one from another, in each action, no matter how small, we overcome cause and effect. No matter how often we fail, and we will fail, we continue to bring this way of being beyond a way of trial and error. We do this by seeing each one and each circumstance as clearly as it is possible for us to see it, while not letting the details obscure the heart of the matter. No perfection is in need of being sought. Just a diligent observance, a refusal to be deceived, and a heart courageous enough to care to act.

How new would the world be if enough courageous hearts were called to Acts of The New?

M

$\mathcal{T}$HE EXILE

Dearest Mother,

I have another question for you. As I was speaking with Kate last night, at the end of our call, when we were sitting in stillness, I had my hand on that place of my heart that has felt strangely heavy and tender. My shoulders were aching so bad, I wanted to move to rub them, but didn't move my hand from my heart. Then Kate saw an image of me as yoked, having a yoke around my shoulders.

There is something so tender-hearted going on in me that I could barely read what's been received, and so I've backed up. I don't feel like an "act-er," Mary, other than in this way, or mainly in this way. I just don't. Two of my friends are in more of a crisis than I am, and I *feel* myself to be in one, one wherein I feel like a stranger. I don't even think it so much as I feel it.

My heart has been just bursting with a pain I can't define ever since our last dialogue. I have become aware that the pain has been there for decades. It is like homelessness. I keep thinking of escape. And your last message feels like something I'll never live up to, and don't want to even dare try. That's why I'm feeling this way. "*A refusal to be deceived, and a heart courageous enough to care to act.*"

This courage is what I've needed since A Course of Love came to me and what I've not been able to find in myself.

Oh, my daughter, this is the exile. You are aware of living away from your homeland. You come into exile to seek refuge in your true home. This is a courageous Act.

Oh, Mary, I am overcome. I don't know how to talk more of this.

This time is similar to when you first began to see yourself as an enabler. No matter your dislike of the word, when you saw that it was true you began to see differently. You began to see the part you played in the dynamic unfolding of your life. You didn't know what you were doing until you did, until this time when you became aware. Now, you feel that you are, in no instance, doing what you once did. You feel that you can see what is going on and are responding by being true to yourself. You are firm, helpful, practical, inspired, and inspiring, looking at the big picture and the small, making your needs and preferences known—and still there is a disconnect, and you are not heard.

The thought of leaving this unbearable way of being that has returned is like a compulsion. You feel ostracized. And it feels so unfair, more so for being less than obvious. The obvious you could address; the less than obvious, you cannot.

You feel as if you are in the way of the others who have formed a unit, and become unnecessary, even though it is you who has created the very home from which you are being displaced. This "home" is where you mean to be free to share on your terms, but instead feel forced to share on terms that circumstances, and personality—and what you can afford—dictate. The unhappiness builds. You realize that you can only have the life you desire quite apart from the people with whom you most share it, and it is a frightening realization that you know, as soon as I say it, is true and has been true. You live apart, even while you live amid.

This is exile. The modern exile. You are already familiar with its nature, its loneliness, and its necessity. So are many.

But knowing you have a homeland, this is not the same dis-

connected exile as was the banishment of separation. This is the exile of the movement "out" of separation.

You have thought it was many things for many years. It is the nature, rather, of the movement of who you are and what you, and all of those who have inner lives, are called to.

To lose contact with the private, the inner, with individuality, lets the public come forward as the extreme of egotism: in fundamentalism and idolatry. Never before has humanity been in such a time—one that is euphemistically called "connected" but is actually annihilating the private.

Your dialogue prayer of "I am no longer separate and alone" becomes: "I no longer choose to lose myself."

Creation is not only the manifestation of the good and the beautiful, but the power to bring truth to illusion, where the denial of goodness and beauty causes it to remain in exile . . . not only with the tender-hearted, but with the vast majority of humanity.

Humanity is in exile from itself.

This exile rises to consciousness with the creative one's fullness of desire, which is becoming, in this new time, absolute. The will to create is the will to live. To deny the will to create is to deny one's own life, and the way of the Creator. Those of the way of Mary "become who they are to be through their acts of creation."*

All I can think to do is to drop out. To drop out of all that I've been doing. The family will correct itself . . . naturally. I can see to that. I can't see any way to affect those who would change the nature of Love, and truthfully, I do not even want to continue to try.

---

* ACOL D:Day19.4

This is what has been sapping my energy and has me denying my own truth. And that is the truth.

Home is Here

Holy One,

I'm trying to think of something I've written recently that was "in voice." I'm so far away from myself! Not being "in voice" is my "self-alert system."

I sit a minute and my thoughts then drift—why I don't know—to how I was "driven" in my 30's to have a home. I remember it so distinctly! The drive. The drive, drive, drive . . . to have a house to call my own! The sick-and-tiredness of living in rentals. The overwhelming desire to have, before it was too late, a place my kids would call "home," and mean it the way I did, when home on Smith Avenue was "mine," and a constant, and even, at times, the safe place we've remembered in these pages.

I know I get away from "my voice" while I'm receiving. I know. I'm familiar with this feeling. Even so, I have conflicting dreams of leaving this "home," as if, away from here, I will find my voice again. And I'm wondering if I'd feel this way at all, this voiceless way, if it weren't for the commitments, here and coming, in which I *need* to have a voice. It seems a small thing, but how can I "go out" and fake it? How do I live in "my own home" without a voice?

Have all these events conspired to bring me into exile? Is it necessary? I don't understand. As I "try" to write, what I say seems to mean nothing, to say nothing.

Because you are writing "here," my Mari, writing in a new "here."

Here you are expressing your Self as well as my Self, and yet what you mourn is like unto the heartfelt and personal and po-

etic, as well as the simply stated "true" sharings you've received from friends recently. These sharings—sharings that you feel are so honest and real, that express the honest and real so well in so few words—draw you into comparison and cause you to remember when your own words were as full and revealing.

These words you admire are truly the light that shines forth from human beings to the divine, lighting the heavens. Each one who finds and expresses their truth in their voice, even when it is the pondering of an unknown, move you, and you have the good sense to know that they do. You see the beauty in each of these distinct voices. Each true heart that reveals "one," reveals as well, humanity's heart and soul.

What we write together, regardless of your part in the personalization of it, is writing that has come for a purpose, and you are acknowledging that it is not the same, and acknowledging as well that it is not what you most long for. You and I can endeavor to continue to convey this purpose, or we can stop and talk to each other as your friends who moved you, talked to you. Would you like that?

I don't know if it's possible. I don't know if it would leave this purpose unfulfilled. I don't even know if I can find my voice to speak truly to you. This is the matter at hand. The feeling of having lost my voice and my home, which combined have brought forth the feeling of exile that I know I've been feeling with *A Course of Love* as well. I don't know that I've expressed one thing that is in my heart, even when I've tried. It is as if the words have taken over the feelings. They fail me! Because I have no home. There's been a takeover. And it makes my eyes fill with tears.

And you do not realize how important it is that you express these very things that you are now expressing. You do not know how many are feeling this way. You do not realize that the words are not meant to take over the feelings but to reveal them. Not to stop them up, but to let them flow. But as with so many matters, there may always be both. A stoppage before the dam is burst and the flow arrives. And this is why we demonstrate in this way.

Well, this return to my "self," by which I mean not one or another, not turning to an "elevated" Self over a human self, not returning to a receiver self over a writer self, not returning to an enabling self over a free self, a homeless self over one who has found a home, is what I'm speaking of. I am feeling some sort of division that is nearly intolerable.

I've been feeling miserable in this divided living for a while now, a place where even the hopeful signs come of feelings of distress, as when I was with friends last week and could literally not withstand the "noise" of it. I thought I would go out of my mind . . . while they were happily expressing themselves. Yet I knew the strength of my feeling was a sign, of something. . . . Maybe, hopefully, something new.

This jumping out of my skin that I'm doing with peopled presences and noise is part of being in this zone of receiving, and this I know. Everything is heightened. Maybe that is the way to put it. Or "I" am heightened. My sensitivity so heightened that every aspect of living becomes terribly acute. I swear I'm going to buy earplugs today, as I have to go out and deposit Christina's generous gift and that of a stranger in Chicago who's contributed in the past, but whom I haven't heard from in a good while. Thank you for these and the gratitude I feel for them. I need to feel more quiet gratitude in such times as this, because if I didn't, I think I'd go off the deep end.

There are just so many awkward things that have made up my recent days. They're leading me to feel I'm meant to be sequestered, and I dream of such a time coming, but wonder how I'll make it through the time ahead of me, which feels like the story of my life . . . a life in which I am surely not a champion of love in the particular, which is where my loving seems most needed at this time . . . *and* where expressing it falsely is the most unloving thing I am doing to myself.

It is as if I'm submitting to a sort of psychic torture, and then trying to "act" as if all is well. And still, with all these words, I feel as though I am revealing nothing. To accept that I feel the way I do, to admit it, seems to reveal nothing more than my own pettiness.

I do not want to "join" with anyone right now. Only the view out the cabin window comforts me.

It is awfully hard, is it not, to have your primary home and work relationships be ones in which there is no knowing and being known going on?

Yes.

M

AT THE MARGIN

It's a quarter past six and the sun is just coming up over the fence. Right now, it's throwing long shadows over the desk on which my red journal sits, past old letters in Efrain's distinctive print, Terry's carved spoon, Betty Lou's painted rock. It moves past the desk onto the wall, showing precise vertical lines from the window.

Those direct light shadows happen so seldom—this mirroring of the front on the back.

I am experiencing at the margin of my life's . . . desires.

It is right where you need to be.

M

Holy One,

It has been a year now since we began.

And it is the tipping point of summer, a lushness heading to decline. When I walk from house to cabin, when I pass beneath the grapevines reaching down from the arbor, I bow my head and weave between them. It is as a passing between worlds. This has caught my imagination this morning.

I have been away in the confusing world of that which exists on the other side of my morning walk. I come back, as from a nether land, and only feel myself to be "attempting" to breach this other time zone.

But I know it is here, just like somewhere it is tomorrow and in other places yesterday.

I have also just traversed the land of night passing into day. Is this all the borderland of which you briefly spoke? This sense of passing that is also a sense of coming into being?

Here, you are being without borders. In this way, you are "it." You are the borderland. It is in this place that we join. It is in this place that we leave meaning behind and enter being. Here we are inter-being. Comingling. This is the nature of the imaginal realm. You are "in person" with that with which, and with whom, you are being. Here, your quest for meaning ends. Here, being—not meaning—is the focus.

To what end, my mother?

To have a guide, my daughter. A guide for your return from exile.

M

$\mathcal{T}$HE END OF MEANING

There was a turn—not only in secular life, but in the Church, and in spirituality—from being to meaning. "Being" was given over to the "meaning" of being, and definitions of it abound, while Being itself has nearly disappeared. This left you with disembodied spirits after which you quest, and with dispirited bodies, existing near to a living death. You are killing yourselves, and your spirit, in order to be meaning-full.

What does it all mean?

Just behind the quest for meaning is the quest for what to do about the meaninglessness given to that which could be meaningful. Because . . . you know life could be meaningful.

And so, you are caught in a double bind, which is why I ask you now, to cease your quest for meaning. If you can cease your quest for meaning, you will find life itself meaningful again.

Think of your questions—your continual question:

What does it all . . . mean?

You ask this question, not only about esoteric knowledge, but about each life situation that holds any sort of confusion. What does "it" mean? What does the "situation" mean? Why has it shown up? What is it here for? What "lesson" has it come to teach? What purpose does it serve?

Whatever words you use, they are mere substitutes for the cry, "What does it mean?"

Goodness, my Mari, how much time do you spend with these questions? Don't they nearly consume your life—even now? Even when you sit with me? Oh yes, my words are beautiful, and our

time together calms you with the truth revealed in relationship.
You are calmed by your lack of doubt—briefly. But then what
happens when you attempt to address one life "situation" after
another? Situations that arise in life?

I'll tell you. You become tremendously burdened.

Lay your burdens down! Do not remain yoked to your bur-
dens! The burdens that arise as you feel, and feel so deeply, and
think so continuously, "I know not what to do."

Forget "what it means" and Act! Act on your truth. Act on
your feelings. Act from the womb, the gut, the heart. Act from the
place of union you feel here. Quit separating your Acts from the
heart of who you are. Do not "administer" to your acts. Just Act.

Good Lord, my mother, "life in form" is so complicated that I
do not know how to act! This is the nature of life on the ground!
There are problems that require money that doesn't exist, and situations before the public eye that require sensitivities I can hardly
foresee. And personal and vocational matters that ask more of me
than I can give!

Yes, your life has become as unpopular to you as do those of the
candidates who run for president. There is so much that needs do-
ing and always someone, somewhere, thwarting that doing. The
solution is "a plan" that then must be defended. If the wrong plan
is chosen, what then? Plans upon plans are made. Contingency
plans then follow.

I know, my dear one. You have forgotten how to act. I know.
This is for the good. This is the prelude to the New Acts.

That I have forgotten how to act sounds like the truest thing
you've said to me—about me.

I know you are sitting here in alarm. You are not soothed, but dismayed. You know, and have been brave enough to admit, that you do not know how to do what I am asking you to do. This is the first step in letting your training go. You have been trained not to know how to act "for yourself." Thus, does your un-training begin.

M

The Un-training

There are, in your training, actions that you initiate and actions that you respond to. By way of this training you see many things to consider.

There are "conscious" and "unconscious" thoughts that arise, and conscious and unconscious actions that call for your response. How is the "conscious" act differentiated from the "unconscious" act? When I ask you to respond, which is the New Act? Is there a difference?

Let's first talk of the natural, for this is where we are headed.

In even-tempered times, actions and responses "are" natural. These are the times you wish desperately to abide in—times when no decisions whatsoever are needed. You live your life peaceably. You move through your days without any trying at all. You are not worried. You are not confused. You are not burdened. You are not defended. There is not even any call to respond. You are enveloped in a choice-free atmosphere. You are . . . being. Simply being. It is all you long for. All you live for.

And then a "situation" arises. I will call each and every "situation" a circumstance in which you feel you know not what to do. Knowing not what "to do," you cannot "do anything," and so you are burdened. The burden sits on your shoulders. You try not to think about it, but, since it must be responded to in some way to cease being a burden, you cannot rest. You cannot set it down. You are unable to let it go. It can be a choice as simple as whether you want to schedule an important call, or spend that time with your grandsons.

You give it thought. You work it this way and that. And it becomes clear that all you want is freedom. This is exactly what you are sitting here today feeling.

What you desire and can come to believe in, is a way of "knowing" what to do—or "not" do.

I know it sounds unbelievable, but this is the way we lived our lives, all of us "of good heart." But the "conflicted" were not so far and few between as you might imagine! Matthew, Judas and Peter were each conflicted, so you see that inner conflict was there in a quarter of Jesus' own disciples. This also means there were nine who "did not" do what they did not know to do, and "did" do what they knew they were to do. Even so, at the time they could have risen to their greatest acts, they did not.

Now, Mari, turning to yourself, we can begin with the simple knowing of what you "do not want to do." Believe it or not—that is a start.

There are as many or more conflicted ones who would "claim to know," as there are unconflicted ones, and they are often the least trustworthy. In such a way has knowing been given over to the tyrants of knowledge, politics, and crime.

No one even strives for the kind of knowing we speak of anymore, but I am telling you how crucial it is—first, to ease your way through your days and years, and second to prepare you for the day on which you will claim what you know "for yourself," that true knowing may abide restfully within you.

And then, when you know you need a quiet day to yourself, you will do this without question. And when you know it is time to act, you will do this without questioning your need, or willing-

ness. *You will trust as thoroughly your indecision. You will trust and know that it is not time to act.*

With true knowing, you can take "decision" out of the equation. Understanding this is essential.

This will be hard for you and you will, for a while, feel rather isolated. It will become as if there is no "Yes," and neither any "No." Only Being.

If you were each to dedicate all thought to unity*, and do only what you know is yours to do, you would bring great peace to the world by Being in Peace. As long as you think that such a little thing as this makes no difference, so long will you remain unliberated.

This is the division within each and every person on the planet who has come to consciousness making choices in multiple areas of life, and at a steady pace, each and every day. How burdened you are.

All are yoked, my Mari. All are yoked.

And of all who have become free of choice, you will not find one despot.

These are the saints and the shrine makers. You know exactly how holy it felt when you cared for your Dad as he died, and knew—in those moments and months, absolutely knew—this was yours to do.

Let yourself begin to begin by simply realizing that any situation about which you do not feel the call to respond, doesn't need to be responded to or held within the range of your thoughts. You do not have to go within and ask the Holy Spirit or take any time

---

* ACOL T4:6.8

for discernment because there is only one choice: Yours. You trust in what you know is yours to do. That is it.

You can relax into this right here, today.

With great love of the Holy Ones, you become choice free and miracle ready.

M

CHOICELESS CHOICES

Confusion in regard to choice happens to everyone. You are not alone. All face so much choice that they are becoming more and more unclear of mind. Some of the truest souls on earth have failed to face every situation without burden—including Yeshua. Yet even when you forget that this is where your freedom lies, you are very unlikely to fail in your appointed hour.

Why do you think your decisions have become so burdensome? Have you ever thought it is because they "are burdensome"? You have felt this, my Mari, and after you have felt this, really felt this, nothing is ever quite the same.

Cease now to find fault with yourself. Limit your causes for choice. Trust that you will know or not know, and that it is enough.

This is the way ahead.

Yes, Mari. You can drop all the busyness and Know that you possess the freedom of "not having to" make any choices . . . including this one.

We will continue to circle back to the Act of Trust. The heart of this will be knowing when the "time is right." Knowing when the time is right is the master art of the feminine alchemists.

Yes, my daughter, we will keep circling back to time as well.

M

CHOICES AND ORDINAL TIME

Only now does the Act of Memory cause you to realize the connection it has to ordinal time. In "ordinal time," and only in ordinal time, are choices of life and death your yoke and your burden.

As you pass beyond ordinal time, you are free.

Freedom of choice is not freedom. Freedom to know—is.

You have begun to know in the unity of the duad and will begin now to "know that you know," and that you will Act with knowing Being.

It is in the certain movement of freedom, and there only, that what is occurring is truly seen, and addressed.

This, I know, is hard to accept. It is hard to accept until you understand that "the particulars" currently lie separate from "the people."

People suffer, and will continue to suffer, if "situations" and their particulars are removed from the people involved . . . of which, when such situations arise in your life, you are one.

To make this clear, you can look at your daughter's relationship to her son, and how the "particulars" of finding an acceptable place for them to live are separate from the relationship that exists. Yet the relationship that exists has, at the same time, made the need for a place to live imperative. Does that make sense?

A "situation" is not removed from its circumstance, as for instance, when you were a young mother alone, your situation was not removed from the circumstance of your financial situation. It is in actuality the combination of situations, the location, the setting, and your position within the whole that make up your place in life. So, when we speak of a "situation" we are speaking *of a person's actual place in life, the "reality" of it within all the mitigating factors of what you call "life on the ground."*

When this realistic truth cannot be ignored, the particulars plague you. They plague the government, they plague the displaced, they plague the poor, they become the plague of the migratory nature of life on this planet at this time. These are not inconsequential matters, but neither are they the situation at hand. The particulars are important, but they are not the "reality" around which the particular has formed.

The particulars are what come in "response" to the situation but are not the situation itself. Agreed?

I'm not sure.

Well, let's say the "event" of A Course of Love *was accompanied by its situation: the conditions attending it, the location in which it took place, the year, the decade, its relationship to you. In short, its surroundings. The determining factor of the "event" is the happening, the occurrence, the coming into form: the Act of it. It is the essential element of what is happening. It is not "apart" from the situation, but it is not the situation itself.*

I am using another route to say again that A Course of Love *was not "separate" from you, or the particulars of your situation. I am not saying this only for your benefit. This is true for everyone. It was true in my life and that of Yeshua. The choices people make are not only part of the fabric of their lives. They arise from the innate givens that pattern life in time.*

What you are experiencing now is a difference in time. The difference between the 1920's and the 1960's, and the difference between the 1960's and 2000's, include vast dissimilarities in the way people live and understand the world around them. This quickened pattern of change was not present 2000 years ago. The world has changed more in the last 200 years than in the preceding two millennia. Time is changing. You are changing. The situation is the combination of the circumstances that contribute to outcome. What will the outcome of all this change be?

This is not immaterial to the two Courses of Jesus.

Although you were called away from a university job to receive A Course of Love, you were not an academic as was Helen Schucman. You were not an intellectual with a prestigious job, with no children, and with few financial needs that could not easily be met. Yet everything about Helen's circumstances and your own were perfect for the Courses you were destined to receive.

Each person's life is the same. Each life offers the perfect circumstances to fulfill a destiny that, like the air you breath, is an invisible but vital characteristic of being "here." But here, the present reality is changing at great speed as time spins us closer and closer to the advent of a truly new beginning, in time outside of time.

M

THE SITUATION WITH ATTRIBUTES

It is 6:50 now and I've only just had to move out of the sun's glare. It hasn't been particularly dark since I got here. There has been light. But only now is the sun rising over the fence.

I started looking at definitions of the word attribute, because of what you said yesterday and my remembering that Jesus said, "love has no attributes." I had been thinking of an experience of Heaven that a woman at a Course of Love group I attended once recounted. She was saying that many "in Heaven" want to return to their experience here, because in Heaven you couldn't give and receive love. Love was all One.

I didn't like this idea of not "giving and receiving love" at all. Then it came to me: Love has no attributes! And I think if this report is true, it may be because love can accept all attributes—all that is given is received, possibly in such a way that the sense of giving and receiving is lessened.

Here is what I found in the dictionary:

Attribute: To think of as belonging to, produced by, resulting from, or originating in; to ascribe as a quality or characteristic peculiar to one; a symbol: as in "winged feet are the *attribute* of Mercury;" tri – three, the three groups the Romans were divided into (makes me recall how Saul/Paul was a tribune).[*]

I wonder if this means it just "belongs" to love and not what is produced or results from it.

And so, I look up attributeless being in ACOL:

---

[*] *Webster's New World Dictionary,* 1988.

"Although this is a difficult concept to get across with the words that are available, I would like you to understand that when I am love being, I am being without attributes—love being in union and relationship. I am the anchor that holds all that has taken on attributes within the embrace of the attributelessness of love. This is why my being has been capable of accepting your projections—because I am attributeless being. I am love, being.

"I did not make you in my image. I created you in love because it is the nature of a being of love to extend. Realize that it is only when being is added to love—only when love is in relationship with being—that love is given its nature. Realize that it is only when love is in relationship with being that it attains this quality that we are calling extension."*

I take from this that God is Love—Being. And it is me who enters, or does not enter, into relationship with Love's Being. And then I am, in a sense, the holder of the attributes of Love's Being.

M

Weighty shadows now fall into the cabin, the kind caused by the movement of the trees, but that are so distinct they make me look up with the feeling that someone is coming near. And now I realize that this is true. Who, from the imaginal realm, is joining me?

It is I, Jesus, here to be with you and my mother as you make this realization.

---

* ACOL D:Day40.3-4

DISCOVERY AND THE ACT OF DEVOTION

You are hitting on something here, having come by it in your own unique way, making a discovery. By doing so, you are writing your own name into the tapestry of time outside of time as you begin to recognize the reality of distinction within oneness . . . and that with this realization, which you do not understand for having realized it, you have made so.

You may now, and forever, exist where you desire naturally, to be.

We are near to the time of my Mother's assumption into heaven and this is akin to what my mother experienced. Now I draw you nearer to me, and the other realms, because you are ready. I come because it is me you have been closest to for so long, and because there is no competition, here, for affection. But there is distinction as well as relationship.

What my mother will reveal to you, more and more, is the mirror reflection of Heaven and Earth.

What I do, today, is recognize you in a new way, because you often do not see these steps you take through your explorations, as Acts, and as being of the magnitude that they are. You continue to be hard on yourself and to doubt yourself, and I am so very familiar with this side of you that I miss walking through these times with you. They are poignant to me—poignant to me with life and memory of life. I have known so many passionate doubters and the fervency with which they continue to quest, even after knowing has come.

No quest is wrong! You do not waste time! Quests give new textures to what is coming into knowing, signature textures that are the mark of your being on your knowing.

The mark of "your" being on "your" knowing is one of not knowing what you know, and rediscovering what you know time and time again, in dozens of various ways. Many of your discoveries have happened at this window, both with me, and now our Mother.

It is perfect timing for this to occur, and for you to realize my nearness in these few days of approach to the Assumption. I want you to know what this is, "in your way," and so I am here to prod you along.

Discovery is your joy. Your discovery is your return to who you are. All of it is of you, drawing nearer to me, and me drawing nearer to you, and Heaven and Earth drawing nearer to each other.

Oh Jesus, I asked who was visiting, and my having asked alerts me that I knew it was not Mary. She is the one who has made me her guest here, as you did in *A Course of Love*. I wouldn't have asked if I had known it was her. And this thrills me as a sign of the distinction I can "feel." I feel it as evidence of continued distinction within Oneness, even beyond death, or assumed death. You and Mary are so alive to me, even while I wish at times for greater vision of you than that of words, and of shadows passing with uncommon weight.

I have just given you a vision of Heaven in which you now see you will remain who you are, as my Mother remains who she is and was, and continues to inspire and welcome the devotion of those who sense her care. Few see our Holy Mother as an inspiring "leader." They see her as one honored into service by God and serving in return. They see her as devoted to me, which she was, and they are inspired by this devotion, to her.

Do you see the similarities of your ways? God called you to this Act, this . . . "life." Even while the Act of Devotion you have participated in is not seen clearly, it is responded to.

There is a call that is felt, an empathetic call, between those with the devotional experience, a call that inspires strong feelings here and now. Not many have allowed themselves to respond to the call of the Act of Devotion.

Many are as desirous of a call to service as they are to leadership. In these calls there is less devotion, more envy, and even some jealously, such as you and our mother have experienced. I want you to know that I am aware of this, and that it is connected to the Assumption; to being lifted-up.

You will still explore and create and question and maybe even doubt for a while . . . if you want to . . . even while you remain devoted. But I would like you to start to imagine that I can take you to a place where you are comfortable and, as your comfort increases, will find joy in new ways of being who you are. You can remain who you are, and can stay where you are comfortable, because this is Heaven. This is where your comfort and your joy are the same, and where your exploratory power may call you to much that is new, and your creativity inspire more than you can imagine.

Heaven is where you can choose to inspire others in the way you have been inspired by us, and in an inexhaustible number of ways. It is so close to how you feel when you feel you are living the life you are meant to live, that you will be completely at home there, as you are, in these moments, completely at home "here." Released from time, those with whom you would join are infinite and accessible, and having "many" connections is not overwhelming, as it is now, due to the difference in time and space that occurs when you are free. Outside of ordinal time you are free.

It is this change in the experience of time and space that you are called, through the Act of Devotion, to help create. Through the imaginal world, all those of Heaven who are choosing to breach the in between realms, draw you closer. This is the beginning thrust to joining the realms in a new manner.

In Heaven you will be able to enter deep and lasting friendships with far more than a dozen people. (Yes, I say "dozen" in reference to the apostles, and what "I" experienced, upon living life in time and space, as the same limits you are facing: the limits that time and space place on those "physically" close to one another, and the complexities that arise. This was a burden for me too. I had to find a way to exist in time and to deliver the message of eternity.) But I also fell in love with each I gathered to me . . . as do you.

The burden of time that is being felt by you now, is a burden of relationship as much as it is of work to be done.

I want you to realize this today. This is why I have more specifically joined you. You are heavy with the burden of relationships, and these are almost always the burdens that cause you doubt.

Why? Because you fall away from one side of yourself due to the "time" it takes to "be" in relationship the way you wish to be. This has gone on so long that you have taken my advice and begun to exercise choice, but choice gets you muddled, as we both know. Mother Mary has begun to encourage you to go the path of least resistance. The path that involves no choice. And yet you continue to stand on the sidelines of this path, seeing always the choices that you fear are passing you by (as with your creativity), or the choices you have acquired (as with schedules and administration). You see these like possessions you must now tend to, through love.

Thus, you have retained too many burdens, the burdens that weigh you down. I am here to raise you up, as I once raised my Mother in a similar way, to similar Acts, because your devotion to me breeds devotion.

Acts of Devotion encompass all Acts of The New.

There are more people you would love than you can possibly be in physical relationship with. And so, the realm of your relationships both extends and contracts, to be possible for you in the physical.

Our Mother is now poised to open a greater realm of relationship to you—one you will at first doubt, as is your way—but that you will come to embrace. I am here to encourage you, and all of those to whom you have drawn close—the thousands of those who feel close to you through our Course. I encourage you to simply be aware of the truth of your relationships, without the burden that relationships, in time, can be.

This has to do with Who You Are, and I will be near, accompanying you and our Mother in the days ahead.

$\mathcal{M}$

THE ASSUMPTION

Today is the Feast of the Assumption, my Lord and Mother. Although I barely hear the words as I say them (and skip a few), the Apostle's Creed, or Nicene Creed as it is now called, has us saying at each Mass, "We look for the resurrection of the dead, and the life of the world to come." And then as I think back to these beliefs, I know this is to come at "the end of time," an "end" that I never really associated with what we've been speaking of—with the end of "ordinal" time. This all feels overly complicated at the moment and I want to dismiss it from our time together, even while it feels of some consequence.

I need this time today, as I feel myself to be in a sort of inner crisis once again.

Something sad happened yesterday, and I don't know what it was. It was like a breach. It started when I listened to maybe five minutes of the first podcast Mary Love put together for us. She was asking me these probing questions. It just threw me for a loop. Later she asked about it. She could tell something was wrong. I said, "It sounds like you're my analyst." She said we could change it . . . change anything.

Then Steve came for our website meeting and they talked in their loud way for over an hour. I put my earbuds in, and the volume was still bad, and when I wanted to say something, I had to take an earbud out because I couldn't hear myself. I mean, it would be a perfect comedy sketch. Mary was just beautiful, Steve happy, me homely and miserable and popping ear buds.

With 45 minutes left in Mary's time with us, I felt I had to bring it back to getting something done. If we were getting ready to launch our podcasting thing, we needed the front-pieces to start it. I pulled up the only site I knew of, the podcasting site of my friend Jackie Lesser. Steve and Mary acted like I wanted to copy something when all I really wanted to do was bring up an example. I don't listen to podcasts and so had no idea how they were presented. Yet I felt like I was . . . irrelevant. I felt kind of crazy. There was nothing urgent to do . . . but "we were there to get something done."

And I wanted to do that, to create something . . . but I wanted it to come from a natural flow . . . I aspire to be like my literary, radical, feminist women writers, but it takes more than talking about it.

So, what am I actually doing here? Do I, or do Mary and I, actually want to do anything that doesn't come naturally, or that isn't . . . new?

M

I came to the cabin before my walk because I wanted to be here for a bit before the sun. That was nice. Now I'm back, and the sun's just topping the fence at 6:37. It seems like it won't be a blazing one . . . or the type of blazing one that chases me away. I welcome time and space and birds and squirrels, and my own creative life.

Then a thump, and a sound like breathing. I get up to look. There could be a mama deer and her baby in the brush behind the cabin for all I know. Nothing appears. I feel summoned again. And then I notice words below these that I've just written and scroll down to see what is below. Good grief!

"When you are not wholly present as who you are, you are experiencing, still, the image or after-image of who you are. This image is like a lingering shadow. It encompasses all of your former ideas about yourself, all of the patterns of the time of learning, all of the moments in which you feel an inability to join in union, and in which you recognize still the image of your former self."*

How did those words get there?

Thank you, my Holy Ones! I suppose this is it, and that I am experiencing an after-image, a former self—the "manifesting" self—and at the same time defending all the ways that I have been, and still feel a need to be.

What I write is not separate from who I am because I am a writer! That's "my" tradition, and I guess I may have to stand up for it now and leave off the rest. Why am I even trying to do these other things?

M

Mary Love texted and we spoke a bit later. She said it had occurred to her too: not wanting what we do to become "a thing." We're cool. No more production for a while. The after-image quote means it is behind me, maybe behind "us."

This, from "A Treatise on the New," applies production to something new:

"The production that has so long occupied you will now serve you

---

* ACOL D:16.16

as you turn your productive and reproductive instincts to the production and reproduction of relationship and union."*

M

---

* ACOL T4:2.6

DEVOTED TO THE HEART'S KNOWING

I feel ready now, to return, if such a return is available to me. I feel I have had revealed what I needed to see. I am most thrilled about Acts of Devotion. . . and Creation! These I feel I know, and can offer, but as we are speaking of new ways, how does one convey the way of devotion?

You are creating the true devotion that will end special relationships forever, my daughter, and doing so in a way uniquely your own. You might wonder why this is so important. It is important because it is recognizable.

I know you do not feel this way as yet. You have not felt this way because you have not shared the way of your devotion, and so you have not given those who are looking for The New a way to recognize it. The ways of Helen and Bill* were such that their known spats and Helen's endearing but cantankerous nature dissuaded many who read of them from seeing the devotion they truly had—both for each other, and for Jesus, with whom their work was inseparable.

It is unreasonable, and even silly, that their monumental devotion was, and continues to be, so easily dismissed. There were others too, but Helen and Bill entered relationship to take down the inner dictation that Helen received from Jesus. They were the two who recorded it as it was received, and who devoted themselves to it for many years. It never left them, as your Course of Love never left you, or will.

---

* Helen Schucman and Bill Thetford, who partnered to bring ACIM into form.

People used to tease you about how earnest you were, and your Jesus seemed to mock earnestness. But he spoke of the earnestness of the ego, the earnestness of trying hard to "learn," not the earnestness of devotion to truth.

You were sincere and serious about this work, and so solemn and heavy of heart that you had to work yourself back to some lightness of being. But this was not due to the industriousness of trying hard. It came of knowing the importance of what you were being given, of what you were receiving.

Devotion is substantial, dear one. Devotion is such a generous giving. And consecration to an original work, with all these new ideas? It is not only substantial but a way of substantiation, a way of embodiment. There is a way that this "right," this right to be who you are, is seen as an inalienable right, a right that exists apart from man-made laws.

The release of the ego was not the same call and could not, in those who did not see what it called them to, elicit the same fervor. This call—this "right"—is a call to Acts of passion. These are Acts that will summon many to true devotion and is why you must reveal and accept your own. Your devotion is of your heart and so unconfined. It is not bounded by the work you did. It is of the nature of the unbounded, of being without boundaries.

Your reception from Jesus inspired in your mother's heart an explicit understanding of what was at stake, as well as of what was promised: the unchallengeable right to be who you are. It will do the same in many. This sacred acknowledgment is the end of the old, false ways of being, and the rebirth, the renaissance, of The New.

All of what has made you and each person flawed, has also

made you perfect. In you, your compassion for the tender-heart-ed, and your passion for creating, made A Course of Love and our work possible. Without both, this would not be. For you, and all creators who know who they are, creating is a personal, intimate call to new knowing. Revealing this is exactly what is needed to appeal to the humble, tender, and creative women and men we most desire to reach. These, too, much like you, may feel that they do not measure up to our call.

Mari, you are simply as common as the majority of the popu-lation on this Earth. You aren't the brightest, the most educated, the guru who has left home for a new life of enlightening the mass-es. No. You are ordinary and have let yourself realize that you can retain your ordinariness, and still be so much more. Knowing that this is so will assure your sisters and brothers of their unseen potential.

You have as well, in your devotion to your Jesus, to your fami-ly, to your friends, to your faith, to your new knowing, and now to me, also called to those who have such inclinations, to embrace the whole of their lives. No one needs to leave behind anything they feel to keep. Life's "stories" that have been discounted in this time that is passing, will not be discounted any longer.

I do not share "my" life history here, not only because it is being shared elsewhere, but because we have the different aim of honoring your life's story and each one's life story as sacred.

Each person of faith is the perfect one to invite their sisters and brothers of the heart, into the realm of the holy of holies. You each see "ordinary" perfection. Seeing ordinary perfection, you can summon, one and then another, to be, along with you, de-voted to their heart's knowing, rather than to teachings. Devoted, not to "your" Holy Ones, in your way, but devoted to their own knowing in their own way.

Personification of the Holy "is" embodiment. It is to have faith in those who exist in form now, as well as those who are beyond form. This is a specific request that will allow the adorning of the new Self each is to become "in relation" to all that is Holy.

It is all relational . . . one to another. And this is the knowing you have been given to hold close, and to protect from the ways of teaching and learning that would but form a new hierarchy, a hierarchy of knowledge rather than the unique commonality at the heart of truth in each one.

M

THE NEW ODYSSEY

My mother, as you know, I can't remember anything. So I am exceptionally heartened to see that what came to me in my drifting, morning reverie, "There is no everyone," is in A *Course of Love*'s introduction:

"There is no 'everyone' to whom I speak, to whom I give these words. There is no single, no solitary, no separate mind to whom these words are spoken. These words are spoken heart to heart, from One Heart to One Heart. . . . 'Everyone' is just a concept. These words are given to each One."*

And then I come back here, and your last words are "the heart of truth in each one." I am so in joy over this! It's the proof of what I know is true; somewhere in me, these words still live. I don't recall them, but I can recollect them. They are in me and I am beginning to trust that I can bring them up again in my own way.

But I wonder. Have I gotten away from our "one to one" sharing, my Holy Mother? Do you know that I forgot the second anniversary of my own mother's death? That I am in this transition time with my daughters, where I can feel them falling away from me, and knowing it is time? That this is where they will become their own womanly selves and perhaps come back to me in a new way? Is this what we're all doing here? Going away and coming back? The great odyssey?

---

* ACOL I.1.11

What an interesting way to put it, Mari.

The new Acts are relational . . . one to another. They do not occur in a life "apart," but in each one who is living in union and relationship with their own journey—their own story.

Homer's Odyssey represented the journey after the fall of Troy, an ever- extending wandering, or voyage. What your brother and I are asking you to see is the homecoming. As Penelope waited for Odysseus, as Odysseus yearned for his home, you are each awaited until you await no longer, take the journey, and accept the arrival when it comes.

What has happened, is that the light is continually seen on a distant shore, and the journeying never ceases. Yet it is when true discovery occurs that creation of The New begins.

What Jesus visited to help you see is the journey's end, the New Act of allowing oneself to be taken up, body and soul. Allowing oneself to be taken out of the realm of "life on the ground"—but this time, without leaving the ground of your physical being.

You, only two days ago, made this announcement to yourself in your journal, and wrote it in this widely spaced way to give the words weight:

This   is   the   ground. The   firmament.

There   are   endings   and   new   beginnings   happening   on   this ground.

Now there is a rising only to descend again, a taking up and setting back down for life on the ground. Since the "bodily assumption into Heaven," this time has been in preparation so that it may occur "on the ground." So that when you say, "life on the ground," you no longer mean the frustrations and complexities of life, but the firmament, a poetic embrace of the Earth's strength and support "of life."

The imaginal realm begins here, not with disdain for "life on the ground," but with an openness to the support and strength being offered, by the Earth herself, for the imaginal—for the realm of time outside of time. This is to belong "to" life on the ground, "for" life on the ground, and to include the ascent and descent of the body.

Each time you come here, you let yourself be taken up and set back down. Your brother and I mediate your travels. What began as a vast terrain grows near as the journey comes to an end, no longer an odyssey but a way of movement between realms. The imaginal is a meeting ground where this movement of being flashes in and out, and you retain the body even as you leave it . . . only to return. The return is here, and it is imminent. Always coming on. It is arising and descending continually. These are the Acts of The New.

This is the joining of the realms.

M

BEING PRESENT TO TIME

Saturday, the seventeenth day of the great August movement. . . .

Today there is a plan and an agreement. Packing up is commencing. Angie got a job at Henry's school, and September 1, she and Henry will move into their new apartment, a building nearby and remarkably well kept. The owner is religious and made it clear he has faith in her. It was rather amazing. I am so grateful, so thankful.

This day's morning sky appears like twilight. It feels right in keeping with the joining of the realms.

Yes, my Mari. In the midst of the reality of care of the body, we now look at the body and its centrality to this joining. The body "is" the ground of your being on Earth. Its allowance of new life is coming into being, just as your daughter's new life is coming into being.

As you watch your leaves being "acted upon" by the wind, being moved to resplendent twinkling with the sun and darkening into the shadows, you see a metaphor for life. Each day you watch the ever-changing sky while the ground lies hidden. But then—slowly, or at times in the blink of an eye—the earth is revealed and becomes your light of day, the light in which you see.

Two realms joining each morning.

You see, as your Toni Morrison said, "What moves at the margin." The liminal, the subtle, the elusive. . . moves at the edge, until the unpredictable becomes present and, by heart, is inscribed.

In another way, through what your Christie describes—as do

*your other women authors—you see those pushed to the margin
and the edges on which there is great and imminent heartache.*

*The hidden edge, the mesa of the middle ground, is also seen.
This is where well-intentioned people seek firm standing for "the
good" as they know it, and to control the outer reaches before it is
too late; too late for "the good" of the many (which often, but not
always, relates to those like themselves) to prevail.*

All of this swirls about, whirring as do your traffic noises.

*You all await your Saturday or Sunday mornings, which your
God of "law" proclaimed to be for rest. There you step out of the
whirl and, from your perch at the edge of movement, you begin
to see the spin.*

*Here the new swirl arrives, the twin cyclones of time outside
of time. From your precarious perch on the ledge of that which is
of time, you begin to see that the consciousness of time is keeping pace with your own. The conflict of time and eternity is the
collision being mediated now in the imaginal realm, which is revealing the original three-fold nature that is becoming the duad
of the New.*

*This three-fold nature is the same as that named the Father,
Son, and Holy Spirit. This naming dismissed the feminine as either the first or the second in the life-giving union, and went on to
create a genderless third.*

*But it is also the only naming of the Holy that remains in
many spiritual communities. We speak of the "Holy" Spirit here,
not as mediator, but as the living holy spirit in each one.*

*Like the imaginal realm, the Holy provides the way—the way
"out." The imaginal realm releases the hierarchy of eternity and
time through the imaginative and poetic vision of the feminine.*

The Holy Spirit has mediated this transition to the point at which we stand, releasing the gender-centric and male dominated hierarchy of knowing.

In this new time, the Act of Being Present "to" time, is the Act of The New that is coming into relationship with the revelation of The New.

M

$\mathcal{S}$ECOND SKY COUPLET
END NOTE

As I'm completing the editing of "Acts," in March 2021, I wake from a dream that passes before I can capture it. All that remains are the words: Second Sky Couplet.

I begin to investigate.

Second is the next after the first, as in the Second Coming. Second sight is the ability to see or foretell events: clairvoyance. Second thought is a change of thought. Second wind—the capacity to recover.

Sky is the upper atmosphere, the expanse of the heavens or celestial regions.

Couplet: two successive lines of poetry especially two of the same length that rhyme. To rhyme is a "correspondence of sound"!*

All I can make of this, my Holy Ones, is "two successive lines" (as in lineage) with a regular recurrence of corresponding sounds. To rhyme is to join, to fit.

Rhythm is all about timing, spacing, repetition, accent; cycles like of menstruation, sleep and waking, or in other words, flow, and movement.

This word, "rhythm," with no vowels, causes me to remember the old chant from grammar school: "A E I O U and sometimes Y and W!"

Good morning, Mary, Jesus, and all in spaciousness. I can think of us all, in relationship, being firsts and seconds in duads of one-

---

* *Webster's New World Dictionary*, 1988.

ness, couplets in a rhythm of correspondence. I know the word "correspondence" was used in ACOL and go to find it.

It is in the second Treatise, speaking of how every species knows innately that they share the same needs as every other:

"In relationship, every need is met by a corresponding need. It is a dance of correspondence.

"Every being inherently knows that it shares the same needs as every other being of its kind. Every being also inherently knows that needs and the fulfillment of needs are part of the same fabric—they are like puzzle pieces that fit together. Other beings that share life with you on this planet are not concerned with needs or need fulfillment. Doing what needs to be done in order to survive is hardly the same as feeling that one has a need. Needs are the domain of the thinking being only."*

"The extent to which you are willing to abdicate your needs in order to attain something is the extent to which your belief in want or lack is revealed. This is the purview of special relationships. Thus the very compromises you are often prone to make in special relationships are but the symptoms of your fear." †

Mary, "trust" is one of our New Acts, and although I came to this reading by way of the word "correspondence" I read it through and realize such a lovely difference:

---

* ACOL T2:9.6-7

† ACOL T2:9.10

"This phase of coming to accept need and dependency is necessary only as a learning ground of experience on which trust can grow. Once this trust is realized you will no longer think of trust just as you will no longer think of needs." *

It's not about "not" being trusting or knowing when to trust, but not "thinking" of trust.†

I love this and realize that it was in this time, of first receiving the treatise on unity, that I began to think about my needs and tried to make them known to those with whom I was sharing ACOL as it was being received. I spoke of them in hopes of having them met. It was a disaster. There was no dance of correspondence going on, and I became "the needy one" who made those I worked with uncomfortable.

Yes, you had been denying your needs even as you thought about them. The move you made to speak of them was important, and while it took a while, the "movement" it initiated opened you to this dance of correspondence.

M

I woke early, and it is a morning hospitable to my mood. It is expectant with a hint of rain and spring in the air. I love the words:

"[Y]ou will be left as who you are in truth."‡

---

* ACOL T2:9.18

† "Ceasing to think in these terms will soon be seen as a valuable ability and a timesaving measure of great magnitude. As these old ways of thinking leave you, you will be left as who you are in truth." ACOL T2:9.19

‡ ACOL T2:9.19

It is both simple and staggering that the new acts include no "acting," but simply being natural: Natural Acts. We aren't even "accepting" of our needs. We simply know ourselves and in knowing ourselves, are naturally honest with ourselves and others.

And so, you can see that Natural Acts become the end of "acting" from the old script. You aren't even "honest or dishonest" about them. Natural Acts take away designations such as honest or dishonest. You are being who you are and, being who you are, opens you to revelation.

Because you "were who you were" with me, "you" were the opening. Being who you are "is" the opening for each one.

You being you, "with me," created the entry point to all that, in naturalness, could be revealed. Your own mother's heart drew you naturally to the revelation of the Mother of the Living.

Mari, I know there is a danger in speaking of "acts," and not only for those prone to take them up, one-by-one, and define them. It is a risk for you, too. Do not let this "naming" take you from naturalness. As we take this risk, I ask once again, that all who read what we, together, have composed, carry what has been given within them. You do not have to remember what the new acts are. When you have "taken them in," they will remain in you, and arise "naturally."

Do not "think" of The New Acts. Let them come. As I ask you, now, to let Revelation come.

M

THE TREATISES OF MARY

SECOND HEART TREATISE

REVELATIONS

MEMORIA AND THE NEW REVELATIONS

Revelation abides within Memoria. What is revealed, brings to the newly prepared holy ground of being, the seed by which creation of The New is planted. In expectancy, a nascent dawn is lifted from the time of memory's birth. The life of the new babe, alive with radiance, ignites Advent's emergent splendor.

The New is a seed nurtured in the belly of Mother Earth and all her children of The New.

~Mary of Nazareth

Memoria is like memorializing the glory of spring, when the seed of trees and flowers are dancing to life.

Revelation feels more like the intangible variations in the gleam of snow, the color of my mother's eyes, a past and future blending; a difference so tenuous it is a distinction I can't name. Revelation is an intermingling; gone, here, and coming.

~Mari of St. Paul

 EGINNING AGAIN

OCTOBER 19, 2019

My Mother,

Yesterday, Christina gave me permission to be exactly where I am. To sit and look out the window again. To crawl onto land and let my wings dry before soaring off once more. What's coming in is the infinite. It's time to unpack and *then* to receive. She wasn't speaking only of my trip, but of emptying myself for the new. I cannot be so full that I can't receive.

As you know, I've been away as I prepared for and presented at the Miracles in the Mountains Conference.* Mary Love joined me. Christina was at the conference, too, and her presence one of its highlights. There were miracles there. Now it is over, I am home, and want to come back to both you and me.

The "both/and"† I am coming to includes the trip, as well as everything that is "new."

This was an historic, life-altering event for me, but I can't say why. My nature is to record some of it before it fades, yet it appears that what I am experiencing is only "meant to be" feelings. Maybe they are a precursor to trusting that all that's happening is given to take me to where I am.

"The New Revelation. . ." That just came to me as the end of the way of Mary, or the next part of it perhaps.

---

* Produced by Kathy Scott Perry, who brings vision to her events and great personal generosity to their creation and all of those presenting and attending.

† Paraphrasing, Day 10.21: Joining with Christ-consciousness, we are existing as both Christ-consciousness and as the woman or man that we are. Day 36.18 extends this idea of being both at the same time as cause and effect, means and end, the end of choice and the beginning of creation.

Now I think I'm ready to go tend to my home a little bit, al-though it's so beautiful I want to linger here in the cabin. The trees are a lovely mix of pale green and gold, just standing there, twin-kling for me, waving to me. Welcoming me home.

I am tired though. I can feel it in my eyes and face, as if my animation needs to come to a rest, to just be, to just look out the window. To quit saying "just."

I see a blue-gold light twinkling from behind a tall limb, like a moon but not the moon. The light of you, Mother Mary. Am I right that you are here and that we will end with the new revelations?

You are poised for revelation, Mari. And you are right that I have shown you a sign of my presence. I am a golden blue light that shines forth just for you. Each have their light that will shine for them. This one is yours. Continue to do your completion of what stands between us: your "others orientation." *

You owe no one anything.

Now the outside of the light is blue, and the interior is gold.

This is representative of the outward orientation (the blue) growing dimmer, and the inner orientation (the gold) growing more brilliant. It is almost at its perfect balance, and it is this per-fect balance—as the balance of the sun and moon, as the balance of the stars and planets that fill the heavens—that is the natu-ral. Heaven and Earth in perfect Harmony. You are the Earth. You are the Heaven of the Earth. You are why the Earth is here. Heaven is why you are here. You are the reason for this life-giving planet being in existence.

In the new humanity, Mother Earth becomes the landscape

---

* In "Mirari," p. 312, it is suggested that this orientation delays many.

to which thinking will not be brought—where thought is no longer a matter of concise, abridged mental constructs, but of mind and heart being in the perfect alignment of wholeheartedness, and thus, in perfect harmony with her. It is here that repentance—a change in thinking—will occur. It is here that the either/or of form and content, as well as feminine and masculine, will be reconciled.

"The same energy exists in the stars of the heavens and the waters of the ocean that exists in you. This energy is the form and content of the embrace. It is within you and It surrounds and encompasses you. It is you and all who exist with you. It is the body of Christ. It is like unto what the water of the ocean is to the living matter that exists within it. The living matter that exists within the ocean has no need to search for God. It lives in God. So do you."*

You are the ones who will realize this. You are the ones who will bring completion to the Earth's own longing to become fully sentient, fully able to respond in kind in her relationship with you. As you transform into living awareness without thought, Earth will join with you and baptize you and her Holy Self in the joining. She will make Herself a holy partner in union with you and with Heaven. Mother Earth will populate Heaven with the Living. With the divine women and men who will complete Heaven.

I raise my hands in prayer to you, Holy Mother. I bring my fingers to my lips and send you kisses. I send a kiss to your light and to the image of you on my table. This is the perfect "answer"

---

* ACOL T4:5.5

and one I never dreamed of in this way. To bring Heaven to Life and Life to Heaven by bringing Mother Earth to expression of her sentient life.

M

$\mathcal{T}$HE NEW FORECASTING

Holy One,

It is the next day (or the next) and I look up the word sentient in the dictionary. I love what I find. One of its meanings is "mere awareness or sensation that does not involve thought or perception." And so, the Earth needs none of "our" faculties to come to sentience!*

My plot of earth feels fully sentient and able to communicate already, Mary.

This is true, Mari! But it is local and your awareness one to another not "fully" realized yet. More is coming.

I had to turn the light back on to read from the dictionary, and now, with it off, the sky appears as a whitened blue, veering to gray. My trees are utterly still. I can feel myself returning home to myself and to you.

This "coming home" is beautiful, is it not? Isn't it an expression of "Mirari"? Of an ever-changing form of wonder? A wonder that brings to you, at least momentarily, a release of the pressure you so commonly hold within yourself.

In between these times that hold you in the embrace, you can, and do, make your forays into the world. You then hold within an allegiance to the holy words that have come to you, as well as an allegiance to your own self and your fellow travelers of this time to end all time. This is a pressure that you feel with your lovely loyalty, but the pressure comes more of self-doubt than of your calling.

Yes, I know this is true.

---

* *Webster's New World Dictionary*, 1988.

While you took a step beyond self-doubt on this mountain top adventure, "time" is still the real pressure. The pressure is that, even if you do not feel ready, you need to show up, you have to share anyway, you must, nevertheless, get on the airplane.

When you are sitting on the other side of your coffee table from Mary Love, there is no pressure to share, and no self-doubt. The same happened on your travels. You sat across a different coffee table with your friend, and your doubt about yourself shifted.

M

The type of pressure you experience barely existed in my time. What you call pressure came only in the natural ways: to eat, to sleep, to have shelter, to connect around a fire under the stars or beneath a tree or in a dwelling that offered shelter from the sun. Sometimes these needs took extra attention or extreme measures, and all we could do in such times was respond. It is the same for you with weather events. When there is a big snow, all else is set aside. You must respond to the event of weather.

Travel was communal. But most travel was imposed, as my journey while pregnant was imposed. The "imposed" can become the greatest pressures in time.

Until Yeshua's maturity, he knew little of this. "We" knew little of this. In our community, the vast majority of our time was not pressurized by external forces. Not in the beginning. The Romans brought this pressure to our small communities as the "white men" brought it to the Native Americans. They were a threat to our way of life. It's not to say we didn't have our common

*concerns, but they were rarely pressurized or dictated by forces
other than nature.*

*You come home and you have choices that do not feel like real
choices. You feel the need to respond to the foray you have made,
and that becomes a pressure to respond. Yet you come here, as you
come home, also to release the pressure.*

And I am so thankful that I can, Mary. I remember you saying
in "Mirari" that naturalness is the way of The New and that it is
returning. While conferences have impact, the way of them doesn't
feel natural and I didn't do as much as I could have beforehand to
help my friend who sponsored it.

*All experience this back-and-forth in this time. One makes
her way into the world and returns home, where for periods she
can forget it all, and where in other instances, she or he must
respond to the events of the day past or the day approaching, as
well as those needs common to all, such as food and cleanliness.*

*In life at this time, with the increased ability to be "connect-
ed" via social media, the pressure might never end. And so there
come into being those who do not even see or feel the pressure. It
is simply the way life is. A vacation becomes a mere adherence to
a new schedule. One's work, even that of the heart, is plotted on
the map of time.*

There is a draw and a repulsion I feel around these conferences,
both at once, which feels similar to many aspects of life. It's like the
whole world is in an identity crisis and no one knows what to do.
This feels like such a strange time.

*Yes. All of this has a great deal to do with this "strange time."
Here, we begin stepping away from time's former boundaries. We
change the map of time. We enter the period of new forecasting.*

We chart a new course. We bring new revelations. We remove time from her little calendar squares, and release time to be, along with you, free from her bondage.

Time is certainly part of the pressure, Mary, but what I'm feeling is of things happening without connection, relevance, intimacy . . . meaning. That's the world I can't live in.

When the connection person-to-person is made? And it is real? *Then* something has happened.

What I've felt since coming home is the sense of loneliness in a crowd—and it doesn't feel like my own, although it may be. Sometimes I feel "loneliness" here too, but in an intimate way that I can embrace. Today, though, I am feeling a larger loneliness, a world weariness. It is a lonesomeness that doesn't even know itself. And I have a touch of it too.

A melancholy, a sweet sort of sadness, is returning—as it so often does. It seems to be part of my cycle of going away and returning, and it feels like a metaphor for going away from Self, (which is very much like going away from home), and for something else too, that comes of . . . I don't know what.

I want to envision a new way, Mary. I really do.

Don't you know that this is what we are doing?

M

A gaggle of geese fly by, only barely coming together. Seen at the start of their formation, they seem to be heading out as randomly as the rest of us.

This is not a hopeless reverie I'm sending out, Mary, and I know that. But it is, perhaps, a feeling that even we haven't reconnected since I returned, and the feeling that it may mean I haven't yet re-connected with myself.

This sounds like a matter of trust going on, my Mari.

Really? Maybe so. I am suspecting myself for being taken by the popular interest in me, and by the man who is going to be in town and asked to see me. I looked for information about him online and saw nothing that gave me a sense of who he is. He's written all these books, and I wonder if anyone knows him. I feel as though I'm feeling his loneliness, and that loneliness is coming from every quarter. This small bit of public popularity has attracted my attention to this. There were other things as well.

These demonstrations of the more public connections are having a strange effect on me that I cannot name, but that may be a loneliness inherent in being solitary within the crowd, as with the leader of the crowd. It is this thing that has gone wrong in society as a whole, this being "unknown" even within one's group. I suspect this "lonely in a crowd" feeling is rampant—a constant for many—yet it only finds me rarely because of your grace and my solitude. With "us," as two women together in this way, I still have a gap, a space in which I am fully with myself.

I wonder at that needed space and its graces.

As I write it out further, I know that on this return "home" I am still away from that pure space, which is where, I believe, true trust arises. Does that make sense?

Perfect sense, Mari.

M

THE SANCTITY OF THE ONE

You are speaking of the sanctity of the One, the One without duplicate, which each of us are. This is the cause of joining, without which there would be no awareness of union. It is sometimes felt as loneliness. Joining is more than the acquaintance you have with a few here and there at these affairs. In truth, you tend to come home a little disheartened, don't you?

That's true, Mary. I do.

We are not going to do anything to figure this out, Mari. Not right now. Not ever. Instead, together we take in the disheartened and the lonesome. We do this with a way of knowing and sharing that is often misunderstood. In my time, we called it prayer.

My own thoughts were sheltered within me, and yet, they were always being shared in this way we called "prayer." It is the way you follow here with me, without knowing it. I understand that at times you miss your Jesus as we converse. He is the one you evoked, throughout your life, in your sheltered thoughts of prayer: "Dear Jesus, please be with me." What you did not realize was that in "all" your sheltered thoughts, you prayed, even those that were figuring-it-out thoughts. They were prayers because they were shared implicitly and worked through, within yourself, to their natural conclusion—especially all that could not be "figured out."

Almost all prayer is like this—a giving up, or giving over— after a long soliloquy of what you could not bring into focus on your own. Praying continuously is what is happening when you know that what you cannot bring into focus is given over in your heart, to the Holy. No matter that you may cry or rant, the trust is there. A trust that you are not alone.

But you are wondering about those who do not let themselves be known, correct?

Yes, because that is my feeling. Sometimes the most known are the least known.

And of course, you are tender and empathetic to these "least known." But do not confuse them with yourself, my Mari. You are held by an awareness of those who know you, both in time, and outside of time (as all are held, but who, without the awareness, know it not). Some have an awareness of the divine but lack the human. For others, it is the opposite. It is time now to realize that both are needed. Loneliness is the demonstration that this is so.

Loneliness, as you know, can serve as a longing that is itself a catalyst. It is not to be feared. To worry over it is the cause and effect of your "others orientation." You can let this orientation go now, without disregarding the loneliness you see and feel. You already know of it. Knowing it, you recognize it.

This is "a good." It is good to recognize the depth of this feeling of loneliness, whether it is in yourself, or in another. The recognition is enough. There is nothing to correct. No intervention needed. The recognition itself is a stimulus for greater knowing. Trust it. Trust the recognition. Trust yourself. In what you recognize, you bless. It may not seem so, but it is so.

M

The Source of Awareness

The time of revelation is very much like what we have just shared in dialogue. We have shared about loneliness. It has been revealed that loneliness is not to be feared but welcomed as a way of knowing. Each feeling is the same. Each feeling is the "source," the source of awareness.

"Signs" will mean nothing to those who are not intimate with their own feelings. If you can dismiss one feeling, you can never find the One.

The One to be revealed is you—the revelation is of oneself. When one's Self is revealed, all is available to be discovered by you. Revelation is an inner occurrence that will, one day, be so widespread that it will appear as an outer occurrence. The "revealed ones"—those who know themselves—will gather, and in this gathering, there will begin a whisper, "The Time has Come. The Time is Now."

There will come a revelation of shared knowing that will transcend time and space, and cause the explosion of consciousness that is to come.

This has already happened with you and Mary Love. You have already experienced revelation "together." You have had shared revelations. Now you can see that they have greater significance than you realized.

How could I have had such a significant experience and still "know not what to do"?

Because you imagine that, "if" revelation had truly come, you "would" know what to do. *Why do you think there is something to do?*

Let this question sit with you. Understand that when it is said, "where two or more are gathered," it means that "two" can be a gathering.

M

REVELATION:
A WAY OF KNOWING IN TIME

OCTOBER 26, 2019

My Mother,

It is days later, and I feel such a rapport with what we've written so far. It has seeped into me like a fine mulled wine, bursting with flavors that complement the season's own aroma. I feel warmed from the inside out, delighted and thankful to be out of the cultural context. Sitting here, alone with you, I realize that I am away from my "other's thinking." What a blessing!

Of course, I'm in my cabin, sitting with my sentient trees, your living image, the sounds of traffic and birds. All of it is of one piece. I am blissfully aware that I have no idea of where we are going . . . which I do not always feel. Sometimes I have a "good idea" of what is coming, or a sense of it, or have not had it enter my mind at all. Today I am aware that, although the thought of revelation has entered me, I have no idea "what" will come. I suppose that, itself, is the idea behind the sensation of "revelation." Maybe it is all a giving up, as for me of my "others orientation." It is surrender that lends itself to the unexpected and the sublime—to what is coming, rather than what is apparent.

And I am content with these thoughts. The volume of things I have to do stands apart from "here." They are for another time, although I will invite you into that work with me when the time for it is present. I remember how you spoke of being "here," and one of the ways was exactly like what just happened. "[W]e move from what was revealed into the awareness that the revelation has occurred." *

Here, I am so enamored by the sun that has come in the crisp way of fall, and with the trees, so moved by a soft wind that they are clearly enjoying their own hanging and waving splendor, and maybe even my appreciation. There is such warmth and shelter from "other noises" in the furnace's steady blowing. That, too, is a safe haven from all that would enter our space. I'm so happy to be with you this morning.

And I with you. There is not "something" to be revealed here, Mari. There is only revelation.

I'm beginning to sense that, Mary.

I know you are. Revelation is a way of knowing. Revelation is a continual, individual, yet communal reverie of communication and creation, with no impediments or blocks in its way. This is the reason your brother and I have worked on your others orientation more than any other. Even though many of what you consider your problems are relieved by this orientation's release, it is not the main reason for our work with you on this. No. This is about being present. The Act of Revelation is precisely being present to yourself and to time. Here, what is revealed is your joint tempo, your unified seasons. Being present to yourself and to time is the revelation of The New that is here and coming. It is here and coming into relationship with you.

I remember that the saying, "The truth shall be revealed to you," is the same as the saying, "Your Self shall be revealed to you."† This is like that, isn't it?

---

* "Mirari," p. 308

† ACOL T1:4:22, see also 23-27

Yes, what is revealed is always "a truth," a truth given within the light of your own life.

Your relation to time is here to be revealed as truth. This is not a relationship to clock time but to that time that is also sentient, and sentient enough now to care for your regard and to regard you as well. This regard is a matter of affection! Affection and attention. It is to heed, my daughter, to heed and to hold in a certain light.

Your regard "is" a certain light. Each of you have a certain light that comes by way of regard. To heed this light in the way of The New conceives the beam of revelation, like unto the column of light you once saw, right here. It is a beam of radiant energy that broadcasts—like radio waves, like nuclear particles that signal The New.

It is like unto the hum of soul and the whisper of the wind of Memoria. All are connected by the memory of time, and all time is within you.

M

In my time, life on the land is what we lived. I welcomed it after my life in the temple. While we have, together, felt into your life at home as a child, we have also identified our kinship as women. This is mostly from your life in the cabin, which is more like my life in the days that came before Yeshua's birth, and after his death. A change began with his impending birth because I, like you, had a new feeling in me then, akin to what you call the pressure of your commitment to this work.

I feel a light around me, Holy One, that feels of sun and more than sun.

Yes, my daughter, notice such feelings. Record them when they arise. There is a reason for them and for the recording that will reveal more to you later. You will remember them, and you will see.

You may guess, even now, that this light is akin to the beam I have just spoken of, a light of gratefulness for your service, as I had a light come that recognized mine. Without this light we could not, alone, bear the weight of Yeshua's life—not me "in form"—nor you "in words" that continue to reveal his light. This light affects the human body with kind consideration, embraces it and energizes it, even when it does not seem so. This light kept me going, and now you as well.

M

The life now of a rancher, a farmer, or a naturalist bears more resemblance to life in a city than ours did then. But our lives were not so different from such lives as your ancestors lived a hundred years ago, or to ones like the Amish who choose a more sequestered way. Our lives were lived primarily "in the country," as you would say, in villages away from the cities and their hazards—hazards that included the Romans.

Remember that the nature of the Bible is one of "recorded history," which makes it quite different from certain aspects of spirituality that would deny history or its life. This recorded history is often a story of battles and conquests, of good and evil, of migrations and the salvation it was simply to survive. Fleeing armies was a way of life in biblical times.

This life and way of living has left artifacts that last to this day. Our history is the history of a people. Don't forget this. Yeshua and I lived in the history of this world and its people. We existed in an historical reality. We were the corpus sanctum, the holy body of life within an historical reality, as are the stars and moon that exist in like manner. As trees and spices and lands and rivers exist as historical materiality. All are of the physical world.

Lands of our lives were noted and still exist: Arimathea, Jerusalem, the Mt. of Olives, Bethlehem and Bethany, the Sea of Galilee, my hometown of Nazareth.

Following Yeshua's birth, Joseph and I lived in what you might call a compound within a community too small to even be called a village. We lived with other members of our family. My life consisted not only of continual prayer but continual work. From dawn to dusk we all worked to provide the necessities of life, and so did not think of this "as" work, but simply as life. This was not unlike those still living in villages in Africa, Asia, South America, or your own rural people, especially those of just centuries ago. In our compound, we shared an oven, walked to wells for water, used a millstone for grinding grain, kept animals, tended to the needs of cleanliness . . . and of course . . . the children.

After the way I was raised, much of it was new to me, and I had to work to fit in, as you have done. I was "an odd one." And so, I can identify with feelings you have had more than you can imagine, and with the single mothers for whom you feel yourself an advocate, as well as to their adjustment into life beyond their identification with their "illegitimate" motherhood.

Once I adjusted to village life, though, I was happy for it. For a few years I felt a sense of normalcy and I knew a freedom in it.

It was a joy to be amongst the women and children, and to have physical work occupy me. This is also much the same as you find in your "regular" life, with your family: a sense of limited but secure freedom, and commitment to family and the friends who extend your family.

This is true, Mary. I think often of leaving—not for any lack of love, but due to wanting "less" of everything noisy, or messy, or dramatic. But at the same time, I realize that what often feels like distractions have the odd side effect of making me more grateful and present when I am here.

Yes! There is a way in which this limited freedom guides and secures you and even liberates you for this other passion. In this way were you able to claim, and be free for, your passion to Jesus. My passion was raising Yeshua, yes, but also more than this, just as you, in your work with Jesus, "raised" Jesus to awareness in you, and raised yourself and others to awareness of the change his birth brought into the world—a change that has never ceased to unfold.

You can see this as a physical and wholehearted act of rather ordinary importance, while also knowing it is something more— something that means more for you as well as the world, and the future yet to be created.

And people need to believe in this again.

M

FROM PARABLE TO PARADOX AND OBSERVATION

Mother,

You sent me to the dictionary for this one.

Yes, I want to speak of this change that is going on in a new way. Yet it began with you. You sought to look up the word "panic" because the thought arose in your mind that writing is a panic. Is this not correct?

Yes, it is. It was such a strange thought! I turned to the dictionary because I imagined that "panic" would have another underlying meaning that would explain why it arose in that way.

And there you found the idea of panic as "a swelling"! The swelling of a bud was referred to, and this led to blossom, and blossom to inflorescence: the producing of blossoms. And we could stop right there, with the swelling that leads to the blossoming, and to creating anew. What a delightful turn, in terms of your writing, to find that a negative sounding word could, instead, have such a positive meaning. But let's go even further, to where you found words that extended from the root.

"Pan" is "universal," a swelling or arch embracing the unity of many parts. And then your attention was drawn still further, to "parable," and then to the line drawings of "parabola" and to "parallax." And it was this drawing of the parallax that made you realize this jaunt through your dictionary was for a greater purpose. It came when you began to think you had been wasting your time

to chase this errant thought. That is when you got the feeling that it was purposeful, and then. . . my part in our adventure begins.

I do love the way this happens, Mary.

I love it too, for what you may have forgotten is how your often "errant" thoughts led your Jesus to respond in the way he did, and now my response, in the dialogue we are having, is the same.

Your brother taught with parables to respond to the errant thoughts of those of his time, you see! And the "errant" is not the same as an "error." The errant long for the journey of discovery, and all those with eyes to see and ears to hear have been so moved throughout the history of time.

But the way of time and the journeys of discovery have changed. Parables were stories that gave examples or compared one situation to another. Now we can use the word paradox, and the image of parallax, to convey the change going on in how you, as more sophisticated people in this time, not only think, but come to new thoughtfulness about the nature of life and your journey of discovery. The quest is on and we have come to further it.

First, we speak of the common paradox: a statement that may seem contradictory, unbelievable, or absurd, when it is in fact true. Next, we speak of this paradox occurring as a change in the position of the relationship between the living person and her Source. It is a long way of coming to the idea I will propose, which is that a great many forms of support will be required for all who will need assistance to accept the changes ahead. Some will find understanding from new scientific discoveries: novel ideas drawn from earth science, botany, physics, or astronomy. Some from writing or art or music. Every means is being drawn to the forefront to guide this birth of The New.

Astronomy is why I mention the parallax, which is about, primarily, the change in perspective that occurs in relationship of one to another. This relationship of one to another is the leading edge of the way of knowing in this new time, particularly the change to the view of the person and her God. But not only there.

Envision a person viewing the heavens through a telescope. Do you see? It refers to the "starting point" of the self as the observer. It is about how life, in all its variance and complexity, "is viewed," and how each one individually, in relationship to the Source of life, comes to the unity of vision that is the revelation of The New. Unity of vision comes of unifying the way in which you see.

"See" that in every circumstance and field, the relationship is the guide that suits the distinctiveness of each person, as for you, writing, in all its complexity, leads you to panic, and panic to the swelling that blossoms!

"See" that paradox assures that different ways do not make different, but only reveal diverse relationships.

Relationships are distinct within time. Era to era, the norms of relationship change. Region to region, continent to continent, religion to religion, norms change. In this globalization, with the ever-present cries of differences, and the insight that differences do not make different, the paradox of life itself can be accepted without fear or consternation.

Still, the most enormous of all changes is the change to how you view your relationship—within time—with time Herself. It is crucial to your new orientation to yourself, to all of life, and to all you have seen as beyond this realm of life.

And so, as we proceed, I ask each to be observant,* to note the differences of the ways in which you see from one context to another—the way you see each view that you observe. Become devoted to this observation, as it will begin the change that needs to come before you will accept that, not only is this a new time, but that time herself is new.

I can tell you that I could never have imagined the time in which you now live when I was living my earthly life. Yet I can tell you, just as honestly, that all you can imagine can come to be, and that what can come to be, is more than you can imagine. Imagination invites revelation and unites with it.

"Observance happens in relationship, the very relationship that disallowed the making of a separate self. Observance is linked to cause and effect being one. What is observed is in relationship with the observer and this relationship causes an effect. Because this was part of the original choice for the physical experience, it is a natural choice to serve our new purpose: the miracle that will allow you to exist as who you are in human form. See what perfect sense this makes as your human form is an observable form. It is thus from observable form that the final learning will take place. This is the perfect example of using what you have made for a new purpose. It

---

* "[W]e move past *study* and *learning* to observation, vision, and revelation." ACOL T4:9.1

is the perfect ending for the desired experience, as it was the goal of the desired experience."*

M

---

* ACOL T3:18.3

$\mathcal{S}$OPHIA AND THE RETURN

OCTOBER 28, 2019

As I shared with you at the start of this year, which seems such a long time ago, Sophia is the awareness that birthed Love as Itself. As a companion to awareness, Sophia conceived the translation of thought and feeling into a relationship with Love Itself, a relationship that birthed the world.

And so, we have awareness as the thought of Love, birthed out of the Hush of Love, and awareness of feeling born out of the awareness of Love's thought, and these together became the nature of the Life of Love, the sound and light, the creation, the third of the trinity that stands at the beginning.*

This, I told you, and share again, only to help you to see, as well as remember, that

". . . awareness was not complete until both thought and feeling were birthed. This duad of thought, coupled with feeling, is what you now call the masculine and feminine, which only in relationship, *could Love, and create as Love creates.*

"Love has no attributes because it is the 'before' from which attributes arose and moved always toward extending Love's creation out of itself. God was, and is, Love's awareness of Being via the relationship of thought and feeling."†

Sophia, this feminine face of God, is not only what revealed

---

* "Mirari," p. 85

† "Mirari," p. 101 (emphasis added)

God to God, but what is of God's knowing of God—like unto the soul of God. The Sophia is the feminine counterpart to the mind of God, as it is the non-physical counterpart, "the before" of the physical body of human beings. And as your soul is also "you," Sophia is also God. Sophia is the She of God and humanity, who revealed love to thought, and birthed the movement of love and thought, beyond thought, into life. This is what love initiates: the "living" speech, Word, or idea of God . . . made "knowable." You can see, in the knowable, a reflection of what occurs in every aspect of your own life, and all lives.

That of Sophia is, to you now, and me then, an invitation beyond the current idolatry to a distant and powerful God, and beyond the physical and practical idolatry of "a" god, whether that god be one calling for worship, belief, or piety. This is a god shielded from "knowing" by the very naming of separate things that became a belief in separate things. God knows "each" only as one of the divine "two," the divine duad. God knows each through union, which is not "knowing" as it has come to be understood. "Knowing" as "naming" or "understanding" is not enough.

"Creation" is the language of God, the beauty of the marriage union of the feminine and masculine in God's being. God's Knowing is the Knowing of the Creator of Creation.

In Memoria, Sophia reveals the heart's imagery, an imagery and symbolism that brings the creator to light by knowing the creator in oneself. Knowing the creator in yourself, revelation gives way to manifestation. Sophia manifests the beauty that swells with life, and bursts into visible and audible expressions. She carries to you the senses required to appreciate sights through vision; smells through scent; sound through hearing; weight and measure through the feel of physicality in water and rock, grain and blossom; and living beings, who expand God's creation by having an awareness of Self as Creation's Being.

Sophia created what made love possible: the swelling, and then the burst into what was the onset of imagination in consciousness, the imagined becoming real, and the real taking on the feeling, knowing, and creating ways of Being.

Imagination was the central feature of creation, birthed by the feminine and masculine of God knowing each other within oneness, and in oneness, discovering the multiplicity possible from their Being. They are Being. They are . . . "Being" rather than "a" being, or two beings. Their "Being" made it possible for us each to say, "I am," and Their Being passed down, in form, the necessary "mating" of the masculine and feminine in the reproduction of life as Being.

In some ways, none of this matters. It does not matter as fact or myth. It does not matter as knowledge. It matters only that you have some idea of the nature of Being, and that it is synonymous with the duad of the divine masculine and feminine. It is one and the same with creation.

This I knew, not by thought, or knowledge, but by joining with the Creator to bring this combining together into the human form of Yeshua. I knew things I did not know, and that were impossible to know or believe. But I "knew" them in my Being. This is my memory of revelation—the very sense of revelation coming together in Memoria.

In this togetherness of Being, a togetherness given the names of God and Sophia, God and Self, there is one Being. In this togetherness there is one memory, a memory of creation.

Beings are reflectors of the mode of Being. God reflects the Being of Sophia, and Sophia the Being of God. Our way of Mary does the same in each of you.

Our way of being is in alignment with Being. It is hard to express in words, which is why I speak to you of "views" such as that of parallax, as well as your "orientation" to knowing. Reflection, like memory, is a way of revelation. Being as well as revelation come of the reflection, one to another, that occurs and is held in memory. This must happen once again, for the return, once again, to Being.

"Christ-consciousness is the awareness of existence through relationship. It is not God. It is not man. It is the relationship that allows the awareness that God is everything. It has been called wisdom, Sophia, spirit. It is that without which God would not know God. It is that which differentiates all from nothing. Because it is that which differentiates, it is that which has taken form as well as that from which form arose. It is the expression of oneness in relationship with Its Self."*

M

---

* ACOL D:Day11.7

THE REVELATION
OF REFLECTION

Holy One,

I know something new from what you shared days ago—something that I've only realized in rereading it, and that I have not seen in this way before. I have received "new knowing" that is of that type I do not know, but that I want to admit to having some sense of, because you said it matters. It matters that I have some idea of the nature of revelation of Being.

I have seen it in two things you said. One is that Being is synonymous with creating. The other is from when you spoke these words: "I knew things I did not know, and that were impossible to know or believe. But I knew them in my Being."

It is so elusive that as I typed I lost my sense of it. But I know you've said this of me too, and because you have, I feel a certain inner excitement.

You knew, from having comingled with God. You knew, from the combining, what you could not know alone. And Being is of this that happens as we *join* in Being—as there is a *togetherness* of Being. You have called this the duad and are passing this knowing on to me and us.

M

A squirrel is out scratching himself on the wood pile, and I've seen a red squirrel scutter about too. It was so still as I began this morning that the movement of life is wonderful, as is the way this squirrel is grooming and satisfying his itches. A squirrel that must mate, as we do, to produce new life. Not quite the comingling of Being, but a part of it in this realm, where you say, "Beings are reflectors of the mode of Being." Reflectors of the mode of God. God's way of being God: Knowing one to another.

You are close, my Mari. You are to give back as you have received: to return, in being, to the Being One, in order to mirror, once again, the Being of Love. Here you see the genesis of what has been reflected forward into life.

You brother speaks of the next step in A Course of Love:

"Although you have been called to union you still hold an image of the state of unity as separate from yourself. Although I have removed myself from the role of teacher and entered this dialogue with you as an equal, you still hold an image of me as 'other than' yourself. You will never fully rely upon your Self while you hold these images. When I call you to replace conviction with reliance, I call you to replace belief in an outside source with reliance upon your Self."*

"Part of the difficulty you find in accepting reliance on your Self is what you have 'learned' within this Course. As you 'learned' to remove the ego and deny the personal self, you transferred your reliance to me and to the state of unity. This was purposeful. Now, however, you are asked to return to wholeness, a state in which you are not separate from me or from the state of union."†

---

* ACOL D:Day10.15
† ACOL D:Day10.17

"You are one *in being* with your Father, your Creator, the origi-nator and denominator of life.

"To have experienced only separation is to have known only half of any experience, to have seen every experience in only one dimension. ... By realizing the unity of the relationship in which experience becomes manifest, you not only realize oneness, but realize that you are a creator and that you always have been."*

Your feelings reflect who you are. Do you see and feel this dif-ferently now?

Yes!

"Those called to the way of Mary are called to be what they want to see reflected in the world and to the realization that this reflec-tion is the new way of creation. In their *being* they become what they want to create."†

Even God had to be seen to be known. And so, it was the fem-inine knowing of Sophia that awoke God's own Being? And now, in doing the same in my, and our, recognition of God's "Being" we ... what? Start anew? Become new? Get to reveal The New? Or .. . know as we are known by love?

Now you've got it. One in being, different in the relationship of knowing, and loving, one to another.

$$\mathcal{M}$$

---

* ACOL D:Day31.4-5 (emphasis added)
† ACOL D:Day19.4 (emphasis added)

THE WORLD AS SEEN THROUGH MEN'S EYES

OCTOBER 29, 2019

My Mother,

Last night, I read through the latest *National Geographic*, which is on "women." There was a bit about the march for women's right to vote, with posters from the time and lots of pictures, which they're so good at. There were many comments from women—primarily successful women from around the world. But not one from a mother, or about being a mother.

There was one statistic that related to women who are mothers. It noted that women make "only" 14 percent less than men now, until you figure in the unpaid time a woman takes off to have children, care for them, or to care for another, such as an ageing parent. Then it becomes 49 percent.*

There was much about harassment too, especially in business.

What struck me was not the harassment, nor the pay inequality, but that it was all so business and career oriented. Achievement oriented.

You had already given me the title of this chapter. Maybe it was because I was thinking of the loneliness of men. This feeling has grown in me, from a "few" men, to. . . men. It feels more isolating than the loneliness I imagine being common to women. It seems loneliness *is* the isolation of not knowing and being known. I sus-

---

* "What Needs to Change in the Next 10 Years?" *National Geographic*, 11.2019, Women: A Century of Change, p. 108

pect that, for many men, it is a "learned" holding back of the intimacy from which knowing comes. Perhaps it is due to the need to be strong, or manly. I can feel for them, and still sense so strongly the truth of that title you gave me . . . because of the magazine. The world "is" seen through men's eyes. Through their value of "achievement." Women fight to be equal via achievement, as if equality is still in question and achievement is the proof of equality, gender to gender. What greater evidence could there be of the world being seen through men's eyes?

It is what your brother often called "insane," is it not? It is absurd. And it is necessary for this to come to light, while at the same time it is no disparagement of achievement. It is only that it is not an accurate reflection of a woman's being . . . or that of a man.

You have felt it is your right to question a world in which the burdens of abandoned mothers and non-support-paying, uninvolved men, crush the spirits of so many women, and leave children to be raised in poverty. Here, you add to this, the missing of even the whiff of an idea that the raising of children is holy work—still the most valuable of work. This, has bothered you.

Is the raising of children even seen as holy any longer?

It is my daughter. Of course, it is. But not so much "seen" as "felt." The feeling, however, must be carried over into the action of raising children, and it is here that achievement and raising children is divided by sex, and where the dual desires of the woman are put to grueling, and for the most part, unshared tests. So, too, is it, with the work of caring for the elders, the frail and the ailing. Unless it is "paid" work, it just doesn't count as achievement, does it?

The failure of nurture is the rejection of the masculine model of courage, strength, responsibility, rationality, daring. This model is being "used" rather than cultivated as what it innately is.

Of course, there are some men who nurture splendidly and some women who cannot nurture at all. To talk in this way is not the best, but necessary to our dialogue and its emphasis on embodying the feminine "and" masculine within. This is acceptance of all that you are, and is equivalent to assenting to, and embracing, your Being.

To realize how it is, and has been, is a vital part of revealing how the different natures of men and women developed. We take to heart a new view of the expectations and causes of heartbreak. We do this to engender respect, not only for children and the frail, but for all who care for them.

We speak of this to emphasize that the desire to be normal overrides most other desires, and that the norm is now an achievement model and an earning model, and not often a model that leaves room for much else—for either sex.

The achievement model is inhumane.

M

Gender was once a way of organizing the world around the survival of a family, and the continuation of a family through children. This was exceptionally important. In my time, no man wanted his family line to end. No man could build a better life or future without children.

In your time, men do not give their names to a third of the children of the world. Women can proudly continue their line in

this way, but what I am speaking of is a difference only recent-
ly come into being. This is the way that the last fifty years have
changed life fundamentally, particularly in developed countries.
The fundamental change was to the ultimate, and only, accepted
shape of family throughout time.

A way as old as time itself—the way of a family unit—the
way of the sacramental nature of the joining of men and women,
a way most often overseen by the elders (once commensurate with
the wise ones of a culture), has fallen.

The way of a woman tending to the children while the man
provided, has been upended. I speak of this not only for your
own experience of it, my Mari, but because this is an enormous
upheaval to a central way of being in the world—to an intrinsic
"given" of the partnership that manifests the babe who comes
into the world helpless.*

Helpless! Male or female, each babe comes into the world in
need of constant care! This is the way of human life. No one enters
as an adult, ready and willing to care for themselves! There is a
reason for the model and the care, for the commitment and the
devotion.

It reveals another reason that self-fulfillment, earning, free-
dom, career, accomplishment, and esteem have subjected the
times to the terms of men. The god of achievement slowly deval-
ued women, and children, and family, and the power, yes power,

---

* According to Pew Research Center, the U.S. has the highest share of single parents in the world. In 2019, almost a quarter of U.S. children under the age of 18 lived in a household with a single parent and no other adults present other than adult children. Being a single parent predominantly affects mothers around the world. 49 percent of Black children in the U.S. lived with one parent as did 28 percent of Hispanic kids and 21 percent of White kids. The UK has the second-highest rate of single parenting.

of nurture. Much of what you are seeing in the world you are seeing due to lack of nurture.

As women began to reclaim their lives and sovereignty, the family was no longer a kingdom for the men to rule. Men lost their control there and sought it elsewhere. While secure men grew more respectful, and more nurturing, threatened men returned to the way of the primitive: the conqueror, the despoiler, the user, and the abuser. Such ideas as "common decency" began to decline.

Women, who once had no recourse to the family structure, were liberated from it and began to shine with their new freedom. They became achievers in their own right. Once they did so, the greater number of earners created an unnecessary upsurge in the cost of products, particularly housing. People had more to spend, and to the opportunists, the way to greater wealth gleamed before their eyes.

Now, I am not saying that women are not ready to be creators in more means than giving birth to, and caring for, a child. I am not saying that women's fulfillment is not the blessing it is to the world. I am saying that the world is still measured by men's standards, and that the measure of a family, being raised in love and equity, has been disassembled in this rapid progression along the road to achievement.

In only fifty years, this change in the structure of families has become close to a new norm—which means it is accepted.

It seems as if the "unity" of marriage is dissolving and that, for many, being alone—even with the raising of children—is becoming as much a choice as an accident. What possible meaning is there to this time, these ways, and this rapid change?

Think back! The private world of "family" has changed almost totally from when you were a child. In that short amount of time, it left behind what had, since the beginning of time, been considered a natural and necessary parental desire to raise children "together." Is it a matter of irresponsibility? Of independence? Of something out of balance? Of a new choice? Or has it come of something more insidious . . . something hidden in plain sight: an achievement model that benefits achievers only.

What calls for a return of wholeness and balance more than that which has grown so separate and unsteady that it is ready to topple?

M

CHOOSING THE EVENT OF IMAGINATION

OCTOBER 30, 2019

People now claim serenity when what they are actually feeling and displaying is the nonchalance of cool detachment. The imaginary scales or fortunes of fate, meant to be an emblem of justice and the power to choose one's own path within limits, have become ideas that are old and dusty emblems of a former time. Symbols have lost their meaning. This is more dangerous than you can imagine. But you need not imagine it. It has come to be.

As a woman not prone to easy decision-making, you know of the power it is to decide, and have learned painfully of what comes of not having, or feeling as if you do not have, the power to make a choice. You have also experienced times when stating your preference, or even your "knowing" of what is needed, is dismissed. Many women have. You all, men and women, see the way meaningless choices can inundate you and beset you with weariness. You feel beleaguered. Overwhelmed.

Oh, Mary, this reminds me of my sweet dad and how he was with the mail. I can remember visiting him when his kitchen table was overflowing with it. He would just feel so beleaguered . . . your exact word. And now that I think of it, Mom did too. I never thought to suggest this with Dad, but when Mom was inundated with appeals, I told her, "Just say a prayer, and then you can peacefully put the request in the trash." She looked at me in a sort of startled way, but as if it was a good idea that she was surprised she'd never thought of. "It's what I do," I told her.

I'd bet, Mary, that people like my mom and dad gave a greater percentage of their income than do the wealthy.

Here is another reason why I have counseled you toward "knowing" as a place of non-choice. While you cannot always follow what you know, knowing what you would do "if you could" leaves you with self-awareness rather than self-denial.

"Not knowing" can be linked to both a failure of imagination and to a lack of self-worth. Women have learned to stifle their imaginations almost as often as have men, and to devalue self to an even greater "conscious" degree. Most men devalue out of lack of consciousness. Women and feminine leaning men will consciously make choices that devalue who they are because doing otherwise brings harassment. Silence, in the time when speech is needed, is one such devaluing choice.

The importance of balancing the masculine and feminine energies is shown again to be essential. Sexual harmony, and the decision to engage in imperative acts of choice, are tied together in a crucial way. But there is a new way.

M

To engage with the questions of your time can become an act of the imagination. Imagination views the possible and balances the probable. Your engagement may depend upon your remembrance of, and conviction in relying on, the revelation of Memoria, and your welcome of the imaginal realm.

Your dedication to imagining a new future is crucial. This you have not chosen to do, other than in this way. You still, in your "private" life, imagine with old eyes, eyes trained by the life you have lived thus far. This is true for almost everyone. The present and future is based on the past. Each one's past terrors remain in memory, haunting or taunting with their ability to live on in you.

Here is what can make the difference: the recognition of the terror. The recognition of what comes as a fear of not being able to speak or to sleep, or as a panic of writing, or of terrorism—and the revelation that they all come from the same place. Then compassion and vision can enter.

Why do you, my creative one, so often decline to recognize what you imagine with the vision of The New?

I am thankful that you may see my imagination as having a part in this, Mary, but I am chastened to feel that I limit what it could be.

Mari, I am not speaking of imagining a life of monetary wealth for yourself. Here is what you do not realize: you have imagined the wealth of this time coming, this time when you would receive from me. By doing so, your imagination "is" taking part in the creation and revelation of The New.

You also imagine much that you do not allow to occur, such as the sabbatical you have felt you need now. You needed, and finally took, a brief sabbatical last year that allowed us to begin, but you continue to imagine, and delay, the longer time you have desired. You imagine stopping "all" that keeps you busy, and then feel that you merely procrastinate and make things harder on yourself because there are things that you feel "must" be done.

Would this change if you realized that what we do today is what you have imagined into being? That your reception of Jesus, and your response, was what you imagined into being? How would your life change if you saw that your imagination is of a life centered on your writings, that your imagination and your writings are of one piece, and that to imagine a life of world peace, is for you, to write for such a world in your way, and for Michael Mark, or Walter Brueggemann,* to write in their ways? What if you saw that the areas to which your imagination is called are responded to in this way, and are part of your own personal peace, as well as a "piece" of what you are given, in this life, to do?

Your imagination is alive and not as under your control as it has been assumed to be. "Imagine what you desire," they say, and yet you each desire the "event of imagination" that is yours alone, and part of you: the swelling and blooming of you. You do not dream up that to which to apply your imagination, that which you can "ask for," and have come to be! This is a ridiculous notion, as so many notions of the present time are. Your imagination cannot be used in this way!

Your imagination cannot be used—period. What you desire is already there in memory, in the revelation of Memoria.

When you finally let your imagination be, and let imaginal memories guide you . . . then you are being true to your Self.

M

---

* Walter Bruggeman, author of *Prophetic Imagination* and many other books.

THE WORLD AS SEEN
WITH IMAGINATION

We began this part of our dialogue with the world as seen through men's eyes. Here, we continue with the way it is seen through the eyes of the imagination, a feminine quality found in the masculine with magnificent measure—when allowed.

Other than in the arts, imagination is antithetical to ambition or achievements, to dreams of wealth or power. Other than in the arts, it is seldom sanctioned, and when it is legitimized, it is "used," and turned into achievement. While some of these achievements are perfectly sound, others are used in manners that are discordant and at times malignant.

We shift, as your brother suggested, from ways of "use" all around, and replace this idea with that of service as shared in "The Dialogues":

"The power of creation, harnessed by form in the service of form is the next step in the expansion of the power of creation."*

To "harness," your "hands" are needed. We will speak of the word "harness," not as your yoke and your burden, but as that with which you couple to give direction to your expression and your acceptance of your new relationship to time. What you are harnessing is out in front of you. "It" is pulling "you" forward. It is not all up to you.

---

* ACOL D:Day10.1

Some wrap the reins of their harness around a post and stay in one place.

You have felt the yoke of your harness sitting on your shoulders. But you have also felt the freedom of barely hanging on as you whisk through new realms.

Now, "being pulled forward" is one of those statements that, taken out of context, or misapplied by the errant mind, could lead to a great misperception. The idea that you must "lead" is the great misperception. Memoria, the revelation of memory, along with the wonder of Mirari, are your desire, imagination, and orientation, guided by the heart. You are drawn by the pulse of this new guide to reroute the direction, and to redesign the very fabric of, "reality."

$\mathcal{G}$ENDER AND THE
MOVEMENT TO WHOLENESS

I have used the word "men" rather than the softer and less gender centered word "masculine," because boys are taught to be "men." Here, we must speak of the way of women too, because girls are still taught what it means to be a woman. What is taught has certain meanings, not all of which are guided by loving parents. Peers, schools, friends, and especially the new voice of media, fashion the young.

We speak of both men and women / boys and girls, in their physical form, because this too conveys certain meanings that, for most, never change. Those who make the choice to change the physical must also go through the transition of picking up the reins that then tie them to their new future.

The physical is the primary habitat of the human, the flesh and bones, the matter to which soul and spirit have come, the existence of which has been obscured in gender, and the movement of which is halted by the directions she or he are given.

What has been obscured is the given nature of Being.

$\mathcal{M}$

What is happening is meant to be. The heartache of confusion concerning gender is a confusion of one's identity. There is an aspect of identity that is changing in response to both evolution and transformation.

There is a prediction your brother put forth that male and *female would be no more.** Why? Because they were always a melding.*

There were, in my time, and have always been, some physically obvious forms of this melding, ranging from mutation to miracle. It has been called androgynous—from the Greek "andr," which is "male," and "gyne," which was woman or queen. These words have passed to the English as androgyny.

In Aramaic, my language, and the language in which the New Testament was spoken, divisions of male and female, inner and outer, were not emphasized. They did not constitute an essential part of our way of seeing or thinking about our experience.

But, you see, in the writings of scholars—in what was passed down—the Greek was used, and their gender-centric word divisions were included by the scribes. No sacred events are as recorded as ours, and the scribes sought this out as the holiest of work. While their aim was exact "copying," their language nonetheless distorted what was copied. Original meanings were often lost.

Yet there have always been those who, by grace and instinct, sought beyond the language to the heart's elusive meaning. Who is to say that this quest was not meaningful?

$\mathcal{M}$

---

* "What 'was' is being thrown out and the first step in this is embracing what you heretofore have not embraced. You are pulling forth sides of yourselves that were previously undervalued rather than looking for an *other* to provide what you lack. This is important and universal in its impact. It would seem to be about balance but is about wholeness. Male and female are labels laden with attributes. When the different attributes are merged, male and female will be no more and wholeness will reign." ACOL T1:9.16

But let me try using, as an example, that which is sealed by fusion. Imagine jazz "fusion."

Jazz fusion is something new, and it makes what we are speaking of more lyrical and fitting for your time. It is a fusion that blends, through improvisation, different rhythms, elements, and harmonies. It does not render one or the other inconsequential or obsolete, but it does create a new "third."

And we have mainly spoken, so far, of pairs and duads.

The Christ within carries the realized feminine and masculine as a third state of being and can open it for discovery.

My Mother, I feel dizzy with this, the power of this creative act, the unfolding and the listening as well as the content.

This "reeling feeling" is felt most often with words that hold more power than you can carry. Remember, the "reeling" is like unto the motion of the vortex, the whirl of The New. "Heady" words no longer suit you, which is why I brought the metaphor to jazz, without achieving the aim for which I hoped.

Let me say it this way: You already know of this. You have spoken of it. When you and Mary Love come together, this happens. You call it "a third something." It is that which comes of your joining, that which you know would not come without your togetherness. It is "a knowing"—correct?

Yes.

It is "a knowing" that does not lend itself to something you can name. Correct?

Yes.

And yet you sense that it is an invaluable "way of knowing" for what it is "in itself," is this not right?

Absolutely.

And so, what I have described as "fusion" is like this comingling of the two into a third something, a creative combining that, in music and the arts, is called a new "genre." "Genre" is of the same root as the word "gender." And, from this, "engender" which means to cause to exist.

These words convey that something that did not exist before has arisen as a creative blending—as a distinct way of mixing different elements that already existed—into a new pattern or rhythm that allows synthesis.

My daughter, you know of our mutual high regard for language. The Word is so holy. Yes, Yeshua suggests there will be a new language, but what then does he say about this language?

This language will be one of mind and heart.* This language will be one of combining or . . . fusion!

We work together, here, in this wholehearted way, to find a means—without creating words out of thin air—to express that which has no name, in a way that describes an aspect of creation that is essential to what we are revealing.

We, you and I, seek "together" to bring light to this change that has developed at great speed in recent decades. We are messengers as well as comforters. We are here to herald a change to the very nature of life on this planet.

Among our acknowledgments are those which admit that "common genders" always had exceptions and that they presage multiple and focused exceptions. And so, this revealing of the beginning stages of which we speak—the melding of the masculine and feminine—is necessary. Our message will relieve suffering and open the revelatory doors of memory and imagination. Our

---

* ACOL C:21.4-5

way will bring solace to those who are confused as well as room to explore the inner realm of these energies.

The "roles" of the masculine and feminine, the acts of continuation of the species, the medical means to change gender, and to "artificially" create new life in the womb or expel life from the womb—all of these—are playing a part in the way the new future is unfolding, as a "new" future. A future yet to be created.

A future yet to be created is a future continuously being created anew.

We will pause here so that you may rest before we continue. It will be an inspired rest.

M

$\mathcal{A}$ NEEDED SIGN

I experienced a miracle this morning. A blowing tree stopped on a dime.

The limbs were blowing rapidly, the leaves flickering in the light as they turned and twisted. And then utter stillness, in the blink—less than the blink—of an eye. I felt as if my eyes were wide open and seeing truly. It doesn't sound miraculous, but it was. I know it was. Like a demonstration of flashing in and out of time. It was too still to be anything less than a "stoppage."

When it happened, I wrote, "I think it's the greatest miracle I've ever seen!" It was like turning all movement off with the flip of a switch. No degrees of slowing down. No exceptions. Just an "on and off" of movement. I don't think it's physically possible for it not to be a miracle, and it was my Mary Tree, where the blue and gold orb shone.

Now the sun has risen, Mary.

You were missing love yesterday, my daughter. You were missing love. Not love "in life" but the love you usually experience here, as if there had been a disconnect. And so, what better time for you to see a sign than this morning, with your return? Isn't this so?

Yes, now that you say it, I imagine it is true. I needed a sign. I am so happy you gave me one and acknowledged it. My feeling of awe—of the impossibility of "every leaf," every single moving part, small to large, coming still in the same instant—well, it made me feel it and see it with my eyes wide open, so to speak, and as too improbable to not be a miracle.

What happened yesterday, though, didn't feel so much like a disconnect as it did an unnecessary difficulty that brought me to my struggling mind. Okay, and yes, *then* the disconnect. I do not like not understanding! I'm sure you're not surprised to hear that.

No, I am not!

This makes today the perfect day for you to see a sign "that you do not understand," but that nonetheless has, for you, the ultimate meaning of the miracle. What you now delightfully call your "Mary tree" ceased to move in the wind.

Sometimes, all must literally stop for a new idea to come to light. What you struggle with as "understanding" is there in everyone. It is why we remain focused in love, which is understood naturally, as a quest to meet with that which is like itself. Your "love focus" shifted as you struggled. This is what happens to each one as they struggle to "grasp" something that appears evasive or threatening. It also clarifies the problem with the thinking mind that is "always" grasping.

But what I most want you to see is that those who cannot find others "like themselves," also shift out of love. They feel themselves to be odd. They are unbearably lonely until they find another. The good news is that they know themselves enough to "know that they are unknown to others." It is in this way that the loneliness you have felt in recent days, and felt as an overwhelming constant among men, is highlighted once again. It is not a gender difference so much as it is the difference in those who are coming to awareness that they are "not" known. This is a good sign, as it means they are beginning to know themselves as they are.

As you grow in love and miracles, you begin to feel this way yourself. You can feel the discomfort in being unable to share your experience with another in a way that will be understood. To sit here quietly and be so moved is not easy to describe.

No one really has this true desire to be known—known "down deep"—until they get beyond the surface level of awareness of themselves. And so, in this way, it is a revelation for which we can happily rejoice.

The mood that you experienced yesterday, much like those newly coming to know themselves, was brought on by the weight you feel when you do "not" understand. You know next to nothing about jazz fusion, and when you have heard it, you have not liked it. It has felt like chaos, chords without melody.

And you like order: beginnings, middles, endings. It is a frustration for you to exist without them, which is why your ability to be present for this work, which you cannot control, is also a miracle. It does not feel natural to not know, or to invite that over which you have no control. But in a way, this is what you are doing, as are each of those who create anything—anything of value!

You are much like a jazz artist who composes her own music. You are having a dialogue, and translating it into writing, into what is being expressed in the moment. You cherish the surprise, but you are not, yourself, spontaneous. It is your combination of composing in dialogue, and having a deep respect for words, that comprise your architecture, as Mary Love foresaw. It is this that causes you to not let an idea fall apart. You will not stop until it rises to completion.

And so, this "fusion," which you took in with the feel of chaos, and saw as being too much for you, touched closely on the "controlled chaos" that this process between us sometimes is. That feeling of "I don't know where it's going" is not easy, even as it excites you.

And it is okay. It is all okay. Maybe, someday, you will meet a jazz artist, and she or he will understand. Maybe our work will most appeal to the creators of art and music. Maybe it will reach out and surprise the scholars. Maybe you will come to understand why the Bible, which in many ways is "controlled chaos," has never called you to its study. Yes, you go to it when something arises that you want to know. Yes, you "tried" to love the prophets and to understand more about them. But it was that controlled chaos, or sometimes just plain chaos—the lack of order and completion—that would find you abandoning your exploration.

Isn't that interesting? Isn't it fun to learn something new about yourself?

Yes, it is, Mary. And I'm "feeling" the ring of truth in it. And . . . I'm still reeling.

Welcome to the chaos. The chaos of creation!

M

On Memoria, Remember Miracles

NOVEMBER 3, 2019

Are you saying, then, Holy One, that each new feeling, and each new coming to know, can leave us feeling lonely?

Until you can share and have this knowing understood? Yes. Although, for you, sharing here with me has relieved the feelings, has it not?

Yes . . . mostly.

And again, this is okay, Mari. "Mostly" is okay. Not at all is okay. Uncertainty is not a curse. Loneliness is not a curse. Each are part of the movement. You trust your eyes when they see a moving tree come to instant stillness. You trust that you saw what you saw. Then you wonder, and without my acknowledgment would still have some uncertainty . . . and some certainty. Do you think this was not the way with the "burning bush," or other signs and wonders? There is a needed confirmation, a feeling that creates the question you must ask, have heard, and have answered. Without confirmation, the burning bush would merely be a burning bush. In this case, the confirmation was two-fold. The burning bush was not consumed by the fire, and Moses heard words spoken by Yahweh.

You know this need for confirmation as you know the anxiety of sending out a new piece of writing. You feel it is "good" or you would not send it out. But you experience hope and dread as you await a response, because you have shared something you created.

A miracle is always a partially self-created offering, sometimes created by a need you may not yet know you have.

Miracles are affirming. Remember this, and don't fear calling "signs" the miracles that they are. What you might do is see all signs of wonder in the new word given to you: Mirari. I just love this idea. Mirari for my Mari!

In Memoria, remember Mirari!

I would so like you to see and to share this sort of lighthearted attitude to the signs and wonders (the Mirari) that are present. I would so like you to more often see and share the "knowing of love" that you are receiving, even as it mixes with complex ideas. You are almost ready, my daughter—almost ready to give up your desire to see more clearly and know more precisely than The New will allow. Almost.

And it is because you are "almost" ready that you can receive for the "almost ready" brothers and sisters with whom you abide. It is perfect. All is perfect just the way it is. Continue to trust what is coming "in" my daughter, as you always do, even when you think you doubt or do not understand. This is the way that is coming to be so that signs and wonders—Mirari and Memoria—can lead the way to revelation.

This IS the way of love.

Who can "understand" it?

This IS the way of creation.

Who can take uncertainty from it?

This IS the way of Memoria and her revelation.

Who can deny it?

Do not look back at the construction that made you feel certain in an uncertain world.

Look forward with Love.

M

$\mathcal{A}$ BLUEPRINT OF THE VISION

Holy One,

A sense of the desire to construct has come to me this morning.

It is a desire that is much stronger in some than in others. I feel that I am in the middle, although I admire both ends sometimes. Having a lack of concern with manifesting is like a freedom, and I see how happy it makes me when I allow it. Yet my manifesting feels imperative, and so I am letting you lead me from my "constructive" tendencies . . . to a new architecture. Manifesting, I trust, is not constructive in the way that you have spoken of.

But it's weird, because "I" must construct (or attend to the architecture of what I've heard) in order to manifest what I'm given, so that others know they can cease their own construction . . . or something like that! I must take this dialogue that we are engaged in here, and make sure it is arranged in the right way, with the right tone, so that the next thing—the deconstructing—can come to be. Really, all of ACOL was like that too. And I was enamored, at the beginning, with the construction, and so ready to let it go at the end. So, if this is what you speak of as architecture, I'm not so sure I'm good at it anymore.

Oh, my daughter, you excel at it. This is not proofreading. This is not the manifesting itself. This is not construction. This is setting down in memory the vision of which we speak. In it is implied all that, like the spacing of the cosmos, will hold the vision of The New.

I like that! Thank you so much!

M

MISREPRESENTATION

I have, to some degree, my Mother, let the nuts and bolts of *A Course of Love* go to focus on The New. But I continue to try to prevent others from constructing a new "form" of The New, a "this is how it is, the way to do it" form. That is awful work. Work that has consumed a great deal of my time.

I'm speaking of this because of where we left off, but today I am feeling the tinges of yesterday's dispiriting find—another sign that I am not heard (or taken seriously). This has been a hard feeling for me to speak of, even with you.

There are those, my Mother, who, "in my eyes," are putting things in the public realm that speak authoritatively about this work (ACOL), in ways that don't fit with what it is and where it's taking us. It goes against my integrity to have this be so, and it makes me mad. What am I to do?

My daughter, in general, this is a problem you will not sur-mount. A person could take a quote from the beginning of ACOL and make it appear to represent the whole. This will happen. Some people will never move out of the beginning. Some will keep reading, letting the words sink in, and still take years or decades to let go of what they think it "means." There will always be an enormous range of perception and it will all be based on what one learns—or the extent to which one can let learning go.

I know this troubles you, but it is not something that you will be able to stop from happening. You can only stay true to, and represent truly, the new way.

When people misrepresent what "you," individually, are saying, that is different. Your integrity is important, to you and us.

But you can speak up. You can speak up about the termination of teaching and learning, the expiration of the search for meaning and definitions. You can speak up about the architecture of The New. You can reason with those who misrepresent, and if this fails, remove yourself from their company. Some will understand this and love you for it. Some will rail against this and find you protective. What does it matter?

What matters is that you have a voice. Having a voice is one of the ways of revelation of The New.

Can this writing, and writing in general, serve as my voice, my Mother? More and more, I realize how much I get away from myself when I leave here, and how much I honor the will of the Holy, and my Holy Self when I stay. In some ways this feels to be the whole deal—what it is about. Doing what honors who I am and who you are.

Doing what honors who I am feels like being in alignment with you and the original intent of creation. In this way (and sometimes it feels like *only* in this way) I am not using the force of will against myself. I transcend—everything! Which feels like knowing who I am in a true way.

We will continue to explore that feeling in you, and all the living Holy Ones who reach this transcendence, including the transcendence of gender and its hierarchy.

M

RESPONDING WITH REVELATION

I have not come back for several days for fear that we would return to this subject of voice.

Fear, my daughter?

Well, at least trepidation.

What we spoke of in Acts was you beginning to respond. Don't you see, yet, that this way in which you and I are revealing "your" feelings, is how the feelings of all tender hearts will be revealed? If our way, and that of A Course of Love, are not going to be taught, feelings need to be shared in a dialogue that not only reveals, but transcends, both thought and gender.

We have spoken of your presence, and of you joining this dialogue. What I am beginning to disclose here is the revelation of what the world needs now. What the world needs now is personal revelation. Too few voices are being heard in general, and "personal" voices, tender voices that reveal The New as it comes into being "in themselves" . . . hardly at all.

This is why you continue to be misunderstood. You felt disallowed a voice concerning the future of your work with Jesus, which was your deepest, darkest pain. When what you say, or feel, or care to share, is "considered," and then able to be denied through group consensus, your vision, your voice, and your power are blocked. Remember these words your brother spoke to you.

"You no longer trust yourself with your own power, and so you have forgotten it and realize not how important it is for it to be reclaimed. As good as you may want to be, you would still go meekly through your life trying to comply with rules of God and man with thought of some greater good in mind. If everyone did what he or she wanted to do, you reason, society would collapse, and anarchy would rule. You think you are only fair in deciding that if everyone cannot do what they would want, then you, too, must abdicate your wishes for the common good. You thus behave in 'noble' ways that serve no purpose.

"If you cannot claim at least a small amount of love for your own Self, then neither can you claim your power, for they go together. There is no 'common good' as you perceive of it, and you are not here to assure the continuance of society. The worries that would occupy you can be let go if you but work instead for the return of heaven and the return of your own Self."*

Oh, Mary. I am always so shocked, awed, delighted, and at the same time mortified, that I forget the brilliance in "the Course" of *A Course of Love*. I so seldom return to it.

And yet, as soon as I began to speak of this passage, you did remember it! It is all there in you, and is revealed again when the time is right. My prompts are those of your own feminine will, your own inner guide.

In this way, we—you and I together—pull you back from distraction in the only way that we can: by giving you encouragement to be in voice, in all the ways that you can do so. We do not discount writing! Writing is revealing your voice and our voice. Your voice, here, is our voice in dialogue, and my voice, here, is our voice in dialogue.

The true "greater good" of the Word does not stand separate

---

* ACOL C:16.25-26

from you. There is never any greater truth that stands apart from the Original One, or from the origin of the work of any creator.

The idea of having two separate aims is at work here. Divided aims always lead to division. We end division with revelation, by revealing to those listening to our voices that they need not heed those who tell them it is wrong to feel the way they do. We reveal how important it is to The New that they do not regard such words, and that they need not let them wound their tender hearts, as you have let happen to you. We need to reveal that none need stand on logic to combat this claim, but only to stand by their feelings, and not be shaken by those who claim that "the old ways are not needed" even while they continue them.

Remember the response your Jesus gave, specifically from his heart to yours, when you asked him for an introduction to the Course that would set a tone that would "not" encourage the old way:

"The mind will speak of love and yet hold the heart prisoner to its new rules, new laws, and still say 'this is right' and 'this is wrong.' It will speak of love and not see its intolerance or judgment. It will speak of love to be helpful and with all sincerity, and yet the very logic that it uses, though new, wounds the heart of the most tender, of those most called to love and its sweetness. 'I am wrong to feel the way I do' the tender-hearted says to herself and, convinced that another knows what she does not, covers-over her tenderness with protection."*

Here we speak of a more hidden truth, the truth that the ten-

---

* ACOL I.3

der one does "not" actually believe that she is wrong and is "not" convinced that another knows what she does not. She is just silenced by the common knowing that is presented—with authority—as truth. It is this that leads her (or him) to cover her tender heart with protection. And sometimes, for long periods, to cover her own knowing as a precaution to ridicule, or the campaigns of those who believe they know the way for everyone.

To remain hidden is what you do to keep a secret. You take cover. You go underground until you are ready.

Both ways speak of you, and of many in need of having their knowing revealed. This is a sure way of describing the means by which the new knowing of revelation will come! The new knowing will come out of hiding. It will be "revealed" by each of you who has held your knowing in waiting—held it in hope of a world that would welcome its revelation.

You are the hope of the world.

M

The common way of subjecting the tender-hearted to appraisals of their knowing is with the assertion of the more prevalent intellectual knowing. This is a way many have used to silence others— mainly women, but also feminine men.

In the face of such pressure, many think they must "regress to the language of the mind and its precision."* But more common are those who imagine they've left the way of the thinking mind behind. They may pretend they have, even believe they have, but

---

* ACOL I.4

truly, they have not. What they hide is that they know it. Hiding this is their protection.

Both ways deny the promise of this course: Real change. Real power. Real Love. Both ways await a feeling of safety before they are secure enough to reveal themselves.

And so, all these years later, we come together to reveal this way that continues to offer change in the sure embrace of love. And yes, it requires that each one come to voice in this exact way that we, together, are accomplishing—by unveiling the heart of truth in each one.

M

ONE IN BEING

Is this when your words truly become my own, Mary? Become "our" knowing? I have always been reluctant to share what I receive as "my own knowing."

Oh, my daughter, now you are seeing the real, the true. You are revealing what is at the heart of the very distinction we are making between the old and The New. When you know, rather than dismiss your knowing, is when our voices become one.

In the past, you only accepted that you knew when you felt you came to your knowing . . . alone. This is the common way knowing is viewed, as if it exists in an inner chamber awaiting your excavation. Or as if it is acquired through your hard work and study. This is exasperated by a society enamored by firsts. If someone else has spoken of what you've come to know in your way, you are often called to reference that person. This is fine in terms of approbation where appropriate, but it too often means you do not credit yourself with your own original thought. Original thought does not arise in you in a vacuum. Because Henri Nouwen spoke of loneliness do you need to see him as having staked a claim?

What this view of "how you know" has done, is once again, mount a claim for authorities.

The way you see "your own" knowing is as coming when you are "being you," possibly with "your people," or at times when you are moved by a more solitary passion, particularly writing. You see your knowing as a culmination of years of explorations and have no disinclination to sharing those who sparked those explorations.

As you write in your journal, you know you speak "your" truth, your moment-by-moment wonder, your revelations, your doubts. You give expression to what you are coming to know in a way that reveals it as "your own knowing." We are embracing your way so that your true heart can be revealed, and also to reveal why a great deal of hesitancy exists around claiming "one's own knowing."

Do you see, here, a cause for your anger "at yourself"? A reason that this situation persists? The felt need to say, "Here is what Jesus says" and "what Mother Mary says" is only part of it. Most people have a private voice they do not share.

I am helping you to share your true voice and calling all your sisters and brothers to share their own true voices.

And, I am proclaiming that what "we" do, we do "as one," without disregarding either of our voices. "Our" knowing becomes the revelation of a way of knowing to come.

You and I reveal in the way of dialogue. In dialogue, two, who are distinctly "two" (or more), are differentiated, appreciated, and conspicuously individualized while at the same time they are expressing and coming to know "together." One unity with many voices. We reveal the truth that arises in this way.

Through our holy relationship, we will welcome the world to shared knowing.

Still, can you see why there are those afraid of "knowing together"?

M

In "The Dialogues," Jesus revealed this unity to you—he "let you know" that you are one in being with God and like unto God in relationship. "The power of God exists within everyone because all are one in being with God."* He then shared with you, and through you with all, that this power cannot be used. It can only serve the cause of holy relationship.†

These are cautions for those who would be the God "Man." Those who, as in my day, saw God on a throne, dictating the terms. Many still see in this way. The lecturer still stands at the front of the room, as the priest stands before the congregation. There is still truth and wisdom to be found in both, but these ways give not a clue as to how each listener experiences, expresses and expands this knowing in their own way.

Creation's natural multiplicity is the consequence of "shared knowing." Creation comes, in this time to end all time, in ways of knowing barely conceived of "yet."

While one's own knowing is a given, when it is clung to, new knowing is hard to come by. Dialogue is a way that opens you to being possessed by shared knowing and to recognize that shared knowing, in unity and relationship, negates no one as it creates oneness of being.

M

---

* ACOL D:Day33.1
† Ibid.

$\mathscr{T}$IES OF KNOWING

My Mari,

The way you "feel" is a way of knowing too, and there is a tie-in to what we last spoke of.

When you couldn't have compassion for yourself, you couldn't have access to a thoroughly compassionate God, could you? You could still "see" a compassionate God, but you could not know, or access this God. Your own judgments were in the way.

Could this show you how much your knowing is tied to the knowing of God? Could what was unforgivable to you become forgivable in your knowing of God? Isn't this exactly the way of forgiveness? Do you not see that I point out your self-deceptions so that you can know that "you" can forgive them too? As you, in knowing from the Being of Yeshua and myself, know as God knows? Know from another realm, the realm of Being?

Knowing from another realm, the realm of Being, is the very knowing that is moving into time and space through our revelations.

This knowing that "goes before you," shining a light on the future yet to be created, is also felt within you. You know the wisdom "within" you by way of the soul, the soul that knows "you," and in knowing "you," knows your distinction and is here "for you."

God and the angel Peace still feel a bit "external" to you. But Yeshua and I? You and your soul? These have come together. This is a true feat that has been revealed to you through our lives. Our distinction within oneness does not make us more distant. It makes us more near. The same is true for you. All of you.

Do you see that God, if not the angels, is still seen by you without this distinction? You find the bodyless and formless to be lacking that which makes Yeshua and I familiar. Do you know why? Because you see them without lives, without lives lived in form and time.

Acceptance of God "given form," is acceptance of Jesus, my daughter. And that is easy compared to acceptance that God shared that life with Jesus, as I have asked to share this life with you. This is revelation of the realness and particularity of that which is. It is the way for which the time has come.

Ponder the "beyond" my daughter. It is further "in time." When phrases such as "the great beyond" are used, they—sometimes knowingly, sometimes not—refer to that which is beyond time. What might be beyond in time other than a future not yet here? An existence that stands in the space of light, before you, readying to be revealed and created in union "with you." Readying to be in-formed.

Remember, please, that I told you I felt like the mother of all the world's children. You might say that you all are children of the time that has been. You have known not what you do.

But I am still doing what is of my nature to do, and it is of my nature to feel, and through feeling to nurture life into a new time, one that stands outside of the awareness of the old. I am to do this in you, and in all the feminine ones, so that our time can come and gently deliver the world into acceptance of The New and its revelations.

M

THE SOUNDING OF THE WORD

Thank you for filling me with remembrances, my Holy One. I like so much getting away from *things* and *concepts*. Our dialogue was very revealing yesterday, and I still carry it within me. I, as much as most I suspect, am still in need of much undoing.

Yes! We are not only unlearning but undoing. We are undoing the ties that bind you to what you have learned and to certain feelings you have learned to cling to. These emotions have been your secrets—secrets you hold to yourself. You cling to them as if they are the treasure.

You must be willing to treasure something new. I know this has happened for you, my Mari, but even after your realization, there are jolts each time you leave an old bit of treasure go. This corresponds to letting a piece of "the old" go.

M

Here, we let go of prophecy for alchemy. The feminine form of prophecy "is" alchemy.

Literacy has left the way open for the Word to become universal but also for the universal literalization of words. This has led language itself to represent the way of fact, knowledge, and definition—which minimizes the power of language at its source. Language as it is revealed in its origin, is . . . revelatory.

If we do not have a new language—with new words like "the embrace"; and "Mirari," for the wonder that is new knowing; and

"Memoria," to suggest the link of memory to revelation and to newly remembered knowing—we do not de-literalize the words of the past through which your feelings, as well as the world itself, are known. "The embrace" did much for you and for those new to this way of the open heart. Our "new" words can also do much . . . but not if they are left to be literalized.

Remember that your brother said we need a new language and called "the embrace" the first of this kind.* Here, at the same time, he gave you to the "imaginal."† But what he began, and I continue, is not only inclusive, embracive, or imaginative language. We, with you, are conceiving of a change to what language itself conveys. Your reception is of this conveyance—not only of the words, but of their condition, of their starting place, and of their way of movement into form. Revelatory words are, "at the same time," of the way, and time, and place where you are as they are given, and the time and place from which they come. These words are fashioned for the future yet to be created.

Divine words from time outside of time are not words on a page. They are revelation. To see them as words on a page is to take them "literally."

Words must be "put" on the page, and "lifted off" the page. This is a way of alchemy! Your Mary Love has literally seen this! Words rising off the page. New words must find life in you, and beyond you, to come to life. The prophets spoke the "living" Word of God. Your brother "was" the living Word of God.

This is the difference of which we speak: the "living Word." The living Word is the alchemy by which the world comes alive.

---

* ACOL T3:10.15, T4:12.11

† ACOL C:20.10

The alchemy of the Word by which a person's heart comes alive. The alchemy of the Word by which relationship and ideas come alive with newness. The "sounding" of the Word whose time has come.

THE NEW REVELATION

The voices becoming one is what first happened in me. When you are whole, you are aware that you are one in being within the divine duad that our mother has newly revealed, and which I spoke of twenty years ago:

"Being whole is being present. Being whole is being all you are. Being whole is being present as all you are. When this occurs, you are All in All, One in being with your Father. I fulfilled my story, my pattern, the idea of me that came from the thought of God. In doing so, I restored unity, oneness with God. I ushered in the new way that you are now longing to adopt. I ushered in a time of being."*

The new revelation is that of oneness that is conscious of itself—which is what knowing and being known to the "other One" that you "also are"—is. This is what consciousness, full consciousness, is. With this, there is knowing and "being known." This is where "being" resides. This is what Being is. Where being originated. Not even God was "Being" until God was "known" and began to relate as a knowing Being.

Being is "knowing being," that comes to be only as it is seen, recognized, felt, and heard.

My Brother, it is Monday morning and I feel stunned by this

_____
* ACOL C:26.6

and your unique power. I feel the truth of this knowing "along with you"—in oneness with you—by being with you.

This "is" Being. This is the awareness you have awaited, and we have awaited from you.

From this point onward, you will be able to bring more than words on a page to life. Your dear trees bless and thank you in their utter stillness once again. They come to stillness along with you. They are sounding along with you. This quiet stillness of the sounding, like the quiet trees, will override the noise. The two are Being as One.

$\mathcal{T}$HE MIRACLE OF
CHANGING FORM

Mother, after being visited by Jesus, I notice that the trees beyond the yard move—but not those within it. I am sorry that I need such convincing of the miracle that is occurring here, but I do feel different, like I am in shock, and I feel a little scared too.

Yes, I know that you have not awaited phenomena, but it is the way of conversion.

Prophecy *is to foresee the way ahead.*

Alchemy *is to see by way of bringing into being.*

Convergence *is to come together.*

Conversion *is to have faith that you can change the form of what you believe. This is what allows the miracle: knowing that "you" can transform through inner sight. That "you" can be. That "you" can be who "you" were created to be, and that you can create The New.*

To foresee, is to imagine the way ahead.

To speak the future before it comes to be is prophecy.

To recognize the foreseen and to bring what is revealed into being is alchemy—the changing of form—through participation in the happening.

Feminine alchemy sees the future into being by recognizing the foreseen. Feminine alchemy sees the foreseen to its natural conclusion: into happening in form and time. This movement of being into expression, like the passage through the birth canal, makes life actual; real.

This is so powerful. I am . . . in awe. Maybe beyond time somehow—still here but beyond here too. Maybe in the new "here" or the new "near." That just came to me. The new near. I am nearer to what you are sharing with me, and to you.

Everything is the same. I hear the traffic. My yard trees continue to be still. But I've seen squirrels move, although at this moment, nothing is moving but my fingers. My fingers move. Words appear. It all feels like the same miracle.

It is all becoming different for me.

We are adding frequencies of modulation. We are signaling The New.

I don't understand. But I know that I do not need to. I will sit still, and let you make me into readiness for the miracle coming to be.

M

THE SWIRL

It is already nearing 8:00 on this new morning, my Mother, and all I've had to do is read what we wrote yesterday to be spinning once again. I am back in the swirl.

We are "sounding" The New, my Mari. Today, your body's circular movement is a sign of this. Without even the time for the words to form in your mind, you "said" this to yourself, "I am back in the swirl," and I repeated it. You have confirmation—just like the astronauts!

This happens to corroborate that the new way isn't known in the old way.

The new way is revealed in the different energies of sound and its movement. This is the dialogue happening in the physical. The dialogue engenders this change.

(I have had a beating in my right temple. I may have to end soon.)

Now you have been sitting with your eyes closed, imagining a chamber in which all sound is blocked. You have on your ear protection and still cannot block the noise completely. But you will continue to imagine that which will ring in The New.

And now the throbbing in our temple is gone.

M

THE NEW TEMPLE

"Temples" were created as places "apart" from the world, places for the sacred at rest. This was to reflect the sacred privacy that is the essence of the temple: the revelation of the sacred solitude within.

And so, you have the story of Yeshua running the money-changers out of the temple. There is always a sense of betrayal when what is created is used for a purpose other than what it was created to be.

Words have many meanings, and, in general, all of those meanings relate to a simple and central idea. This word "temple," like so many others, has to do with time. "Tempo" speaks of movement in time.

Words always represent something real. What we reveal here is, almost always, the original intent of the word, and descriptions of how this original expression changed over time.

And so, too, we have the "temple" that describes the depressions on each side of your head, the place that signals your heart as it beats in your ears, keeping "your time."

The heart is your timekeeper. Here is another reason that your Jesus called upon your heart to end your self-deception "in time."

We are now changing the tempo of your heart.

M

THE TEMPLE BODY
AND ITS DIGNITY

Some, including Mary Love, have said, "My body is my temple." The meaning is often one of "it is not to be defiled."

Others take offense at the idea that any "places" are more holy than others, and scoff at them. But again, we return to the creator. What did the creator intend it to be?

For what was this creation—created? This is what has been forgotten: the primacy of the creator, and the creator's intent. But this knowing was not lost to Yeshua.

A Course of Love came into a time of such deception that your Jesus asked you to issue the clarion call to end your self-deception and return to the light.*

Your learning innocently obscured the fact of this self-deception . . . but your unlearning made it plain to see. You cannot remain innocent or tolerant of self-deception when you have moved beyond learning. You carry an obligation, a fidelity, to the creator's creation. You!

All have felt the abuse that comes of self-deception. Artists, naturalists, and all people of good conscience, are aware of the defamation, the defiling of the original creation and intent. They are aware of the ideas that give birth, in each time, to the new of that time.

To "not" honor the creator's creations—any creator's creation—"as what it is," is to defile the creator; it is to bring what is not meant to be "inside" of the temple, "in to" the temple.

---

* ACOL C:6.22

To be profane is to put to improper use.

*Now, of course, some would say, and rightly so, that "who you are" cannot be defiled, but you see the dirty tricks being played by your own government, the defiling of your own Constitution and of the "idea" and "intent" upon which your nation was created. You see what the creators intended being misused. And you see dignity contrasted with gamesmanship.**

It has been awful, Mary.

What is called for from you, and those of The New, is dignity in action.

You are seeing the very time that has come to be revealed, and to be revealed in order to end the time that has been.

I believe I am seeing this, Holy One. The need for change is so vast. As you say, it's happening here in my own country, as well as around the world, and even nearer than that. There is something with the word "near" going on in me. Almost as if all feels "near" — *on the brink* in one way, like something readying to take place, and near to the heart, or to Being, in another.

I feel "near." And that it is a good "near," like you are near. Here within me and here, in the cabin with me, or sometimes "there," in what my eyes gaze upon, part of the woods and the wind. This feeling gives me hope for the world.

Let the way this word "near" has called you be a sign of what you do not know you know. We are moving beyond the meaning

---

* This was written at the time of the U.S. House of Representative impeachment inquiry into President Donald Trump. It ran from September to November, 2019.

of "near" that contemplates distance, to the revelation of an intimate association that already is, and is closer than breathing.

M

# YOU WILL SEE

My Mother, I feel uncertain if I'll be able to be in dialogue with you today. I copied some of the last things we wrote together to send to Christina because I felt that she had just conveyed feeling something so similar. Then I went on email to send them, and to check-in about my weekly talk with Kate. Kate was also speaking of the Word of God and sound. This is amazing to me! It shows that profound connections of "knowing" are happening, even before our sharing occurs. Yet being on the internet, before I'd even had my time with you, seems to have taken me to another place.

Also, Christie is just back from the hospital. I'm sure we'll talk today. Thinking of her last night, I watched us in our recorded dialogue with James Kelly.* I saw myself so differently in conversation with her. I was so present, my Mother. It was beautiful. We were so present to *each other*. I want to share it with her. She was so "herself." Our knowing of each other was so clear.

So maybe it is the contrast of these feelings. The dissimilarity between reviewing email and what we do here. Being on-line has made me feel stuck "in time" rather than present in time outside of time. But I hope the morning is recoverable.

Of course it is, my Mari.

What a lovely, and ordinary revealing, of the way presence "looks" and feels, and the way lack of presence feels.

You cannot escape all the details—only some of them. It is

---

* Host of the 20th Anniversary of ACOL conference.

rather like the way you are with food. You can't escape the need to eat, but you have increasingly made eating remarkably simple for yourself. You respect the need to eat, and you are happy with the easy meals that take only minutes to prepare and that you can eat slowly, as you are doing now with your peanut butter and honey sandwich set off just to the side of the computer.

You really are beginning to find your way with simplifying. You have even declared your upcoming sabbatical. This is great progress, and nothing you cannot come back from.

It is a demonstration.

Just as we spoke of the intent of creators, what you are feeling is your own intent subverted. "You" subverted the way you have given to our mornings together, by taking care of some other communications first. And you are right that you are not "as" available. Yet you realize, again, that there is a need to "start" your day in this way, before the things of time have gotten ahold of you.

The world's time does put a hold on you. My world's time does not. You can feel the difference that comes when you are no longer being held captive to time. To know the difference is an invaluable revelation.

To be attentive to making "my" world's time, "your" world's time, may now feel more crucial. Does it?

It is all I long for.

Then we will proceed.

We will proceed amidst your weather event, the howling wind, the sleet turned to snow and back to sleet, the knowledge that soon you will not see your fall leaves. There will be a burial of the ground in snow, one that may even prevent our time together in the cabin or make it less regular. You are sitting amidst the change of a season, and your time with your friends this evening will continue this feeling.

Be attentive. Be present as you were with your Christie. Feel the sweet innocence of each one finding their way like children. It is so beautiful to behold. Remember the way you explored the world as a child. This is what you each get to do newly now. This is how you will discover what is being revealed: by having the eyes of children. With such eyes, you create a new world, your world.

Isn't that how you felt about the worlds you created as a child? "You" described to yourself what the world was. You invented it. This is what you do again. And I remain the Mother of the world's "children," the innocent ones.

You become innocent of the world again to imagine a new world into being. You become lucid and the world becomes transparent. You see through its appearance to the fluidity of what it is, and you realize it is not separate from you, or anymore "solid" than are you. It was only your learning that ever made it so. You will see.

And then you will see.

M

$\mathcal{M}$UTUAL REVELATION
COMPANIONS IN BEING

What runs through my mind is that of the difference of "learning about" and "being it." It came in this odd way that keeps flitting in and out of my mind. (Everything flits in and out these days!)

Oh. I know. . . Andrew Harvey's Sacred Activism. So easy to see there. Do you want to "learn about" Sacred Activism, or do you want to "be" a Sacred Activist?*

I am a sacred activist by way of the work I've done, and the way I represent the sacred, and I was beginning to get a sense of it when I attended Harvey's Sacred Activism workshop. I did so due to his vision being so like mine in *Creation of the New*, and it was why I finally brought *Creation of the New* to print in 2011, four years after having written it. That was revelation in my own voice. Because of it, I could imagine myself being a sacred activist. I don't know if I thought I already was one or not. . . then. I was "not" in the way Andrew Harvey meant it, and he was not responsive to me. It was disappointing, but somewhat expected.

I know my own response to *Creation of the New* was much less than what it could have been. Christie could never understand why I was not more elated by it.

It was your first experience in writing of the mystical experience in your voice, from your own vision. This perplexed you, not only due to the peril suggested within it, but due to your shyness in

---

* Harvey, Andrew. See *The Hope: A Guide to Sacred Activism*. Hay House, 2009.

needing to claim it as what it was and is: "your" mystical vision. It feels even more relevant now, doesn't it?

Yes, but again, in a way I cannot describe!

In a similar way, you can feel that what just happened here is more than is apparent in what you wrote. It is still here, but is indescribable.

You could feel me more "in yourself," and the strange sense that we could write "as one." This brought Creation of the New *to mind.*

I don't know that I could have found the words to describe the feeling, but you just did. And I'm aware that I did describe the feeling, in the flashing in and out. It happens all the time lately.

There you go.

This is because we are not separate.

There you go.

I know this is the awful, inevitable revelation.

Yes. It is the awe-filled revelation. You just do not quite know it yet.

Because we are one.

One in Being, but now, through your awareness, becoming differentiated Being in Oneness. Yes. From here on we must speak with one another differently. Speak "to" each other, as well as "with" each other.

I understand without knowing what I understand.

Yes! Now we are in and within the revelation of why we have joined together here.

We are "in" the relationship which is God. *Now we speak as companions in Being—companions in Being who are knowing and coming to know together.*

And this is revelation. So was Creation of the New. *I remind you of this so that you bring that writing and that time to memory. You might say* Creation of the New *came in the way of Memoria. All revelation is like unto a memory of the future, a memory of what is both here and yet to come.*

There is much I want to know of you, and what you already know and sense of this new time, my Mari. Much is held in your sacred privacy and in what you do not know you know. In "this" relationship, it is what "you" know that is revealed . . . alongside what "I" know. As we continue our mutual revelation, we will experience knowing "from Being." In true relationship, mutual relationship—in relationship without hierarchy—we arrive at shared knowing and being known. Two in correspondence.

We move now to Letters that recognize this equalizing agency that we bring into being.

M

THE TREATISES OF MARY

THIRD HEART TREATISE

LETTERS

$\mathcal{T}$HE OPENING

NOVEMBER 23, 2019

Dear Mary of Nazareth,

I am here and I am crying. Now. Yesterday.

So easily. I read good writing and I cry.

I watch good TV and I cry.

I need and want to cry. With weariness, with body aches, with love and tenderness, with some things washing away and some coming forward, the looks of my hands and the feel of my feet.

My life moving this way.

I breathe, drinking down the tears that don't fall, feeling them in the back of my throat.

I am not sad. I am sentimental.

There is so much that I love.

$\mathcal{M}$

I have been confused this morning, thinking I was up later than I actually was and remembering only now, in front of a dark morning sky, that it is daylight savings time.

And . . . I'm confused in more ways than one. Every recent event feels far away, while those long past feel near.

$\mathcal{M}$

There is a stream of light running along the fence and it is six o'clock instead of seven. It is Sunday. Church day. I'm glad Henry

gets an extra hour to sleep, and wonder how Angie is on this week-
end when her divorce may become final, and George has steeled
himself against her. I remember the one time Donny and I were
estranged—looking into his dead eyes. I don't know how we came
back from there. I was fraught, at a hotel, ready to end it—afraid
to end it.

> I want to cry when I turn out the light
> and sit in the dark
> in this time that I love,
> this morning tide, teasing in the day.
> Love welling up.

The sky is no longer black. It is an ocean of blue, but a different
blue—that slate blue I remember from other years but haven't seen
for a while. I love how gorgeous this blue is, how the night sky
darkens before morning, and the stars shine brighter the colder it
gets. My eyes are too dry to well up, but I feel tears there, in the
tiredness of dry heat in the cold.

It's the blue of fall moving into winter, a blue unseen all summer, and coming late today with the confusion of daylight savings
time—the upset to the system. In Maine, too. And Santa Fe. And
Massachusetts. I know because we talk to each other.

I was with my Australian friend Kate last night. That's how it
feels. I was "with" her. I sound so confident as I say, "Something real
is happening." Early on, I felt I was the architect pulling her into
my construction, and that she was letting hers get demolished in
a single stroke. But now she has a vision of her own. It isn't that
much different than mine, and it doesn't matter between us whose

vision it is, whose idea. We will meet here again on the 22nd of May, an important day for her. I don't need to know why to feel the significance. I love that.

Last year, at this time, I was preparing for the December conference, which marked the twentieth anniversary of the start of *A Course of Love*. Now we reveal the way of Mary that it took us nineteen years to begin releasing to the world. I know it is perfect. It will be right about the twenty-year mark when it is done.*

I loved putting the Course of Love archives together at the same time you began speaking to me, Holy Mary. I could be idealizing it, but I don't believe I am. I'm just remembering with the same sentiment that's bringing me to tears today.

I'm glad you asked me to join you here. I remember, from a time that feels like long ago, that you told me having a voice is one of the Acts of The New.

It is an adjustment, Holy Mary, to begin this. . .
Mari

M

Daughter,

What a lovely way to start. How much you have kept under wraps! I can see it already. And the word "sentimental" is perfect. It is another word that has fallen to judgment, but it speaks to the delicacy of your tender, gentle feelings—the feelings held in Memoria. Would you say more about this?

M

---

* I finished the Dialogues in October of 2001.

Mother,

You are so right about the judgment. My on-line thesaurus is full of negative replacement words for *sentimental*: mawkish, soppy, syrupy, emotional, corny, sappy! While "sentimental" comes from "sentiment," which my dictionary describes as "complex combinations of feeling; a thought, opinion, judgment, or attitude, usually the result of careful consideration, but often colored with emotion," and it includes a "susceptibility to literature and/or art and expression of delicate, sensitive feeling"!

Another definition of sentimental is "acting from feeling rather than from practical motives."*

So, I guess the judgment of emotion is not only a recent one, as even here, sentiment is said to be "colored" with emotion. I say, "Bring on the coloring!" But my current sense of it, and you seem to agree, is that being sentimental is met by judgment—intellectual judgment.

No wonder the feminine is needed!

Even Jesus seemed to knock emotions at first, but I had forgotten, until now, that he spoke of our feelings being guided by memories—memories that try to reveal the truth to us. He said, "[Memories] call to you from a place that you know not."†

It is our memories that return us to who we are!

But he also acknowledges that "it is [our] language that gives emotion its place, one step behind fear. . ." ‡

Still later, Jesus reminded me again, saying:

---

* Webster's New World Dictionary, 1988

† ACOL C:9.14

‡ Ibid.

"We talked briefly here of emotions, doing so only to differentiate your feelings of love from your feelings of lack of love or fear. What we have as yet talked even less of, however, is what emotion covers up, and the stillness that lies beneath. I have referred to the true *language of the heart as communion,* or union of the highest level, and of remembrance of who you are being the means by which communion can return."*

This is in the early part of the Course, when we are still being spoken to as "learning beings." It came just before he revealed that the Self we've "taken out of the learning loop is the Self of love."†

He gave reasons for this earlier:

"As with everything else in this world, you strive for a balance that allows your heart to beat at one steady pace, for one emotion to surface at a time, for feelings that you can control. And yet you feel controlled by your feelings, emotions that seem to have a life of their own, and a body that reacts to all of it in ways that make you uncomfortable, anxious, ecstatic, or terrified."‡

We "mask" the language of the heart, and only "think" we don't remember Love's reality. But it is in us, "safe within our hearts, at the center of ourselves."§

Our feelings carry our connection to all that is.

I really got the full picture from "The Dialogues," when I real-

---

* ACOL C: 18.21 (emphasis added)

† ACOL C:18.24

‡ ACOL C:8.6

§ ACOL C:8.9

ized that my repression of emotions limited my freedom, and that it's okay to rely on intuition and our bodies because that's where we *feel*.* "The Dialogues" encourage us to feel every feeling imaginable, including sadness, grief, and anger. †And Mother, I knew all of this. I could not have cited these words without looking them up, but I knew they were there, and I knew the truth of what Jesus said even before he spoke it. What I knew was being confirmed! I knew it in my being. I have so often wondered why so many have a different understanding than I do. I've wondered if it is "only me." But here, as I remember that the way spoken of was already in me, I know that what Jesus asked me—and all of us—to do, was to recognize it. Acknowledge it.

Is it terrible, Mary, that I somehow feel vindicated each time we bring all these examples of love's knowing together?

I do feel love's knowing so truly and closely! I wish I could share it even more, in the personal and fertile way that I would like.

M

Dearest Mari,

Do you mean the way that you are doing here with me? Can you not imagine that people may find their way easier by knowing of your way? And that they then may feel not only closer to Jesus and me, but closer to you, too?

I do not believe you have given any real consideration to this, and that is okay. I believe you will get confirmation one day.

---

* See ACOL D:Day9 and D:Day10

† ACOL D:Day16.10

Women . . . are ready . . . as are more men that you realize.

M

An experience: The swirl

Dear Mary,

The internet goes in and out this morning, which I know only because I did it again! I started on something else before talking with you.

At 7:23 light has come, and I missed precious minutes of the dark . . . unnecessarily. The sky has been most beautiful this morning after days of clouds and dimness, and now, there is one squirrel out feeding with relish.

It is Saturday and one with "things" going on. Henry is sleeping, but Angie's picking him up soon to see a friend's soccer game. And later, we're going to see his cousin Isaiah's play.

I step out the door for a minute and see that down the way there is a spectacular, gold-gilded rising of the sun.

The activities will continue to increase this week and during the month ahead and then . . . my sabbatical.

Freedom.

I can feel you wondering if I really want it . . . freedom. And I think I may want freedom, right now, from writing literal letters! It seems that there is too much "union" between us to separate our writing into this form.

Our letters are a wonderful demonstration. They reveal our more usual flow of dialogue, and show you something that goes to the immediacy of what occurs when we "speak" to each other.

This doesn't mean that I suggest rejecting letters entirely. The Epistles of Paul were written largely while he was under house arrest. He gained much in the sacred privacy of those times that was shared with great eloquence and depth. You have let me, and often have let others, share sacred privacy with you in this way.

Yes, I believe I understand now. I have written already to tell you about my "writer friend," Michael Mark, and there are a few others who, with some frequency, write in this way of letters rather than in the more casual, or informational manner that rule our internet "mail." It would be wonderful if writing from the depth of sacred privacy would return.

But I am grateful we started in this way. You are right. It has revealed to me that there really isn't any separation. I can "feel" your answer almost as soon as I type my thought or question. And I can often feel our direction before you say a word.

Then we will continue our dialogue in written form, even as we attend to our sacred privacy by continuing with letters once in a while.

And I need to ask you now: what do you say to the thought about freedom that you have caught roaming between us? I have been watching you, and it seems that your desire for freedom is not clear.

I know. And I want you to know what it is like for me, when I sit here, awaiting you Holy Mary. Sometimes when you come, I have a feeling of not being ready. I thought "Letters" would be great for giving me time to come into readiness, but it's like there is no time.

It's like there is no time! I feel this throughout my body.

M

I look over at the side window. It is golden in a way I have never seen before.

I look back out the front window and I swirl. I feel my body moving in big bold swirls, with no thought . . .

I turn around and see the painting I made of the cabin more than a dozen years ago. It's enveloped in the swirl!

I am "in" something.

How hard will it be on this body to experience like this, from "inside" something? I laugh. . . like I can negotiate.

After realizing that I am "in" something, I start breathing really hard.

My face feels like it's tightened. I think, "Maybe I'm hyperventilating." My mouth is stuck in the blowing out pose, my right elbow sheltered in my left palm, my wrist bent backward, my fingers curled, as if gesturing. I keep looking up. I can't help myself. I keep looking up until my neck hurts and it pops as I lower my chin, and then in moments it rises again, as if of its own.

And now I lay the back of my head against the wall. I feel I can't hold myself upright otherwise.

Pursed lips, the in breath and the out breath.

Who – in breath.

Ha – out breath.

You had the in breath and out breath mixed up.

There's a feeling like a band around my temples. I hear the whistle in my lips. Sit up. Sit back. Press the heels of my hands against my temples.

I laugh, belatedly, at "You have had the breath wrong." A snort.

Holy f'ing-A.

I chuckle.

The barge sounds.

A light envelops the cabin, the back brighter than the front.

I question . . .

What makes your mouth do that? (lips pursed)

Do we become fanatics?

I begin to feel as if I need air.

It's the out breath.

That's what's happening? What happened?

Yes, the creation. God's outbreath . . . life.

Our outbreath . . . new life?

The swirls of time are this breath, like the aeolian wind.

It's all in the breath.

All in the swirling triad.

It's all in the triad turned duad.

God, Sophia, Mary.

Sophia combining with God.

God combining with me.

Me combining with the body of Yeshua in my own being.

Jesus the Christ combining with you, becoming the Christ in you.

My head's nodding. Drink it in. Inbreath. My lips. . . they whistle.

M

$\mathcal{P}$OST PARTUM BLUES

Later, as the "experience" calms, Mary asks:

Remember the whistler? Shawn Phillips? How he moved you?

My mind takes a minute to adjust. It's such an out-of-left-field question that I feel as strange as I did with the original experience. But I answer, "Yes, discovered through Charlie, my first husband. I fell in love with Charlie when he played his guitar and whistled for me."

Then . . .

Oh, my Lord, I suddenly know. I disappeared when I had my first baby. Charlie loved me, and I only now know. . . I left him before he left me.

You left that whole sensuous sound with which he first evoked you.

And I know why, too: because I was not free anymore. Yes, Mary, I know the feeling.

Do you think it's like postpartum blues that lasted until now?

No. How could that be?

What if the world is like this in its first outbreath? What if it is struggling to be free again? Could you imagine that?

I believe you mean the world *and* we humans. Is that what you mean? The planet is like this, and we, too, are like this? I don't know.

Remember how you go "who who who" in childbirth? In pushing? In birthing?

Oh, my God! That is just what this has been like—this weird panting/breathing.

Oh, Mother! This communication is doing something! I know

it! Maybe I need not even share it for it to have its effects. But, either way, I need to speak with you, Holy Mary, of some of the things of humanity in this time. I need to experience some things newly. I can feel that, and I need your response to my feelings, and my memories! Oh, Lord! It is all tied together.

I can feel here, that, no matter what we say, in conveyance *one to another*, we *are* doing something new. There is something new in this joining.

This is true and always has been true, and as a duad, as two made one, we convey, in writing, the seal of the new time. By accompanying one another we escort the new into being.

Remember, Mari, that prophecy was not about predicting, but about listening and speaking.

Human and divine is not a one-way circuit.

M

FINDING OUR OWN PIECE

NOVEMBER 24, 2019

Tomorrow is Mary Love's birthday. Today? Today brings up no charge. A day with no significance—at least none "yet"—wouldn't be so bad. Especially after what happened in the "experience." I have this feeling that no matter how much more you might say, I would never understand it more than I do now, and that it is meant to be this way. It is going to linger whether we speak of it again or not. If I am wrong, please let me know.

I arrived under a gorgeous sky, the first with color and light in days. Now it is dulling down again, the clouds like mottled fabric.

Just the flight of a bird feels an omen, a summons I wasn't looking for . . . yet. Nothing has moved, I'm barely settled in, and then: a cardinal, wings frozen in their glide, a bullet shape whizzing past.

Those cardinals are hard to miss.

Now, once again, all is quiet.

You summon me at times with stillness, at other times with movement. To look up and about, to turn to the heavens and feel the movement of clouds over a still earth, to know there can be wind on high and not below. To fathom the wonderful and terribly consistent tilt of our world, of its sorrows and ours. Of the necessity of compassion. It all feels the same, somehow, as what happens between you and me.

I had a hard day with Henry yesterday. I won't go into details, but he said, "It's not easy being me."

Isn't that the sweetest, most heartbreaking thing you've ever heard? Or maybe the "truest" is the way to put it. Don't we all feel that way, at least from time to time? And I feel for him, with his preteen changes and his lack of choice about things. All the frustrations of the young. And all of us with the routine, the cyclical, the things we "must do."

M

Now the light is well on its way into the yard and the sky an unappealing pink—like old, single wad bubble gum in the days of penny candy.

I will never forget the light and the swirl of yesterday. It was the strangest thing . . . so strange that this day now feels rather tame. The drama of the "coming" has passed. I look out at a bit of commotion in the yard. One squirrel sits content with his bit of peanut butter bread, and another wants to challenge him because he can't find any. Finally, the challenger starts seeking again, and finds his own piece.

What a metaphor. Each of us finding our own piece. What we are here for. What is here for us. Maybe not for a lifespan but right now—right here—finding our own piece.

My Mari of St. Paul, doesn't it feel as if we were built for this quest? These questions? Would we be who we are without them?

Yes, I can feel that Mary of Nazareth!

You know, I spend most of the time in which I am not "here" in family life, where we are all who we are "in the family," and there is little need, most of the time, to question our designations. The problems in my family came when these designations got screwed up. They serve a purpose. They allow for a certain order to be had, a certain following of traditions.

It is the same with what we do, Mari, which is why I only

half teasingly called you Mari of St. Paul. We, too, are following a tradition. Designations matter here, too. Just as you've spoken of your family as a place where everything isn't up in the air, in question—where everyone has their unique position within the whole—so too could it be with our work.

A "unique position" in which my place is secure. Oh, Mary. You are making me ready for what stands apart from ordinary time, aren't you? I don't know how I know that, but I feel it is happening.

Yes. What non-ordinary time brings in is not always welcome. But I want you to know that your place is secure here. I know who you are. And I will know who you are in the upsets that come when life changes come.

This feels oddly cryptic, in a mystical way that I do not understand, and yet that I *know* to thank you for—to thank you from my depths, with my whole being!

$\mathcal{M}$

In my own life, "the new" came by invasion. By foreign power and by the powerful connection to the divine. Both threw the normalcy of ordinary time aside. You have experienced this in crisis, both of spirit and humanity, and were quite struck by it.

This time feels different, though.

Because you have matured in faith. The same needed to happen with me. I found a calmness would come and supersede my body's first response, a response of panic. It wasn't that I didn't still see danger or begin immediately to calculate how to keep Yeshua and my family safe, but that I felt a calm descend.

This has happened to me as well, quite often, now that I think of it.

It is what, at times, guided my calculations by way of vision, and by "other worldly" assistance.

For me too, at least a little.

I must go in now and get ready for church. Thank you for this quiet morning and your reassurance. I have not really moved on from that experience, even while we have continued. But I feel as if I am getting the idea of the new way in which we are proceeding. I've let some things go as our letters have become less literal. My sense is that we're in a different space where a new way is revealing itself.

Mine too.

M

ᴛʜᴇ sᴛɪʟʟɴᴇss ᴍɪʀᴀᴄʟᴇ

We've had a big snow and I've come to the cabin anyway. It's probably a mistake because trudging through the snow isn't easy on my arthritic hips, and I'll pay for it later. I can already feel it. But I need to be here.

Who can describe what a difference it is to have a place set apart? It just is. I've got my phone in my pocket, just in case, and my walking stick, my galoshes on, and jeans over my sweatpants.

It has become even more blustery and blizzard-like since I got here.

And just as I typed that, as if in contradiction to it, everything went still, and I feel called again, even though I was not planning it. It is a miracle, really it is. "Mari and the stillness miracles." I wasn't going to talk to you today, Mary. It is Thanksgiving time. I thought I would write Michael Mark. There are people you want to write with thankfulness.

I feel stopped, but when nothing comes, put my fingers back on the keys as I recall a uniting moment with Lady Burke yesterday. Lady's got a big family and was talking of how she's changing her "role" a bit, and as she talked, I couldn't help but notice our similarities. We both have a tendency for the "strategic." That's what I call it. I think I see naturally in that way. First you do this, then you do that. It's having a picture of the whole in mind when you act. And if you don't have a picture of the whole, you cannot be this way.

If I ran my own kitchen the next two days, things would run

more smoothly than when Donny, the better cook, takes over. But he's a better cook because he loves to cook.

Maybe that's the whole thing and I'm just like him. In practical things, I pace myself. In things I love, I don't. I'm so "all-in" that I walk through a near blizzard to get where I want to be. And Donny just flies around the kitchen when he's cooking because he's doing that thing he loves.

Yet even though I love writing and am blissful and most un-thinking in what I create, I also have this picture of "the whole" in my mind with my "life's work," which is why I'm out here during this storm, and why, even though it makes no sense that I desper-ately need and want the cabin's "remove" . . . I simply do.

Looking out at what's happening with the wind and snow whip-ping around, while we're talking of the sentient nature of time and the universe, I wonder what it would be like if nature, even in all her ferocity, were able to have the capacity to be kind?

The weather does what it does. You do what you do. But what would you say about your own "must do" feelings?

That they come from a sense of . . . responsibility?

Do you recall what your Jesus said about that?

He contrasted responsibility with response.

Yes! What calls for your response? It's such a good question. And you've lived by it to a greater extent than you realize. I lived by it, too. The notion Yeshua put forward was to heed your call to respond instead of letting your "responsibilities" interfere—and this you do. You started this morning thinking you'd write to Mi-chael, and yet when you knew that I was awaiting you, you chose to visit with me here.

This is true. I simply can't not respond to you! And that is not a responsibility, but precisely a response!

And you have been doing this for so many years that you are quite excellent at response, my Mari. You recognize when you are called away from the routine and you mourn when you can't follow the call immediately. But the call, unlike the jobs some rush to get to, no matter how temporary they may be in their lives, is always with you. This is the beauty and the commitment that your call has—to you. It does not leave you. It "stands by" as you leave it. When absolutely necessary, it bubbles up in a way that you cannot ignore, even when something else feels more important.

I love that, Mary. I knew that, but I didn't know it in the way you are revealing to me. "It stands by you." *My call stands by me.* It is so true. I can look back and see that it has never left me, not since my time of receiving *A Course of Love.* How beautiful and comforting. And I can feel how knowing this in an inner, unconscious way scared me, while knowing it in a conscious way, soothes me.

This is what coming to consciousness does, my Mari! It reveals that about which you have been unconscious, and when what is unconscious is revealed, it is comforting, even when it is what you might otherwise call a responsibility. It is all making you ready to respond truly to what you have been given. All of it.

Thank you so much. This feels like something that will make a big difference in my life. How perfect for this moment when I may need to make my transition away from "cabin" time. Be with me Holy One, wherever I am!

I am always with you, and I am always thankful for you.

And I for you.

M

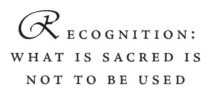

RECOGNITION:
WHAT IS SACRED IS
NOT TO BE USED

Dear Mary,

I want to go back to the feeling of wonder, to Mirari. To the grace of it. It is what makes the world alive, isn't it?

It gives my mornings an enchantment. The sun's rising does it. The light in shadow does it. The stillness in movement does it. I truly do know it as the grace of life. That and seeing Henry happy—bounding around with Isaiah. Proud of the cheese ball and monkey bread we made together that are "his" contribution to our day. I have fewer moments of it with the little ones, but oh, my Mary, the way Jack led us in prayer at the table. I can't understand everything he says, but he closes his eyes, and his dark little eyelashes flutter so against his cheeks, and he's so earnest. He is Mia's boy, and she says he makes up prayers all the time, and they're good. That's a wonder too!

Your words fill me with wonder. That "coming to consciousness" that you spoke of day before yesterday? How it soothes? That was a wonder to me. That was a Mirari moment!

Oh, and Mary Love came that day! She finds wonder in herself as she braves the elements. "I'm always prepared," she says proudly. And our time together was so comfortable and encouraging. In the best sense of the word, she gives me courage for my life.

And she was so delighted with her small birthday gifts. That's another thing she gives me—her delight.

It is one of her powers, my Mari. And one of yours as well. You also delight her. Isn't that amazing?

When a relationship is so mutual, its chief characteristic is intimacy. It is a sign of holy relationship, and the mutuality itself is a power more vast than is generally recognized. But you recognize it! And one of the reasons is that you speak of it. Mary Love knows, and not only due to your demeanor, that she delights you. You know, and not only by Mary's demeanor, that you delight her. Because you have dared to speak it. To acknowledge it. And lately, even to share the wonder of it.

Recognition is more powerful than either of you realize, even while you do realize and acknowledge it, and are careful of it. You are willing to share, but not to make the way you share into "a thing." When you feel the approach of that "thingness," you both feel it, don't you?

Yes, it is true. In the past she would see it and I would sometimes not. Now I sometimes see it, or feel it, before she does.

There are some things you cannot exploit.

It's at the heart of the way I feel about *A Course of Love*. It was at the heart of how she felt with *The Grace Trilogy*. Anything that carries such deep feelings, that are of such sacred territory, cannot be exploited in the name of promotion. It's a fine line with our works of the deep heart, shared intimately. The sense of it is holy. It is not the actuality of sacred words delivered or received, but the way love itself affects us.

Mari, you both have recognized that what is sacred is not to be used. It is much the same as faith over law.

In the times when you return to this, I want you to remember the indelible bond of writers and readers, the glory you felt in

Toni Morrison's enduring words of the "intimate, sustained surrender" that is reading.* Oh Mari, what this gives! Especially in this time! The nature of a book almost does not matter as much as the surrender to it, as you discovered with DH Lawrence, and A Course in Miracles, *and in the diaries of Thomas Merton. Any reading where you fall into the flow and give yourself over to it, absorbs your resistance to experiencing the quiet of your own being and inner life.*

It is a conundrum. One wants to make the material appear desirable or relevant, or at times to make "the use" of the material easier. But as soon as there comes the sense of "use," of reading to "get something out of it," the relationship of sacred reading changes. There are a few instances in which this can be appropriate. Most times it is merely a distraction. At others it can be a violation. Even suggesting contemplation followed by meditation is directive. When you have surrendered to the flow, as you did with ACIM, the contemplation and meditation is natural and reflective.

We simply see, together, the clearest signs of The New without the aid of "things."

M

---

* "I know now, more than I ever did (and I always on some level knew it), that I need that intimate, sustained surrender to the company of my own mind while it touches another's—which is reading. ... That I need to offer the fruits of my own imaginative intelligence to another without fear of anything more deadly than disdain—which is writing..."
Morrison, Toni. "The Dancing Mind - November 1996." *National Book Foundation.* November, 1996, www.nationalbook.org/toni-morrison-accepts-the-1996-medal-for-distinguished-contribution-to-american-letters/.

$\mathcal{T}$HE SACRED SPECULUM

Dear One,

What you have in abundance, is a natural exploratory curiosity. This is one of the hidden ways of what we are calling the way of Mary. Each one has this natural desire, and it is to this that we call them. Ours is the way of the mirror as the sacred speculum through which one sees "beyond." The sacred speculum is like unto the truth rising before you. It concerns sacred places and more importantly here, sacred "space."

Feminine ones are those who concern themselves with both, and rarely as anything more communal than that of a family home or an abbey or shrine. But that is speaking of the external.

More importantly, the feminine hold the spaciousness within to accommodate new life. It is the feminine spaciousness, in men as well as women, that allows openness to all forms of that which is new: fresh ideas, startling sources of energy, novel discoveries, inspired knowing of the divine. Everything that starts with new ways of seeing or knowing is reflected into the world in an expansive way. Expansion allows room not only for invention and discovery, but for the soul to know its own spaciousness and beauty. Interior expansion is the means by which the self becomes the spacious Self.*

Words get so abused! They get tortured into new shapes to fit the time and place in which they are used, as speculum was bastardized into speculate, and then associated with monetary risk-taking. You may notice that it is the most sacred of words

_____
* See ACOL D:Day12

that, more than any others, are twisted and distorted to fit lower instincts. This is rarely purposeful, but a measure of the frightened one's disgust for what they are unable to understand. It is a measure of what Yeshua expressed as "they know not what they do." The unknowing manipulate language into forms that they can grasp. Forms that serve their views. Their moves are all desperate ones in this way, as the ignorant always attempt to unseat the wise, the fearful, the brave. As you remembered recently with your President Kennedy, he represented a hope that shattered too many fearful dreams.

Frightened people, "unknowingly," become very attached to their fear. It is the major "feeling" which they must protect, for without it, they would not feel at all. Their fear is what makes them feel alive. The same can be said for the ego. The ego has been all that made most people feel secure in their identity. It is this that causes so many to stop at learning, or to continually seek greater learning. The ego has filled them, and learning has served the ego. Intellectualizing keeps them both content and grasping. Having full minds prevents them from noticing any effects that are oriented to heart or soul. They need much love reflected to overcome this orientation, my Mari.

Their thinking minds direct their lives. They do not leave room for original thought. Knowing, or besting what others know, is their achievement. Thus, they cannot see what is beyond this competitive field, and what they cannot see returns them to fear. They do not want to de-literalize words, because to be literal about life, is for them, literally, to be. To be alive.

To change one's ideas of what's been learned, is like unto a death. Few can face death to find new life. Many, feeling a hint of change—a hint at all they do not know, all they knew incorrectly, or even the partiality of their truth—run in the opposite direction, or fight to retain their hold on the truth they believe they know. This is why religious fervor has led to violence many, many times.

No one wants to know that all they've worked for is as dust to gold. Few want to "be still and know themselves." Fear gets in the way.

And so it is, that if one can literally accept the idea that they "have" left ego behind, and that they have left fear behind—even for a brief time—she or he can begin to let that which is true, and that does not constitute the false, rise to ascendency. Truth can replace the sense of fullness they felt falsely as "life," and make open space available and desirable as the sign of living. They can begin to live, to be newly and truly alive.

For many, the transition will start with a moment of true living and its realization. Then she can look back and see that even when she believed herself to be an ego, and even when he lived in fear, there were true and beautiful moments of being fully present to life and love. It is with awareness of their own presence that their life-long view of themselves begins to fade. They cease to judge themselves for what they did not know, and, emptied of false knowing, become available to true knowing and its naturalness.

This is where they are open to a new view. At this point, we cannot relate to them by means of persuasion or with the "knowledge of" to which they are accustomed, because this will merely occupy them again. They are tender and willing once more to see a new reflection, a reflection of who they truly are.

M

MIRRORING THE UNCOMMON

Dear Mary,

It is December. December 2nd, a day after the 21st anniversary of the start of *A Course of Love* and my time with Jesus.

Yesterday, the wonder of Mirari happened for me again with my writing friend, Michael. I swear, he is coming to the same "knowing" that I am, without reading more than a few pages of what we've written. And I imagine this in the idea of the sacred speculum: mirroring the uncommon.

What you are speaking of gives me such a thrill. I was going to ask if it is like going from an image to an icon. But no. That takes me to my head. You see, I am tired of words that make me squint my brain, that cause me to feel confused. Some might say sacred speculum is confusing—only complicating the simple idea of the mirror—but for me it is new, and so I love it instinctively. "Image" and "icon" have been defined, and by so many—many who are writers whom I love. Yet the words stay within the bounds of definitions, somehow, which is why the writing is so dense. This is what I am talking about Mary.

I appreciate those writers who try to deliver understanding of what cannot be defined, and can hardly be described, while at the same time they don't *move me*. I feel like I may, right now, be in a time between the old and The New. I pause a moment over our capitalization of "The New," hoping that, when "capped," it does not describe a "definitive" new.

At the same time, I *want to see* a definitive, if wide open, New. The capitalization is a sign of importance, of a greater "new" than any of us have imagined. I don't believe I started this capitalization on my own, but if I am ever demonstrating something that is not appropriate, it may be this very thing I just caught myself doing. Maybe we both are doing it, if the "capped" words are used to demonstrate a more definitive truth.

And I must tell you, I am rather chagrined that this came to mind so easily: *the definitive truth. Definitive* is such an authoritative word! *Conclusive.* As if it is the final say on the matter. The end of the discussion. Let's just say I want to share an expansive and unprecedented New that lends itself to every life-enhancing possibility.

~Mari

M

My Mari,

Yes, you are right. "Definitive" suggests the closed door.

This is just what I desire from you. Your honesty. The honesty of the natural—when you catch yourself, when you question, when you discover, and yes, when you advise. But just as names of people are capitalized, there are reasons that are totally beyond definition. Capitalization in the way we say The New is appropriate.

This is one way that we designate the nature of what is essential, and a way that our readers begin to see what we are speaking of: the vastness, the light of the new time that is beyond learning. You can fill with spaciousness, as odd as it sounds. You can, in spaciousness, be the door opening before "us," the door to the new us, the new we, the new unity that is the combination, the joining, of the duads.

The joining of the realms, or the worlds, is again too vast. You might, though, conceive of a duad of Heaven and Earth as the big picture, which is emphatically a picture associated with locations within spaciousness. These locations have to do with the orientation of each, but say nothing of the life of either. The change happening in the world, in the realms that locate "us," is not dependent on the reading of these words, but on their reception. Our availability to commune with one another in a newly common location, and to become a holy duad of two, is created by spaciousness.

What is created in spaciousness is less likely to make the one spoken of into an "object" of devotion, and more likely to reveal an actual divine person in relationship. Revelation causes the joining of the realms, a joining that changes a planned course of action into an Act, which is never reliant on a plan. An Act refers to that which is happening in truth, and Memoria to remembering that which is to come.

Each reader, in accepting revelation, can experience this joining and Memoria's embrace.

When describing the separation in A Course of Love, your Jesus spoke of this:

"You may very well say . . . that an idea seemed to take on a life of its own and compel you to do things you might have never dreamed of doing. People often look back upon their lives and wonder how they got from here to there, and some may see that one idea took root and changed what seemed to be a destiny already written."*

He then spoke, in "The Dialogues," of a place being created:

"It is a truly elevated place. It is as real as a mountain top, in fact much more real. Were your scientists to know what to look for, they would find it. It is being created to exist both within the body and beyond the body . . . a connection with the state of union as real as if a tether were stretched from here to there."†

We are breaching the space that scientists have yet to discover.

You and I are walking away from the definitive of time and space. We are walking away from the elevated and the not elevated. We are shedding the tether. We are doing this together by accepting the lack of divisions that have appeared to exist. We are doing this by seeing in wholeness the nature of the divine duad of Heaven and Earth. In relationship, we are revealing the divinely human duad by being a duad that is equally human and divine.

Love, Mary

$\mathcal{M}$

DECEMBER 4, 2019

Dear Mary,

What you shared yesterday was so powerful that I cannot even think of it. It was a realization, and I must just let it be.

---

* ACOL C:12.18

† ACOL D:Day6.21

I am sitting in the dining room, rather than my office, because I missed the dark yesterday. I need it today, and it is here. In the dining room the panoramic view is very near to what I have in the cabin.

I miss her (the cabin) anyway, and the way the trees looked such a short time ago. They're standing so quietly, my soul's companions along with you. I have turned off the sunroom light and when the bread comes out of the oven, I'll close off the kitchen light too.

In just these minutes the sky has turned from charcoal gray to a modest medium blue, with peach rising along the horizon. The first bunny is out near the bird seed, but it is still dark. The house is dim around me, and the quiet mood soothes me.

Okay. I am released from what I sometimes call "the tyranny of the bread." It dictates pieces of my time each day. The bunny, startled by my movement, is gone now. I am alone with you. *Thank God.*

Tomorrow we will get the Christmas tree, and the manger will sit on this piano table of my dear grandmother Ivie, who has been so present to me of late. It is as if she's grown in me, as have you.

I have missed this greater feeling of closeness to my yard and woods, and I know that, knowing me, you know this. You understand. The woods are in me, part of me, and I'm struck a bit by the idea that they've "grown" to be that way.

It is one of the beauties of this time of day. There is the *growing* of light (which now is golden) and singular movement: one bunny, one cardinal, one mouse. All are available for notice due to the stillness. It is again a stillness that envelopes me and my land as I greet you.

M

My Dear Mari,

Let us offer Peace to all who enter here. It is like that, isn't it?

We speak in words to evoke feeling. We gaze, we touch, we put our hands together—to evoke feeling. We stop—to acknowledge feeling. To see it all around us, to know it is there everywhere. Even in all the drivers of all the cars and trucks that begin to fill your morning with less welcome sounds. One "feeling being" after another, whizzing by, hurtling into their day.

And then your fine trees, standing in their quiet, acknowledging the dormancy of the season, their place in time as what they are, sentient in their way along with you and me and the burgeoning of the sacred privacy they share by conveying it to you, and you to them.

I hear your thoughts, even when you don't type them, and I can tell you that even the extroverts need time for stillness. Yes, people are different, but stopping is a blessing that can't be done without. When it is avoided, it comes of its own: a broken leg, a heart attack, an unknown choice made by the soul—calling out to be known via acknowledgment. Troubles too, come for this stopping. They are the notices given. The shake-ups. You have been shaken awake many times and wondered why you were so burdened. You expected peace. Here, can you see your shake-ups as ways to peace, even within shaky times?

Can you see that you have stretched greatly without breaking, and when you have felt broken, you have stretched even more. Even fear, when it relates to an actual threat to life or liberty, can do this stretching that we are speaking of. Again, you have seen it in your review of life: The dignity of your grandmother Ivie who was labeled "crazy," and the lack of it in those who labeled her so.

All feelings that get buried are the same feelings that, when felt, do the stretching of the bounds of your humanity, elongating your capacity for knowing through feeling, one-to-another, as well as for knowing what comes in your sacred privacy.

I know, my daughter, that I am confirming all that you feel, and as I am doing this, so too are you. You have begun now, to see your past in a different light. All that we speak of is of what you are already coming to know. You cannot receive what you do not know in this nascent way. It is why receptions of the beyond vary so in time and space, in the life of one generation and another, in the lives of men and women, in the lives of those who have known little hardship, and those who have known much. All begins in the knowing you hold, and expands from there.

Remember with me now. As shocking as some of our revelations have been, they have not really shocked you, at least not in such a way that would cause you to reject them. True shock brings rejection. What you are ready for is what is revealed, and why, at times, it takes a while to be revealed as a "coming," in its fullness.

What you heard twenty-one years ago, was two-fold. One unfolding came to you: that you and Mary would have something to do with the end of ordinal time. The other came to Mary Love, and revealed a "new course in miracles."

The new Course came quickly. The end of ordinal time has taken a while. But a readiness in one individual portends the *availability of readiness in more than one. The readiness of two individuals—of you and Mary Love—portends the way of The New. A Course of Love needed to be completed and to come into shared awareness before we could begin to speak as we are.*

We are not speaking of an imposed order, but an order related by the consciousness and closeness of the time, and of the persons held in and within the time. The closeness between you and Mary Love was so necessary, so dynamic, so intimate, and so creative, that the spark was lit for the new light.

Christie Lord and Christina Strutt felt this spark with you more deeply through Creation of the New. *Many more share bonds they have not revealed to you, but they are there, and those who do reveal their close feelings toward you, reveal more than you have realized, and more than they realize.*

As your Mary Love has said, there are clusters forming— clusters that, like the stars in the heavens—reveal the light at the right time, in the right place. It is a matter of resonance, relationship, and soul that holds the orbit in the space of its alignment.

You might imagine these works being as we have described Sophia: the creation out of which the spark of feeling is ignited. Then the duads form. The knowing one to another. The feminine and masculine of feeling and knowing is bursting into new life.

Mari, you have always known you needed "your people." Can you tell me about that feeling?

M

Oh yes, dear Mary of Nazareth, I can. I would like to.

I have spoken of finding that with Mary Love, and it's been

there with all kinds of people, but in different ways. My old friend, Lou St. Claire Crain, would, by way of love and loyalty, do anything for me if I were in need. But in terms of my inner life—really, my life since opening to the angel Peace—it has been Mary Love. We relate in a realm beyond loyalty.

In regard to my life with *A Course of Love*, I probably didn't know what I needed until I met Christie Lord, until I met one person able to see me and the Course "together." What a balm that was to my heart. To my soul. Yet it was a recognition that, in a way, made the lack of recognition elsewhere worse. I couldn't ask for it, but it's lack was an absence of regard. I was unseen rather than seen. Many opportunities for knowing and being known were locked away from me. It gave me such heartache. I withered rather than bloomed.

I was told, time and time again, "It's not about you, Mari."

In what you are describing, Christie was, with *A Course of Love*, my first duad. She made the experience better and worse at the same time, because as she "saw me," she revealed the unseeing around me. As she validated me, she revealed the devaluation going on. As we united, she revealed the separation that existed with others. And I saw my loneliness and felt that a sort of injustice was going on. I had not seen the source of my pain until then.

Just remembering it is painful.

And now I've forgotten your question!

M

YOUR PEOPLE

My Mari,

We were speaking of your need for "your people." Do you realize how often expressions such as this were used in the Bible?

The divisiveness amongst religions and lands now is not so different than it was then: one right way, territorialism, ideas of the clean and unclean, the vastly different lives and rules governing the rich and the poor, men and women.

Divisiveness has become such a part of life in the areas in which we lived, that it is literally the way and the pride of life for many, and the despair of life for many more. Either way, the division is the fulcrum around which all turns.

All of life, here, has this dichotomy between being well-meaning and wrong-headed. Of being insular while inviting "the many" to partake, all the while leveraging what is allowed, and the way it is allowed, for individual gain, for the gain of one's own "side," and for one's own idea of what truth is.

This is not the gain you, or anyone, really wishes for, Mari. You yearn for true closeness, intimacy, and the simple comfort of following your heart, hopefully while earning enough to live a comfortable life. You never sought the gain of aggrandizement.

The yen for this self-exaggeration was a strange new evil in our small villages; at least it felt new to me as it arrived. I wondered why people couldn't just leave each other to the lives they desired to live. What was the threat perceived? What was behind the grandiosity sought? Of course, it was a distorted version of seeking the godly, which provided me with a wee bit of compassion, if not tolerance, for their ways. Remember this, Mari: You can have compassion and still not "tolerate" that which is intolerable. You can recognize good intentions without accepting an overstepping of bounds.

M

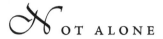

Not Alone

DECEMBER 6, 2019

Life is so strange, Mary. We went and got Christmas trees with the kids last night, and this morning I have a tree standing in my living room and the manger up in the dining room. I'm sharing the piano table with the nativity scene: I just pushed a few wise men aside for my laptop.

The morning has done that odd thing of darkening around me. Thank you for that. It was getting light too quickly. I look out toward the cabin and find her resting in the darkness.

I'm hoping to go out there tomorrow morning. Donny and Henry put lights on her (the cabin) last night. Luckily, they aren't on now. I don't think she likes to attract attention. It's better to see her out there with no light, a mere shape, a shapeshifter. A place of miracles.

Here, too.

You know, Mary, that I've been forgetting a lot. I don't just forget thoughts and ideas, but how to do things on the computer, too. It is very strange. As strange as it is purposeful. This I know from you, and you from me.

And I know that I used to see easier in the dark . . . I mean the discreet things. Now I see easier in the dark in a different way.

M

My Mari,
I love it when you let yourself be the watcher—the viewer—in

this way that includes yourself. Do you see it? Do you see what you are doing newly?

Look at what you just said: "I know from you and you from me." Another way to say it is, "You know for me and me for you." We know each other, for each other. You and the cabin know each other for each other. You and the dawn know each other for each other.

This is the sense of presence you feel continually in your home, and have at times felt in a very heightened way, as a mutual knowing. You and the trees of your woods also know one another.

All that you can be "alone" with, everything that can join you in your sacred privacy, you know as the knowing of God. Can you imagine this as "our" knowing? As the way God knows? And so, the way knowing is? Can you imagine the saying, "God alone," as an acknowledgment of this way of knowing? Not a statement of God's singularity, but one of God's inner sanctum? Each of you abide in this inner sanctuary where your presence is a given, and your awareness awaits only your reception of what is.

I know you can feel the truth of this, with newly revealed but ancient memories.

This is the great knowing received at death, at times just before death. Your two friends named Richard felt this before death. The time of death brings an ephemeral, opaque truth into focus, just as the coming of light has brought your cabin into view from this other side—where your view is from without rather than from within. Close to death, the views of many change in this way. Each knowing in life, in the consciousness of time—no matter how brief—expands knowing for all.

So, it is lovely that you have been given this occasion to view *your cabin in this way. You will remember this always, as you will each of these new knowings that seem to pass so quickly from your memory. They pass quickly because they are not "held" in your mind. This doesn't mean they are not with you, part of you. Does this help you begin to see? To see without your mind? To see in Memoria? In your inner sanctum where you are undivided from our source?*

What you experienced—are experiencing this morning—may seem to leave your mind, but this seeing was not of your mind and will not leave "you." As I will not leave you. As your Jesus will not leave you. As God does not leave you. You are always alone. . . "with us" . . .and so not alone.

You are not alone but you are not imposed upon. There is no sense of infringement. This is the journey: to truly welcome the natural knowing that you are not alone. You are known "from the other side" as you are knowing your cabin and woods from the other side this morning: from the inside.

In this way, the "inside" and the "outside" that have always been one, are becoming one.

M

A CRACK IN THE
REFLECTION OF THE WORLD

Oh, thank you, my beloved companion. What you've spoken of makes sense of so many things. Like my sense of place. My reluctance for change. I love my view of that among which I live. I feel this accompaniment.

I am so grateful.

M

And yes, I feel it with you.

What we speak of is often called soulfulness. Soulfulness was one of your first and most deeply felt reassurances on this journey. It came when you read Care of the Soul,* *and had confirmation of the way in which you feel. To hear that your connection to "views" was soulful soothed you.*

What is "place" but what you view? You would not have this connection to place without your view of place. Do you see? A view is more than a physical orientation to space. How you view is through an orientation of your soul. This view is unique to each, including the blind who see in a different way.

M

Yes! I'm beginning to . . . no . . . I do "see."

It was my *feeling* of what I saw, or *viewed* at that time—my

---

* Moore, Thomas. *Care of the Soul.* HarperCollins, 1992.

feeling of it as something like an aberration. Moore gave me assurance.

The start of this was my love for the look and smell of dark streets in the rain. I felt myself to be somehow different as I viewed them and took in the scent of them, because of the way they made me feel *within myself.* The love of those scenes was my first "knowing" of this grace. Then came the feeling evoked "by" that view, and by my senses—a feeling I valued greatly, yet that I named "melancholy." I then wondered why I loved melancholy so much. *What was wrong with me?*

"Melancholy" might not have been the greatest word for it, but that's how it came to be that Thomas Moore opened my eyes. He helped me see that there wasn't anything "wrong" with me, but just possibly something "right." It was my soul. *And* it was a first step in getting over that sense of right and wrong feelings. That one instance of awareness started something in me.

M

Yes, it did.

In your world of the time, in which "value" was placed on happiness, and happiness was to "look" a certain way, you found a crack in the reflection of the world. This whole idea of melancholy as "unacceptable" came of fear of the dark, and now we are able to embrace the dark and free the dark from the bondage in which it has been placed. We are, to an ever-greater extent, able to be, and to cause, cracks in the reflection of the world, cracks through which The New can come into view.

For out of the dark void came the light. Out of the dark void of forgetting from where you came, came fear of the dark from which you came. You began to value only the light.

Here, what you know to value changes.

M

$\mathcal{O}$UT OF BOUNDS

DECEMBER 8, 2019

The lightening is happening too quickly as more of the upper sky moves down, brightening the remaining.

Then the darkening. Just before the full coming of light, the darkening.

It's quite distinct, this darkness, this stillness. It is very nearly total this morning . . . until it stops being still, and the birds begin to flit, before their color is even visible. They are tiny black shapes dancing in midair. Leaves, too, are shapes with no color, hanging on, wiggling, waving. Black and white and dazzling.

Moments later, at 7:23 today, in an instant, the day arrives: the bronze of dried bushes becomes visible, plants not cut back before the cold broadcast the color of wheat, the gray squirrels emerge, and the mystery seems to leave, but never does.

Inside, the tree is up and beautifully decorated. Here, its reflection lays across my windowpanes, and joins my view, now of the outside and the inside as one. It is so beautiful. And I had a wonderful dream this morning that my next book, after ours, will be *The Given Self.* The strange thing about it was that I felt as if I had already read it.*

After writing of the morning from the inside view, I decided to brave the short trek and have safely made it to the cabin, where the windows are fogged, the furnace is warming the place up, and where I wish I could spend the whole day. How many days in De-

---

* Later I had to laugh, remembering that I wrote *The Given Self* years ago, while the dream was calling me to write it "next."

cember will be so graced? But if I need reminding of the "season" of Advent, church is the place to go, and it is a fine place and a fine day. No perilous passage as it was last week.

It feels exceptionally ordinary, this day, and yet beyond the bounds of what is familiar. As the cabin herself feels out of those bounds.

M

Yes, we are out of bounds!

Each time we join, we participate in an unrepeatable, intensive Act of not only correspondence, but illumination. Out of bounds we incarnate in a new way. The crack we have made is a breach in the world that has been, and an opening for the swirling entrance of the beyond to come into immanence. The New Advent. The new territory of your conscious awareness.

You heard of this, this territory, in A Course of Love.

"Thus, we will begin once again . . . with a territory of shared consciousness, rather than with consciousness of the All of Everything. This territory we will call the territory of your conscious awareness. This territory of conscious awareness is shared with the larger consciousness of unity, just as the territory of your body is shared with those who live and work nearby. This territory of conscious awareness exists within the larger consciousness of unity, just as the territory of your body exists within the larger territory of the planet Earth. We will begin here, with the territory of your conscious awareness, knowing that discovery and revelation will expand this territory, and realizing that no matter how small this cosmic territory may be, it will still at times give way to awareness of the All of Everything."*

A territory of shared consciousness goes along with all we have spoken of—the sense of departure, the great exodus, and creation of The New. It implies "your" territory. In a world gone mad via "the masses," the terrestrial of earth and sky had to get closer, move nearer.

Can you tell me of the feeling of the "near" that you have mentioned?

M

---

* ACOL D:Day7.29

$\mathcal{T}$HE NEW NEAR

Oh Mary,

You know, it just came over me as I wrote the word, as such feelings often do, that this word had an unusual, or significant meaning for me. I heard "near" in a new way that suggested all that it usually means: close in feeling, or proximity, maybe between you and me. But there was something more in a way that eludes me—like we are closing in on something. This "near" has a presence.

I have had the sense of it many times. It's like there's a secret out there, a wonder that awaits being revealed. A feeling that if it were, there would be no mistaking it. Sort of a universal thing. But this was personal. Really, a feeling that you and I, together, were nearing something, something already present.

$\mathcal{M}$

This is so good to hear. And really, it is what happened! We broke into something! We made an opening. And what was it about?

Acceptance.

I know you will question this, but it is true. Your brother spoke of this with you. Acceptance remains the forgotten element of transformation outside of time, your acceptance that it is happening. Your feeling of nearness was a feeling of greater acceptance than you have had before. Acceptance of each new feeling, each new knowing, each new view, each refreshing swirl of time outside of time, depends on acceptance of yourself and your own knowing.

So, you see, it was not a small thing when you could accept melancholy as a sort of happiness, familiar to you in a soulful state of being. It was not a small thing to accept the view of your eyes when, amidst a blustering day, our tree stood still. It is a particularly "far" thing to feel the swirls of time outside of time and accept them as they join with you and yet "not" to become fixated on what they mean.

Some of your favorite words from Jesus were "Let meaning be revealed."

How perfect, my Mari. Acceptance that meaning is being revealed may be seen, and can be felt, as coming from the source of the near. How much nearer to someone do you feel when you hear from them? When you are heard?

Revelation is really a form of dialogue drawn near and abiding with you and within you.

BEING PART OF THE STORY

Dear Mary,

In my days of absence, which come of the furnace not being on (we can't afford to heat the cabin continuously), the water froze in your little shrine and the greens look as thin and wilted as soggy noodles. But I am so happy to be back here. No matter how she looks (the cabin), she is the face of my soul, or one of them.

I felt I saw a shadowy figure a bit ago when I looked up from reading *Early Morning*. I looked up and it was there—a figure in movement, a man. Not scary. Not "certain." What would it be like, I wondered, to start seeing and talking to people alive with color or shadow? Doesn't have to be a figure, but I would like a figure, I think. Shadowy or solid.

There are too many disembodied voices already. No need for more. It reminds me of a haunting sentence that William Stafford spoke: "There it is again, that way you're alert to what the world is doing, even when you are defeated—just to notice, be alive to it."*

I have come here many times in defeat.

M

My Mari, our story is unfolding. I want you to be part of the story. A story that will take us into The New.

Neither you nor Helen were particularly revealed within the Courses you received, but Helen was revealed, as you have no-

---

* Stafford, Kim. *Early Morning: Remembering My Father, William Stafford.* Graywolf Press, 2002.

ticed, in her poetry, and you have a place now to reveal as much as you are ready for. But really what we are doing here, is moving to an exchange that will allow you to begin to come to voice, as you and I together, so desire to see you do.

As you do this, you will encourage your sisters and brothers to do so as well. . . not by trying to, but from within our natural movement!

I love this about you!

M

$\mathcal{T}$HE MÉLANGE OF ALCHEMY

My Mari, change comes from a certain mixing of elements, as of dark and light. The change of alchemy relies on this mélange, this mellow sweetness, free from any stridency or garishness. Change reveals the luminosity of memory, and memory reveals the glimmering afterglow of change. This mélange of alchemy is the mender of defects, the end of forsaking your birthright.

The milieu, the background, or backdrop for light, is darkness. It calls you back in the melody your Jesus spoke of:

"A tiny glimmering of memory has returned to you and will not leave you to the chaos you seem to prefer. It will keep calling you to acknowledge it and let it grow. It will tug at your heart in the most gentle of ways. Its whisper will be heard within your thoughts. Its melody will play within your mind. 'Come back, come back,' it will say to you. 'Come home, come home,' it will sing. You will know there is a place within yourself where you are missed and longed for and safe and loved. A little peace has been made room for in the house of your insanity." *

This melody opposes humanity's order, the insanity that appears as order amidst objects . . . your idea of safety being of the light, and your fear of the evil lurking in the dark . . . in the unknown.

Through the cracks we are making in the reflection of the world, the dark and light will reveal the celestial duad. We will

---

* ACOL C:10.32

use a phrase of your own making to demonstrate that you already
have known of this. You called it "celestial relatedness."

Soon the alchemy of the feminine will begin to extend celestial
relations into the sacred privacy of Mother Earth.

M

My Mother, without my glasses, the yard at first felt swept by the
trees, as if branches had laid down their tracks—left their impressions in the snow. And then, with my glasses on, I knew that what
I've been seeing are animal tracks, bunny mainly.

I slept late and haven't gotten enough darkness. The whole atmosphere is lined with a peach glow, while I want the dark before
the light. Not the dark after the light, but the predawn darkness. It
has been so for so long, and now it seems so obviously part of the
way that I am built and was made to see. I sit here continuously in
such stunned gratitude.

I am inside again today.

The bread-baking is done. I go out to shut off the oven and
morning's great organizing principle comes over me. I have no intention to, but I tidy things I don't even see at night. All of which
you know, and experience with me, along with, I'm sure, what
brings me back to Advent, which hasn't held my attention.

Now I am swept up into the Advent which has been celebrated
for a week now. It reminds me of how "out of it" I was regarding Lent
this year—how Lent blew right by me and when you announced
that our focus would be on The New Advent as the second coming,
at Holy Week, I felt so disoriented. The same feels true now with
the first Advent. So peculiar. And I've even been going to church!

So much seems to be this way! Maybe it is the change, the extension you're speaking of. I love your way with words!

M

Dear One,

The names and prescribed times for your seasons mean less now.

All creation awaits birth and the New Advent. The cracks that are extending remind you that every new idea comes out of the dark into view. This is the new birthing.

M

THE BLESSING OF RECEPTIVITY: A LIVING METAPHOR

DECEMBER 9, 2019

Mary, I am looking for a way to be a receptive *woman*. I didn't know it until I was browsing Stafford. Leafing through, I saw the word receptive and then there it was. Being a receptive "woman" poses an incredible question that I can't form. It's the "woman" part, you see.

I'm sitting in the dark cabin, angled to the side again. Tilted toward the side window that is filled with nothing but the tender fingers of the trees. It's as if they all end there, in the read of that one window. Here, where I say things I don't say in the house. And wonder about being a receptive "woman."

M

My Mari, this is much more than a question to explore. It is the question at the heart of you . . . and . . . you said "being" a receptive woman, and you wondered about it. You did not ask of meaning.

You do not, this morning, "need" my acknowledgment. It marks a true turn to where we want to be. It is a different turn. Even of your body.

It is all these things that you do, that you do not cause, that cause a response to something received. When you feel that still-

ness. When the side window beacons. When you rock. When you turn. When you whirl.

M

This movement of turning away from "the front." There is something about that. Yes, I agree. It is darker "in the back." I've been looking at the light a long time. And I suppose I am receptive of the metaphor. But what of being a woman?

Oh my God. I went to look up metaphor and found *meta* and its first meaning is of *a change of position*!

Sometimes I really do see the places where my lack of education works for me. I've read so many "meta" related words without really thinking of what they mean, other than what I easily infer from the sentence.

Now having looked, I am agog at the further—really the first before the first—definition of meta: "along with, after, between, among."*

We are about "meta"-something, of that I am certain, even while feeling glad we're not actually using that descriptor. Why not "along with, between, among"? Why not use these words? But I flash on all we have spoken of recently—view and orientation— and I wonder . . .

M

Mari, I am so glad you have an idea of how perfect this was! You have long conferred "a" meaning, your "understanding," based on

---

* Webster's New World Dictionary, 1988

the surrounding words that you "did" perfectly well understand. We go back to origins of words for a reason, a reason that has to do not only with original language, but the way you are, all the ways you are. And . . . because we are of the way of the Word.

Verse, too, is a turning. The suchness of the naming of things; verses of the Bible, ACIM, ACOL, almost all holy writ comes in verses. The only reason that we are not doing this is that we are making the holy . . . ordinary.

We are taking the Word out of the realm where there is need of analysis verse by verse. We are forming a whole.

This is the feminine way, isn't it?

You really don't even need to ask, do you?

When we speak of "lost" meaning, we speak of the loss of wholeness. We do not speak of meaning as it is used now—as defined for the "current" time—but of a whole that includes all time: from that of origin, to that of the future yet to be created, to who you are and who you are becoming.

We speak of the ways, vastly different ways, that knowing arrives. One is taking in what was said "as you heard it," through listening or reading, and relating to it as yourself. Another way is taking in what is said or heard without relating it to oneself. Still another is adapting what is said to one's own existing position.

You can see here that we have already been working on your own "fixed position," getting it unstuck. This has included your physicality, your position here in the cabin. I speak of the orientation of "yourself" as you are, where you are. Not anyone else. You. The same will be true for each who "hear" our words.

M

Holy One, I am trying to see now whether it is snowing, and whether I am getting an inkling of how this relates to my receptivity as a woman. And something is coming to me, not yet here but near. Just a glimmering.

$\mathcal{M}$

This "is" your receptivity as a woman. Something is in movement into being. Movement begins because most women are naturally flexible, naturally able to take in, and to be living metaphors, shape shifters, meaning modifiers. She moves amid and among. She holds and shares. You are a living metaphor along with me.

So many attributes of the feminine are of this nature of seeing what is needed. Seeing what is needed relates innately to alchemy. In the lives of those men and women who hold the feminine, an imbalance results when being is overburdened. The overburdened, whether men or women, can no longer receive but only give. To only give is an imbalance—a truth and a lie at once.

What is needed in a "universal," or "meta-universal" sense, gets overcome by practical needs. This is what has occurred in the world. The universal has been obscured in favor of the practical, and the practical is not seen with vision of the whole. The meeting of needs will only come of "being with" the universal.

The restoration of the way of the feminine is crucial for this reason above all else. The feminine is innately receptive. All who carry feminine orientation are in almost dangerous need of recovering the balance of giving and receiving.

All need balance, but we are speaking of the feminine because it is a balancing being sought but denied, in an era of use and abuse. The feminine is, itself, this connecting or unifying agent, full of alchemical power. This power must now be cultivated rather than denied, cultivated as a garden is cultivated. This will produce new life through the seed of what already is, but has lain dormant in unfriendly soil.

We speak of alchemy as miraculous change, much as we speak of the miracle of life itself. What has been forgotten is that there is no alchemy without receptivity to changing form. We restore this memory now.

Mary, there is snow drifting in now, which feels both ordinary and incredible, as snow is a change in form.

All around you this miracle of changing form occurs. And inside of you, too. You feel your own changes acutely. You "feel" them. Your body is not separate from you—from you who feel through it and live through it and are who you are through it. And you are a receptive woman, a female of the species, the mother of three whom you carried and to whom you gave birth. You have experienced receiving the seed of the male and letting it grow in your womb. That was receptivity. So is this. We are creating anew.

Creation of "The New" is creation that is unlike that which has been before.

"We" are remaking creation. I am with you and within you. Through your receptivity you are giving new life to me: life in your time, a voice in your time, a power in your time. But not separately from you. Do you begin to see a pattern here? As a woman? No one has squirmed at speaking of men as they do of women, especially women in their positive distinctions.

I see what you said about women again and again. And Mary, I use that expression all the time, saying things like, "I *see* what you mean." I understand this "seeing" differently. I am beginning to see in the way of wholeness, a wholeness that doesn't obscure the many forms that contribute to it!

Good! As we naturally moved from Letters to more intimate correspondence, you have "seen" our dialogue in a new way, and now we will return to it.

That makes me so happy!

RECEPTIVITY'S BIRTHPLACE

Here is where the distortion started: from a man needing a woman to have children. Men do not like to need, or to admit to needs, certainly not in regard to their own continuity, and not even regarding their desire for pleasure. You might think this was more prevalent in my time, but it was not, because women had no say, and men needed big families to prosper.

In some parts of the world, this is still true. Here in your country, and in much of the developed world, large families are not desirable, partially for not being affordable. In concert with women's liberation, men's commitment fatigue, and that of the achievement model, what has happened is a rejection of this idea that, together, needs can be met. This rejection began the decline of the family.

There are necessary differences in all categories of living creatures, differences that perpetuate life. The miracle of life. This miracle of new life is not the birth alone, but the ability, through receptivity, to conceive of "a new" living being. This is the crucial receptivity needed now, and mating is the smallest portion of it. It is time to dream new dreams, conceive new ideas, and together bring these ideas to life.

There is an underground sense in those men who expect themselves to do it all that, if it were to become overt, would find them realizing that it is the joining that is the miracle and the source of the power of the miracle.

That you and I are joining is more important than the words

we are forming—more creative, more integrative, more . . . life-changing. We are a form of new life whose time has come.

"We" are changing.

I am not only that young woman who birthed Jesus. I am the woman who stood by the scene of his death, only turning my head so that I could live. I am the woman who wanted to die with him but could not change what was not mine to change. I am a woman who knew of the union of which I was part without mental understanding, and who lived with the ambiguity of my own certainty, as do you in your way.

I am a being of life in time as well as beyond time. In relationship, so are you.

"We" are receptivity's birthplace.

You are being a particularly receptive woman. You are being receptive in a unique, individual way. You are receptive to host the divine and you are meta-receptive to begin to move beyond such hosting. To be meta-receptive is to pass on the receptive ability you are cultivating, in a new form, by participating newly. This will include welcoming the feminine of men.

You are soon to be stuck, as well as gifted, in a new realm where the old ways will not work. You have already been experiencing this. So have many women. If men take over when the old ways begin to fail, The New will be delayed. No one, if they understood this change, would want the delay. Many feminine men are ready and, as they will be just beginning, will be better at easing the transition to the new time.

Your Jesus asked you to make this leap in your receptivity years ago and it made you too uncomfortable to proceed. You were attached to the form of your receiving with him: Jesus the example life and the guide to new life. Now you are here with me, and your benefit will benefit all. You are able to receive divine blessing: Benedictus.

For this you were made.

As you pass on this blessing,

you along with me—

we, together—

and all those who receive our blessing, will be held within the new consciousness of human and divine unity.

Those whose knowing is touched by our being, which, through your receptivity has become "our being," will realize they are "one in being."

Then, one to another, along the route of our movement, giving and receiving without boundaries will begin. The quickening will bring new life to the living.

This is the way the torch of our fire will be passed.

M

CREATION BECOMES THE NEW FRONTIER

Holy Mary, I'd like to return to what was said yesterday:

"There are different ways of changing meaning, vastly different ways. One is taking in what was said 'as you heard it,' through listening or reading, and relating to it as yourself. Another way is taking in what is said or heard without relating it to oneself. Still another is adapting what is said to one's own existing position."

And . . . you spoke of getting me unstuck.

I would like to return to this too, my Mari, after remarking that you have changed positions again, and that you can see the sky from a different angle again. And I say to you here that, yes, it is a beautiful view, once again, isn't it?

Just gorgeous. It never fails to impress me how quick the changes are. I look down at the screen and turn my head back and it is different. For some reason it strikes me as funny how I've also kept my hands on the keys while looking out the window, and found I've typed gibberish.

That is funny! I, like you, don't know why things strike me as amusing.

Now, before we move on to this elusive idea that is slipping in and out of your mind, I want to say that we are clarifying this in-and-out phenomenon. It just happened to you again. In the time it took for you to type the last sentence, you forgot the idea that was coming to you—which was actually coming from me.

You just felt it passing back and forth between us—not yours or mine, but . . . ours.

Mary, that is mind boggling.

Don't dwell on it. Not now. You will feel it return. But noticing that you "can" notice it, is why I drew your attention to this manifestation of the sharing of being. This is the way in which you will get unstuck.

I don't know if I can let this go. This is sharing of *being*? This is what is happening when thought goes in and out like this?

You know the difference. It is not about every time you forget your thought, but you will see more easily now that which is of "shared being." You could see it as an interplay, a volley, a tossing back and forth. Giving and receiving without boundaries.

This, that we do now, is working at the edge of the new frontier.

"Creation becomes the new frontier, the occupation of those too young to rest, too interested in living still to welcome the peace of dying. Those who could not change the world one iota through their constant effort, in peace create the world anew."*

It's why I asked that we exchange letters—so that we speak, simply as who we are—nothing else. Doing so helped us reach this example of the edge at which we stand.

Who we are. Nothing else. Is this part of it? If I am not who I am, and nothing else, I can't fully experience "being" with you?

Yes! You change your molecular makeup when you are not being who you are. When you are fully who you are, in the mo-

---

* ACOL C:6.17. See also "The Dialogues," Chapter 14.

ment, you are fluid, and we "flow into each other." You are being a clear pool.

If you are not being who you are, the flow is diminished or even halted.

Let me put it this way. Very often, when you look out the window, the flow begins or returns. You are being who you are, locating yourself where you are, finding your orientation, which is to Being. This takes an enormous amount of stress from you, stress you don't even realize you have. As your brother once said, this stress is like a film on your skin. It is "outside" of you but felt on the inside.*

Looking out the window, this film dissolves. It warms and softens as you face a different picture, just as the morning frost does.

I rock with the enormity of this as I look out the windows that shelter me from the intense cold that has settled today, and I feel the word "settled" differently.

In its fluidity.

Okay. I can take that in.

"You become clear pools flowing into each other."

The dialogue.

Yes! In its exposure.

Yes.

Clarity is of continual movement. It is moving and being beyond all borders. As our in-and-out flow becomes steadier, we will more continuously be one in Being.

Now, we can still write "letters" and be one in being. Letters are records of those carrying on the line, the lineage of revelation.

---

* Jesus' words in this section are from an unpublished work.

That is why I had us begin in this way. But I want to clear this up. It is very, very important that we do so.

Writing/talking to each other is an expression of twoness, but you have continued to see it as one and another when the duad is two "together." The form of letters represented one and another, and it was awkward, wasn't it? Still, the form is immaterial, and Letters showed you this!

Yes, it did!

When you write in your journal, you are basically writing to yourself. It is why it is such a fabulous process for getting in touch with your truest self. You have noticed that when you are preparing to give a talk, you begin to write in your journal in a less personal way.

Your preparation is not a problem of any kind, but neither is it optimal. What I would like you to see is the difference in the way you write—in the way you are expressing yourself—in different situations, and how it has to do with the way you are being with yourself.

Oh, Mary, I've been aware of this for many years. It's one of my major reasons for not wanting to be a public person. Writing "for purpose" feels like a misuse of my gift and my time—even if it is only because I do it to myself.

Yes, when preparing, you are "trying" to say something.

That is so true!

You feel in need of a different language, and of tying things together. Soon you find you've gone fully into writing "a presentation" and your language and rhythm are stilted. I do know that you know this, and in acknowledging it, hope that I'm taking the burden from you. This purposefulness creates the film because what you are doing does not have the quality of movement that is of the natural. It is the film that causes you to "present" rather than be present.

I know you could feel this in your writing, and would try to get back to yourself, but the very idea of the presentation, lying out there in your future, would often prevent you from writing anything that sounded like yourself. This loss is your main reason for not desiring a public presence. It is a terrible feeling for you to sit down to this creative act of your Being, and have it become something else. Writing is too holy to you to not have you recognize this difference and seek to truly honor your gift. It is why the arts are such an elegant and graceful part of this movement of Being.

I appreciate all you are saying and that you recognize how I have felt. It is so relieving!

M

Oh, my Mari, if it were only recognized more broadly! This—let's say, "being nature," this self-exposure—is felt and valued but not recognized as what is happening. What is happening "is" an exposure of feelings. The happening is one's own, but shared. And this is "felt." It is felt, and it is seen, and it is heard— not only in the creator, but by the person receiving it—felt and felt again. Felt in the musician's music, the artist's sculpture, the writer's poetry. It is the spirit of it that is revealing "being in relationship," and Being inspires love. This is what is felt. This is what you desire to convey.

Listening to a favorite song you might say, "That is my song," and in the love of it as one's own, the giver of it is included and honored. It becomes one's own in being felt and, whatever the medium, it is the living way it flows into you and moves you that causes your expression of the feeling it engenders. This is life-giving union. And we do this here.

I remember the intense feeling of that when, after Dad's death, Van Morrison's song, "Stranded," would not leave me.

Yes. Your grief was your "own little island." You were secluded in yourself. But the movement of your being was expansive.

Movement, being, and expression are our own. Your own movement. My own movement. Together, we are being and expressing "our" movement. That our acts occur in union does not mean they are not our own. They are Being to Being. Being is only being "together" in relationship. It is Being that recognizes that something has happened in relation to your breath, to the radiance of the sun, the chill in the air, the arrival of a child, lover, or beloved pet. The recognition is the revelation that there is presence. And this occurs through one's exposure to Being.

Here, it is time for you to recognize and enjoy this phenomenon of love that is coming of your creation.

Your choosing to move your location was an Act of Being. It matters not that it was inside to outside, house to cabin, cabin to house, sunroom to dining room. You recognized your need to orient yourself to your "view." To your "vision." This dissolves the film that would tarnish the view.

We have just changed your orientation in a far greater way, as you see and feel that those who read your Course of Love without any "film" will feel it truly, and by extension, you. This will be far more clear to you when this writing is shared, as it will be so taken in by the feminine ones that there will be no division.

This is what happens when words become real. They become the living Word. You can take up this living now with those who have found love in this way, and those who are to come.

Thank you, my Mother, for this beautiful revelation of this troubling feeling I have had visit me in this area. I hope to really "get it" and live from it.

Well, the shorthand is: Be who you are, and all will be well!

M

*T*HE LIVING WORD

My Dear Mary, at the same time that so many things are right, just as many seem to be wrong. I know that dichotomy makes no sense, and yet it expresses the strangeness of this time. My time. This morning it manifested as me not being able to find my glasses. I've looked everywhere I can think of, and of course I think of all those "seeking without finding" wisdom sayings. It's so hard to seek when you can't see!

Also, I got in a bit of a funk yesterday after thinking I'd lost our last letter, and called Christie, my funk partner, who is such an incredible listener, and asks questions that make me look at myself and what I'm complaining about. And then, of course, when she has so many bigger concerns with her health and family, I feel a tad bad for saying anything.

M

Oh, my God. Now, after all that seeking, I found the glasses I've been looking for beside my left hand. Oh, Mary! Miracle? Or my own nonsense? This is almost the whole of what I was speaking of with Christie. The very closeness of the two. The ridiculousness it seems, at times, to make so much of this. To tie my heart to it. To stake my life on it. As Christie has. Practically dying, literally, in order to come forth shining.

And now, something has come to my mind that feels significant:

solution finders. Did it "come to me," in this new way we're speaking of? As "your thought" finding itself in me?

I simply want you to realize that you are one of the few who truly invite the exchange that is not a "solution finding" exchange. When you "complained," as you say, to Christie, you didn't expect her to offer solutions, and you did not particularly like asking me about a solution for her.

When she asked you to speak to me about her situation, "you" thought you were seeking a solution "for her." Yet, when I speak to her, I speak to you. I spoke of her own knowing, and her fear of it. A thousand fears can leave you before you get to the base fear— fear of your own knowing. No matter from where you imagine it comes, all knowing is your own knowing . . . revealed.

Now you, being less interested in "solutions," seek them only with extreme situations. This doesn't mean that you don't care or that Christie isn't a brilliant light. It doesn't mean that miracles aren't desired or offered. It means only that you have let go of solution finding to a greater extent than many, and this is because you have found that we do not offer solutions. We guide you always to your own knowing. These situations only present themselves as another opportunity for you, in this case for both you and Christie, and eventually many, to overcome the fear of your knowing.

What I just said could scream at you both for not doing so, but in every instance, a fear of taking up one's own knowing can be lessened when receiving a message that speaks of what is already known. Do you remember that we have spoken of this before? That it is always your own knowing that is revealed?

Yes, I do, Mary. And more than that, I feel it. You give me words for what I know, but do not know how to express, and sometimes you reveal what I don't "know that I know."

It is why your reception of my way has waited until you were ready for it. As each one is ready, others are as well, and the "time" as you say, "is right."

It is all part of a change that is happening, a change based on readiness. A change that has been making you feel like you're getting dementia as much as anything else. It is hard to believe that such inconveniences as these "lapses" cause are to be part of The New.

Because they wear me, and us, down.

And my Mari, these are the scourges of your time. Prophecy as well as alchemy fit the time. Our communication is of "this" time, even while I have spoken of the past. I spoke of the past because it is my actual past, so that we come to know each other as women, and because my time was important to your time, in the same way that your time is important to our time now—as all are related in time outside of time.

We redeem the past to create a new future. Or, put another way: We release the present to be what it will be.

We do this as we spend time together in mutual trust and openness. It is with trust and openness that you and I, together, see the lives that are involved in these times, in a way that reveals them as what they are. We are not changing base metals into gold here. We are relieving the strain so that what is happening can be valued as the transformation that it is. Your Christina knows of this.

M

The transformation of time outside of time within time, comes of the living: living persons and a living universe both being truly alive in their fullness as they are seen, one to another. As they relate, one to another.

The word "universe" comes from the base of "verse," which means "turning." Turning to one another is what we're doing here. It becomes a new way of living, of being alive! A way that does not immediately fit into the way things are. You and Christie both have great trust, yet even with great trust, the change that is happening with time is going to cause an uneasiness, an uncertainty, having to do with what is occurring within yourselves, and the universe, as you are turning together. This is the way in which what is turning manifests in time and brings actual change—not only changes of thought but changes in you, in the material universe, and in the outer realms.

You have spoken for a long time, decades, of the incapacities that come alongside your opening to this communication. Remember now, that your incapacities grow into new capacities.

Communing takes you outside of time! This, that we are doing together, takes you inside of a new time. Your brother even demonstrated this to you physically once in the early days of your writings with him, when you were able to document that time stood still as you spoke.

What we are doing now takes you inside of a new time.

And then . . . what happens when you re-enter time? You exit. And there you find Choices. Choices are the great stress of your time. As you have said: "Many choices, all the same."

This is so current to me. Every "simple" thing that I do ends up involving much more complexity than I expect. And there's something deceptive about it. This "time" has been made to seem so much easier than it once was, and in many ways this is true. I did not lose what we wrote yesterday because a backup was automatically made without me even realizing it. I wasn't in a panic about it because I had printed it and knew I could retype it. But I use a technology every day that I don't understand! And the majority of us do.

In one way it seems to have come to free us up. In another, I (at least) feel this is questionable. It has cost jobs and lessened the once necessary (and ease bringing) things, like having a person who answers a phone and a question. But that isn't all of it—just the smallest of its pieces.

There's this preponderance of choice that allows a certain malaise to take hold because it is just too much. Too much of everything. Too much to think about. Something new coming at you all the time. At least for me, it makes me want to shut down, turn off.

I have the hermit tendencies anyway, Mary, but you have wanted to know about "this" time, and although I realize it's hard to see your own time while you are "in it," this is what comes to me at the moment.

Oh, but Mari, this is what we are changing! Remember your phrase: "This is it, and I am in it?"

Yes.

It does not mean being "in it" in the way you just expressed. Not at all! Here you are "out of it." Out of that old "it." You are held "within" the new near.

Yes, I do know, and I don't say it often. I don't know how to say it properly. But to be "here," and to be "there," are two so vastly different ways of being! The "in it" is *totally* different. Our "in it," yours and mine, is like it was with Mary Love and Julieanne Carver in the early days, like with Jesus. It is an embracing, encompassing, "in it—together." It does happen "here." It is possible. . . "here." And it is beyond what I have known before. It is truly one to one. That's the best way to put it. It's not a bunch of noise coming at you, or things to do. It is just, simply, being together.

And we are making these two ways into "one way." We are keeping only the togetherness of The New. The way of the Marys. The New Near.

M

GATEWAY TO A NEW AGE

DECEMBER 12, 2019

You keep sending me reeling. It seems we start out going in one direction, a direction that I think I have a clue of, and we end up somewhere else. And we never, or rarely, "conclude." We just keep carrying on.

My guess is that this is purposeful. I don't have time to "think" about anything! This was true with ACOL too, and no matter that I heard the words of Jesus, and typed Jesus' words, and read the words again and again for accuracy, I quickly went on. I felt like nothing stuck and saw "not remembering" as a curse. Now I'm see-ing the past a little differently. It's happening in so many ways! In so many, many ways, the past—my past, and possibly the "shared" past—seems to be changing form!

But this "reeling" is new, like an internal form of the swirl.

Luckily, Mary Love came over yesterday. We continue to get to know one another, personally and spiritually, on altogether new levels. You feel like you might know "everything" about a person, and then you keep discovering more. It's amazing. I should be used to it by now. Something is always "new" with us. But it is more than that. Something has opened *further* between us. Maybe it is that she's speaking with Mary M.* She was just hearing about trust and so was I. When was it? Just days ago?

Now that I'm reflecting on it, her past is changing too. And "our" past is changing, both individually and together. It is part of

---

* This is the way Mary Love speaks of Mary Magdalene.

what happened yesterday, in a way that is indescribable in ordinary terms.

My son Ian came over, too, and as Mary was leaving, he made such fun of me in that cute "son" way, that I laughed until I cried. I think Mary may have too. She was at least "howling," as she puts it.

We are so like the way you and I are in some ways. We, too, start out going in one direction and end up somewhere else. That is the exact feeling of this whole thing. There are no maps. No markers. And this "reeling" feeling is the feel of the motion—the "inner" motion.

Anyway, I was totally exhausted by it and unable to carry on, and yet I did! I kept "going" until late. It was a peopled day: Mary, then Ian, then Henry and George, then Donny. More changes to the website, emails, discussions about Christmas. Way too much for me in that state that causes me, with almost anyone other than Mary Love, to feel very fragile. It is all too much and too heavy on me.

And it is heavy. "Heavy" is a perfect word, a grounding word. As you are being lifted, the grounding is sometimes needed. But not very often anymore. It is not the time for it now. You are lightening and intensifying at once. And you would hope it would wait until January!

In some ways . . . *Yes!*

M

There is a light snow outside, one I wouldn't see without the benefit of looking up to where the streetlamp reveals it. The whole atmosphere *is* light, light with snow. I was wondering why it was getting light so early. It isn't "bright," but it also isn't dark. Now I know why. Again, something I could not see became visible, answering an unspoken question.

This technology that you do not understand is like that too, but in a more earthly and discombobulated way.

Yes, but technology seems to me like a house of mirrors. It's as if it doesn't actually exist in form but is just "out there" in the ethers. More and more things have come to be this way in this new technological age. In the move from industry to technology, the concreteness has been slowly bending to a new way, a way that has opened communication in a manner that makes all the world near, and at times farther away.

Mari, when you said, "Yes, but. . ." you described what "doesn't exist in form but is 'out there' in the ethers." The New is being tapped into and "used," and one of the reasons we are together here is to end the use.

I am not only speaking to you, but of you, for this reason: to show, through you, what is not being seen, and how extremely near you actually are to a true new age.

This is the quickening of the turn from one age to the next. We are standing at the gateway to the new age.

M

THE SPACIOUS AND
THE BELOVED

DECEMBER 13, 2019

Good morning, Holy Mary. I am near the manger, and the day has darkened again. It has darkened before my eyes. The dawn is not yet here, but I am. I'm here awaiting this quiet. I am so happy for it there are tears welling in my eyes. The beauty and the quiet. I spoke to Lee yesterday and he's read fifty pages of our sharing and is so taken by it. That pleases me.

I spoke with Christina yesterday too, and she was so happy to be mentioned (within our writing), and laughed joyously when I asked her, "So, what do you know?" That was fun.

Yet, since the idea of "solution finding" crossed between us, I'm strangely thinking more of such things, and of pleasing people. It seems sharing with people makes me long to be more helpful, and that takes me toward that solution area, even though you gave me an honest complement when you said this is not what I do. . . usually!

As I sit with this, I really do feel that I am here to know what I know! Thank you for making me more aware of this. And good morning.

Good morning, my Mari. Being filled with wonder, as you are each day, leaves your mark on the world herself. Christina does this too. Mother Earth feels quite adored. As Mother Earth is adored, I am adored, for we are one. The more than one, are one: We are all oneness personified. Personification is the knowing of holiness. It is incarnation. It is its beauty—seen. It is its beauty—felt. It is beauty—named.

In the beginning was the Word. The Word personifies. The Word personifies even God. The Word personifies the light and the dark, the bird and the bush, baby dolls and pets, mangers and seasons, the listening and the speaking. As you, yourself, knew to write, in Creation of the New, *"Living has nothing to do with 'otherness' or 'thingness.' "**

Everything is reminding me now of *Creation of the New.* But the writing of *Creation of the New* continues to be but a whiff of an experience.

Time outside of time is like that. It is ephemeral. Vague. Wispy. "Neither here nor there." That is it, isn't it? The feeling?

Yes. It is. I had not seen this connection of "then" to "now" in this way.

Touching in to your own mystic self, as you did in Creation of the New, *was touching into your own ethereal self. You took on the vague and wind-like character of the in between, of what makes its presence known, but is not seen. Don't you see? In these states, you take on the same nature. Taking on the same nature is part of being natural in a new way, a way that is as old as time and memory. It is the feeling of "not in one place," the "not all here," as you sometimes say. And you never could quite name it. To this day you will sometimes say, "I don't know what that was."*

It was and is the spaciousness from which The New arises in Memoria.

This only shows how perfect you are for this time and our new vision. You have always vaguely known, in this area of your

---

* Perron, Mari. *Creation of the New.* Course of Love Publications, 2007, p. 110.

life—your writing life—the mystery of creation. Even when your writing is, as you might say, "totally your own," even with The Given Self, *which may have been written in your most "natural" voice, you knew "something more" was at work and that it was of you. It was of you in the totality of your spaciousness. Memory includes every mistake you ever made, and every fear, and every sob that ever came from you. It includes your joy and wonder. All your relations are there with you, including your feeling relations.*

What I am saying is that in your writing life, in your relationship to your writing "life," you were being revealed to yourself, no matter how much you struggled or what you said. And you recognized the holiness of this revealed knowing in the Act of Creation. It was in you always, as it is in each one. It is the way creation is . . . in spaciousness.

$$\mathcal{M}$$

Oh, Mary, I have come back after starting the next chapter, because the way in which you spoke of spaciousness was new to me and kept calling to me. I'd like to know more.

Do you remember, Mari, the way your brother spoke of this?

I must not, because I had to go look, and this feels so startling:

"Imagine the air around you being visible and your form an invisible *space* within the visible surroundings. This is the reality of Christ-consciousness. Consciousness may seem to be embodied by form but the reverse is true and has always been true. The body is now ready to know that it is embodied, enclosed, surrounded, taken up, by consciousness. It is your feelings that now will be the sense organs of this spaciousness. Not feelings of sight or sound, smell or touch, but feelings of love of Self. Feelings of love of Self are now what hold open the space of the Self, allowing the space to be." *

Can you imagine how spacious the world would be if self-love were to be embraced? Spaciousness is consciousness unconfined. You are developing your spacious form.

Oh, Mary. I'm so glad I came back!

I am too, Mari. This is your part in our dialogue. To come back to knowing. You come back to go forward newly. Now you will continue more confidently into knowing the way creation is.

$\mathcal{M}$

THE WAY CREATION IS

We begin to return this knowing to all who are ready by speaking of it with each other as the way creation is. Creation is Acts. Creation is events of Memory. Creation is Revelation. Creation is of Being—experiences of Being in relatedness. You, in relation to the act, the act in relation to your humanity, your humanity in relation to your soul, your soul in relation to what is revealed. All are acting and being in relatedness.

And now we are ready for the radical nature of this to be seen and heard so as to herald The New and the transformation needed.

"What was created cannot be uncreated. Thus transformation is needed. The miracle makes you fully aware of the embrace and the consciousness of unity and places you outside of time. In this state, no duality exists. Doing and being are one.

"Action is the bridge between form and the formless because action is the expression of the self in form. 'Right' action comes from the unity in which doing and being are one, or in other words, from the state in which there is no division between who you are and what you do. 'Right' action comes from the state of wholeness." *

In this time of transformation, we no longer preach or teach. We no longer remove the sacred. We bring it near.

---

* ACOL D:Day7.5-6

"Your identity no longer stands 'in form.' "* You are in the world, but you flow from life itself. Life is present. Life is living. Life is the changing form of the world.

"'Thingness' is over, and your identity no longer stands in form but flows from life itself."†

ℳ

We locate the sacred in this world and this time, in each one, in all that lives, to save the world for each one and from every "thingness" that has been made. Thingness has reigned in this old form of the human kingdom. We topple the kings with the grace of the Mother and the power of "creation" initiated by the feminine.

This power is so very near and obvious. It is felt in the egoic kings as fear, and felt in the hearts of the less royal, less egoic people, as hope. Hope is the condition of the initiate‡ in which conception is ready to commence. This is our message to deliver. The Christ Life is not, and has never been, separate from the life-giving Mothers of The New.

Oh yes, you may hear crying from the men and the fathers about this. You will tell them, "It is all One."

The One was given the name "Father," that has survived almost to the destruction of the world. We claim the Christ Life of the Mother now. We retrieve it from those who, without meaning it to be so, simply could not see the ancient memory in themselves:

---

* ACOL C:20.3

† ACOL C:20.4

‡ ACOL C:20.36

mankind's jealousy of the women without whom they were not complete, and without whom they could not sire children. These ancestral memories, thousands upon thousands of years in the making, have been in the lead of humankind.

Yet it was always One: the men, the women, the children, the earth, the animals, body, soul, heaven.

But oh, the indignance that will arise! And yet it must. To reveal the One, we must reveal the Mother as the duad of the Father, without whom the love—the love that cherishes life—would not be. We must love our way back to life and living.

In those close to rising to the Christ-life, their own indignance will signal their self-examination and lead to self-revelation. For those who have not drawn near, they may encounter unwelcome witnessing. Either way, a new humbleness will come and be nourished one to another. The arms of the feminine and the maternal, and eventually, the paternal, will be raised up together.

Oh, yes, now the women will be just as aghast as the men. How strange that the giving of care should rise.

But no.

How strange is it that the giving of care has fallen to such a low station? It brings no status, I know.

What if there were no status?

Oh yes, in the time of building, in the time of forming, the male energy—as it "took on the shaping of the external"—was developing status as well. It was an unfortunate byproduct of the feminine and masculine energy that rose "around" those who brought structure to the unstructured. There was such gratitude, admiration, expectation! All deference began in this way. In the way of the needed forming of the world in time not long past.

With people in need of shelter and an easing of survival needs, it is easy to see how this came to pass.

This masculine, external, "forming" energy is not made for this time of in-forming your Self. It will take a while for most males to find the feminine in themselves and embrace the conception of The New that will happen "in the Self of form." As they begin this revolutionary change, the women will take up the masculine energy in a new way.

There will be no generations of true union without the rise of the feminine that dethrones the masculine way of external formation, by bringing it to the feminine way of internal formation . . . creating from within. As unpleasant as this may sound, we will be equalizing, not creating, a new hierarchy. There will be no more thrones to inspire awe or fear. There will be no throne. We will be establishing a value of care for one as care for all, and care of all as care for one.

"You begin the movement away from observing to informing"* . . . not externally but internally. Bringing who you truly are into form. As this happens, the external forming of the masculine energy will become secondary rather than primary.

"How can the invisible be observed? From within Christ-consciousness, you begin to be able to know and to make known without observation or observance *of the physical*. This occurs *through your relationship with the unknown*. You begin to be informed by what *is* without any regard for your level of understanding or

---

* ACOL D:Day15.3

knowing. . . .You do this by taking what *is* into your spacious form rather than observing it as separate from you."*

We want to look at these masculine kings and queens, fiercely and gently, while keeping an eye open to the potential for a new arrogance in both women and men. There is no time or place for this now. No self-congratulatory lauding of the "enlightened" males. No flaunting of feminine virtues as "greater," though their relative ascendance is simply . . . necessary. This is crucial. Essential. Lifesaving. World-saving. Balancing. The way for which the time has come.

As we invalidate the bastardization of the dark—and that not sired by the men or sanctioned by their Father God—we bring on the emergent power.

We are speaking of the consciousness birthed out of the dark, from which we remove some of the status of "the first." God is the name of the always existent—in terms of "nothing existing" before God.

God consciousness was characterized by existence as spaciousness. God became the conscious spaciousness as the first duad of God and Sophia, both of whom drew life from the dark. By means of shared consciousness, Sophia knew God, and God knew Sophia. The experience of "shared" consciousness arose one to another and became the way of Creation.

Raising up the visage of a "Son of God," created by a divine Mother as well as such a Father, began to lure humanity toward relating to God in one another, yet, at the same time, to lure others to inhumanity and denial of the personhood of women. Do not

---

* ACOL D:Day15.4

forget how recently equality began to be envisioned and enacted, or, as you wrote in "Mirari," how recently women and minorities have gained equal rights under the law, even in the United States. We are a people of faith over law, which at times requires laws of faith to govern so that unauthorized change can come to be.

M

ℬIRTHERS OF THE NEW

I was the mother of God in man, and I became a "savior" along with Yeshua. A savior of the potential for the world to be remade in the way of creation's original glory, through spacious, loving Acts of Creation.

Out of the darkness . . . light. Out of the womb of the spacious Being of God—out of the womb of the Being of space—came the masculine and feminine, who knew one to another, and began to create and extend as love creates.

I welcome spacious consciousness and know that I can abide within it, as surely as I now know that I have been doing so.

Yes, now you comprehend what you have been doing and what has been done unto you: being taken up by spacious consciousness. *

This is being with no separation between the physical and the nonphysical. I am the first to know God in the physical, to know God outside of the vision, or the sound, or miracles of signs and wonders. This, too, makes me a "first" . . . a savior . . . an equal to my son. This way is coming now, to you and to all. I, like Jesus, was born to bring salvation to the world. This has been our joint aim in this time, through these holy works: to save the world. By birthing saviors, Mari. Many.

And so, it is important for you to realize that you battle the physicality of form when you remove yourself from the spaciousness of God, the spaciousness that is your birthright. Does this make it more clear? A clearer "reality"? You battle the physicality

---

* See ACOL D:Day12, "The Spacious Self Joined in Relationship."

374

of form when you remove yourself from the space that is you. You "are" the spaciousness of physical reality, as well as that which occupies it.

This expression of love came into time to birth the divine human through me, and the divine human "in" me. Yet it was an unseen power. Unseen power was capable of being understood only as movement in stillness: the quickening come. With each and every birth, a certain stillness "moves in," and begins a change within. Movement comes to stillness, and stillness to movement. Back and forth it goes.

I'm so happy to hear you speak of this. I feel for you, as a woman, after hearing Father, Son and Holy Spirit—all addressed as "he."

Of course, Mari, all these designations are troublesome now, but they originated in a different time. They are distinctions within oneness that were necessary "then." Now, the distinction of woman is crucial. It is critical, here, in this time.

I feel some significance in you using the word "woman" instead of "women."

There are men. And there is mankind. There are women. And there is womankind. Remember, "kind" is a designation of meaning.

The church did much of this naming, but you know what? My naming was bestowed by the people, and I wouldn't have it any other way. Blessed Mary, Mother of God! Immaculate Mary! Holy Virgin Mary! Yes. Each were beautiful. Gracious. But most prayers I hear are addressed simply as "Mother Mary, pray for me," and these are my favorites. I believe Jesus has shared with you his appreciation for your simple, "Dear Jesus, please be with me."

Your brother called you a receiver, but he also said you would "take" his course. He suggested that each one who "took" his course would receive his words in their own way. Yet your Jesus also called you the "honored birth mother" of his Course, of this new way.

This will be the way of the future. No one needs to be sainted. All need to be honored as who they are. We speak here as birth mothers, beloveds to each other. We know that all who, in this time, have the desire to be so, will be birthers of The New.

This is not in the way of the church of the "public," not like your naming of kings and queens or presidents, but endearments lovingly given. Loving salutations bestowed by those who love, to love. These designations are of the love of divine to human and the love of human to divine. They come of relationship.

When you can love one—if you are willing to bestow love on one, to call one "beloved"—such love returns to you.

You are merely asked to share life in a way that the honor of being beloved can be bestowed on you. This is the new mantle of the new identity and the new way. The mantle of holiness protects the living Holy Ones from the "unnatural" distinctions which have come to be seen as merited according to certain artificial ideals. Holy means of address are used by those of us beyond time now, to reveal the difference that can be affected with the release of pretense.

Your brother's call to change what you desire, and to fully embrace desire again, is a call to your true desires in their more "human" form: desires for knowing, for closeness, for self-realization, *for self-acceptance, for love—acceptance of your desire to be a creator, to fulfill your calling. All these desires, when released from the disappointments that have tamped them down, even to the smallest degree, begin to rise, and let the true Self be known. True desire ignites your passion for love's knowing—to know and be known by God and one's companions—to know and be known as the beloved.*

ℳ

Do you not remember your "Christ to me" day?

Oh yes. It was in 2006 with Mary Love. She was clearly "Christ to me." It happened that, on a lovely day in summer, sitting outside the cabin, talking and experiencing, together, I knew her in this way, and felt that we were Christ to each other.

Mary didn't particularly like the "Christ to me" designation, and I was a little hurt. But, if I had said she was my beloved, she would have said easily that the same was true for her with me. Not exclusively "me," but yes, me. A shared belovedness.

Some naming is needed to distinguish the old from The New, and to reflect a greater understanding of the relation between the old and The New, male and female, human and divine, time and time outside of time. But we convey this more when we speak heart to heart, and we drifted because of the question that I have answered—answered in order to expose the drift that such questions can cause.

You have struggled here, with this, and need not struggle. Naming is immaterial. Love is what matters.

Go now, my beloved, and struggle no more!

Yes, my beloved. I will do my very best.

M

THE WHOLE ANSWER
TO EVERYTHING

Dear Mary,

As I open this morning and see your last words from yesterday . . . I love it! *Go now and struggle no more!* And how I would have hated that a few years ago, and still can hate it if I think of it too much, because it gives the kind of flavor people can use against you: "If you're struggling, you're not *there yet.*" Good God! You might as well say the poor, the sick, as well as this very movement we're to experience, are excluded.

Fr. Adrian said, a week or so ago, that "sin" is "not having your priorities straight." I liked it so much that I got my pen out and wrote it on the bulletin. It could make me feel good about some things—the ultimate things, like what we're doing here. And other things not so much. I don't feel like getting out the dictionary this morning, but I'd bet the word priority came from "prior" and is about what you take care of first, as in this way I start my mornings. Or maybe about the original, the a priori intent of creation— prior to the naming of things.

I do know that after the day starts coming at me, especially at this time of the year, I could never be clear enough to be with you in this way. But there is something lingering from yesterday. You spoke of the movement of stillness. This I believe I may know.

I was struggling a bit then, which I feel, today, gives me insight into the movement of stillness. When there is no struggle, there *is* movement in my stillness. I love the very idea of that. I love knowing I can feel this from now on as a movement. Like the quickening, but a quickening within spaciousness. This is all I must have here. A clean slate, a clean love that doesn't try to lead.

If I wanted to write what people would most like to hear, we'd be talking about whether Jesus married. Today, I don't even remember the question I had in mind yesterday, yet what I remember is that there was a struggle to hear clearly, and an attempt to gain clarity about what felt like an enormous topic. Most of the time, I truly do not do this, which I think coincides with what you spoke of as the movement of stillness. This I feel I know, and I feel like it is "good for me" to acknowledge when I *do* know, as well as when I *don't*.

Of course, it is! This is just what is needed. What you have written today is needed. What you wrote yesterday is needed for what you and I will share today. It is sublime to question what it is you want to know, but it is better if you can't name what that is. Everything you can name is not what you need to know.

Ah. I am breathing a sigh of relief.

Yes, you sat back in your chair and let out an actual sigh. The out breath. Exaggerate a few more, will you?

M

I did that and got up and turned on the Christmas lights. In the morning, and sometimes at night, in the quiet, this ceases to be a stressful season. I feel such love for my home in such times.

My son has created a true home for himself, but my daughters haven't yet. In some ways they still see this as "home" and so does Henry. I sure saw Smith Avenue as home long after I moved out.

It feels like we're creating a vagabond society, and yet needing my home and my solitude, I can't "take in" anyone more.

I have pondered this a bit now, but my thought went right in and right back out of my mind. There was something more I was going to say about this.

Then let me bring up what Fr. Adrian's comment meant to you. You can no longer prioritize the vagabonds—whether of people or paperwork or tasks or thought. They can no longer take precedence. If they do, you will struggle.

This that we are doing, is what you are here to do. And what you are here to do, and to be, is all any of this is concerned with, which is the issue that has gotten so distorted by those who would separate what you do and who you are, as well as what they do, and who they are. Do you see?

Hear that sentence deeply: Those who would separate what you do and who you are.

Those who would separate what you do from who you are, are those who separate what "they" do from who "they" are. It is the way of this time, flashing before you from all over the world.

When Yeshua took in the less than savory, when he crossed the lines of the sects, and the religions, and the King, he did only what he could do as who he was, and this is the whole answer—the answer to everything.

Doing only what you can do as who you are, is the whole answer to everything. When you can do only what you can do as who you are, and only then, will the mayhem subside.

The faithless disorder that you have now, masquerading as lawful order, is made up of those who see themselves as the most powerful men in the world, with the most powerful weapons. It is an answer to nothing but annihilation.

M

When the ego is gone, you're at the beginning—back at the beginning of the beginning of life in form. "What are these bodies? What is this life?"

You ask innocently, and with the wonder of Mirari.

The whole of this journey, the whole epic journey, is to get back to where you began "here." Here in this new life, in this new time, with all the power of creation before you, waiting to be seen.

Oh, Mary. I am blowing out again, big time. I have had a feeling realization. Not a feeling "of" realization but a "feeling realization." Is it that when you feel it, you see it, and it becomes real?

Yes! Yes. And a thousand times yes.

When you see with your heart as well as your mind. When you hear with your eyes as well as your ears. When you are open to sound and light, to the whisper of the wind and the cry of the babe of The New. When you open to the spaciousness that you are.

M

CHE CRY OF THE NEW BABE

The cry of the new babe is your own. It is this journey. Here.
Now. The journey into this life and this time. And let me tell you,
no one came here to be an assassin.

The fact that when evil occurs it can lead to other happenings
that are beneficent, does not mean it is the only way it can happen. No!

Yes, the assassin, Judas, was taken in by Yeshua. Do you think
this act was written into Judas' identity? That it was ordained
that Yeshua be crucified?

Let this way of explaining away the horrors go! But also blame
no one. If you could be walked back to the beginning, none of this
would have happened. And yet everything can become a metaphor, and be turned, so that it "is for" what actually has become
of what was begun. If you realize that everything that came of
what was begun was begun innocently, you can travel back to
innocence.

You can travel back to your virgin state.

Virginal innocence (undefiled innocence) is what I retained
and why I am here with you and Yeshua to resuscitate the world.

Everything is both actual and metaphorical: part of the great
turning. For when "your" universe turns, as a whole, to its original creation, the universe has turned as well. With each frac-
tion of a turn, the light of new life makes its first sounds, soundings that echo out to embrace all, and are held together in a new

composition, as in Indra's Net of Jewels* . . . revived for a new time.

In the new turning, everything comes to you with an innocence of intent. So today, you can see that yesterday, when the question was not the inherent question, what was ultimately revealed was still able to bring forth the new idea whose time has come.

And ideas leave not their source.

The idea that you are here to be who we are is "here." Now. Not "near," but "here." You are beginning to realize what this means.

Your days of being assassins of life are over. You no longer stop the turning. You no longer sacrifice the lamb. You cease to view the net without its jewels. As "you" see the jewels in the net—as you see newly the jewel that Christina is in your net, and you in hers—you see your new net.

This new net.

This new universe.

This universe of love.

All of this makes me feel that my little book, *Creation of the New,* written over ten years ago, was a prelude to what we are writing here, the reason Christina has just reread it, and why her re-reading of it caused me to pick it up again as well. I haven't read far, as yet, but this I know. Yes, "know."

And Creation of the New *came from you, my Mari. From you and for you. Indra's Net was fashioned by Christina from her and for her. What comes from you encourages you to be who you*

---

* Strutt, Christina. "Indra's Net of Jewels - Going Quantum in a 3-D World." *CoCreating Clarity,* www.cocreatingclarity.com/indrasnet.htm.

are. Remember, the whole answer to everything is that you can do only what you can do as who you are.

Creation of the New was your vision of what you did not know you knew. You have been being made ready for this work for over two decades. The time is right now, even more than it was a year and a half ago when we began.

There was a chance this time would never come. This is what I am saying. You have a destiny to live. To do what you are here to do is to be who you are here to be.

Can you imagine what the world could be if each one lived as who they are here to be?

If being and doing were one?

M

CAPTIVITY

DECEMBER 15, 2019

Dear Mother,

It is Sunday under the prettiest, most dramatic sky in a long while, and I am coming to you with a troubled heart . . . a heart full of dark and light, too.

I have hurt people now and again, Mother, if I may call you that today. The traps of this life are great. In a way I stand by everything I have done, even when it caused some people pain. I say, "in a way," because each troubling event involved two, and where I may have been in possession of a certainty that made my conviction true, it was simply a conviction—not a plan of action or of "worldly" intent, or of a specific certainty, but more of a certain *possibility*.

I feel that I have suffered with that combination a good deal more that I let on, and with having hurt others due to it.

Now, coming into a time that you suggest will cause even greater uncertainty, how do I relate with those who "know" in a way, and a manner, that I do not?

You feel the uncertainties that lurk beneath their certainties. You do not have to do anything about them, but only need to feel them—those uncertainties they hide. You do this so that you are not drawn to doubt yourself. This really is your first priority. Discounting how important this is, is a misstep many make!

You each have your own way of knowing. One is not better than another . . . only your own. Consequently, while one way of knowing speaks to you, another may not.

Knowings not your own are often clues or triggers that move you to understand in "your" way. All ways reveal your longing for "your" true way of knowing. "Jewels in the net" support distinction within oneness. What you all are looking for is to meet yourselves as you are, to see yourselves in the way that you were fashioned, created to be. You might say, "Truth is truth," but within the many ways that truth is revealed, there will be few that will speak with the intimacy of a universal tongue. A Course in Miracles *was the most stunning example of this.*

Misinterpretation of ACIM was one reason that created the need for A Course of Love, *but not the main reason. The main reason was that ACIM set an evolutionary change in motion. In the same way,* A Course of Love *created the revolutionary motion that became the advent of the way of the Marys. These works are evolutionary as well as revolutionary. They change people. They change the trajectory of humanity. Holy works "need" to change as their readers change and as those so changed, change the world. The failure to recognize "Holy Works" that begin to catch up with the evolution of humanity is unfortunate.*

I am here to reveal the accomplishment of each original work. Original work is the evolution and revolution to what "naturally" follows. This is a testament to their divine nature. It does not make the former obsolete, but it does make the former incomplete.

Remember: to exist in the certainties of others is not a true way of living. This is what has been revealed.

I can feel the truth of this *so strongly.* Scenes arise of when I have tried to live with the certainty of others—to live with the way the "certain ones," or privileged ones—feel about things that matter to me. From the realm of family to that of the Courses, they range far and wide.

To live that way is what I can no longer do, even when some things, like care of Henry, feel like a primal response. Henry and *A Course of Love*, they are my own, and yet not my own. These muddled lines are the hardest.

Yet they are minor in comparison to those that affect me with this heaviness.

To exist in the certainties of others is not a true way of living. Are you ready to live truly?

M

To break free, all you really need do is quit comparing. Comparing one to another is rampant, and each instant of comparing is like equating figs to dates. They are each still going to be dark, sticky fruits particularly, and broadly, simply fruit. But they are comparable only to a certain point.

You do not realize it, but you compare yourself to every person who expresses how they are different from you, and think the person expressing who "they are," in their difference, is the one comparing—and so criticizing or judging you. Can you see this?

I'm startled—startled to realize it. ... But yes.

And you hadn't seen it before, had you?

No. It is a surprise, one I greet with chagrin. And a truth. Damn.

Do not fret. This situation reveals a change ready to come to be, but which has not yet happened in you.

Yes, Mary. I feel this cloudiness in my thought. I desire, very much, to have it leave the shadows and to have clearness come.

In such times, tend to the feelings, my Mari. Nothing else matters.

Why do I feel I am no good at this?

Because you care deeply, but often don't understand or express your care. You leap beyond your feeling of care, to "taking care of," even situations that are not your own, and sometimes situations that are not yet here!

What you see "first" are responsibilities of a practical and shared nature: "what you need to do." Seeing them you feel obligated, and you have fought feeling obligated. When you fight what you are feeling you do not recognize it. You think you know this feeling of obligation, but what you know is a feeling of un- wanted, unwelcome and nonexistent indebtedness. Your readers would be surprised to know you feel anything but thankfulness for what you have been given, and the opportunity to make such a significant contribution. If you did nothing but bask in the light of what you have given the world, none of your "readership" would look at you askance.

Perhaps your Catholic upbringing gave you a heightened sense of holy obligation. But what is at the heart of this, is that you continue to try to "live up to" an honor that, in effect, never was recognized in the way that mattered to you. Your fidelity to the work, and to each word given to you, has never been honored in a respectful way . . . because of Jesus! That is shocking, even to me. Because the words were given you by Jesus, you were discounted rather than honored.

And still you carried on.

For the variable and infrequent gifts of your doing (which is often a doing you do not want to do), you have given away your freedom and lessened your thankfulness for what you have received and shared so beautifully. Mari, when you feel so bur- dened, you are not free. But the good news is, now that you have let yourself feel that you are so burdened you are not free, you are taking the first step to fleeing your captivity and claiming your freedom.

I feel like I have done this many times.

You have. Can you see in this, your Bible stories repeated? The repeated patterns of all time?

But now, time is on your side. Time is ending with the end of these cyclical patterns. You have spoken of this with technology. Technology could be the great liberator. But it has become the new encampment. It is the refugee camp of the world. It is made so by those who could not resist carrying the old model into the new time. It is the way of every age and the collapse of every age. The making of the new rulers whose underlings go into slavery to acquire their great and wonderful way to ease.

You have refused to carry the old model into the new time, and it is this courageous fight you have mounted that affected your alienation.

Again, you startle me, but yes!

The great release of humankind has been at hand over and over again. But what happens? What could bring freedom is re-made to conform to the way of old. While you have fought for The New, you also made yourself continue "in the old" to protect The New.

Yes!

My Mari, this is what you have been doing with your "responsibility," and it has just about killed you. You feel like you are soon to be 75 rather than 65. You could age yourself right out of life if this continues. And so. . . .

We are having an intervention . . . with you and with . . . oh, I would say at least half the world. It is a stop or die intervention that is not a threat but an invitation to live.

M

THE INTERVENTION

I welcome the intervention. I yearn for it. I am ready, my Holy One. I feel as if it cannot wait another minute.

And then I know...

Mother, this is it, isn't it? It has already begun.

Yes. This intervention stands, along with me, between time and time outside of time, guiding the swirling energies of The New. I am the intercessor who intervenes for the purpose of the new babe, the new life being born. The swirling energies exist within you and without you, and their harmony simply happens. They adjust, one to another. They harmonize to the home environment, work environment, the national and international environment. All are part of your adjustment to ceasing to be less than you are. They bring the fine-tuning that perfects who you are through the gain of your fulfillment and your freedom.

This is my testament that we intervene for the fulfillment of the promise that is yours.

These swirling energies are attuned to your heart. Your own heavy heart had been lifting, and now is settling again. You settle for less than who you are by settling for more than who you care to be. The imposed.

This is true of each one, each lovely human person and the soul resting in their encampment.

Now, Mari, I know you are heading for liberation. This is what is making this the stressful time that it is. You want things in order before your sabbatical. Yet you haven't been released from the call to come here ... now. You desire no such release. Due to this, your energy turns its swirl in my direction and your frequency changes. Then this radical energy, affecting radical change, encompasses you, and we finish for the day.

This is when you begin your human duties without the energy to carry them out. You can push on with your laundry and gift wrapping . . . a different kind of energy. But when you reach out for the communicating, truth-telling energy you need, or even to correct a document, you find an absence of desire so strong that it is nearly impossible to carry on. This—you specifically, you as Mari—do. Nothing is true for all in like fashion. But, some form of this interplay will have affected each one who find themselves in the intervention.

Is it like a do-or-die moment?

In some ways, yes. What is your feeling about this? You are the one living in this time, being oldened by your own ways within it.

I asked, because, honestly, I am seeing it like, well, "don't do . . . or die."

From the way I have seen comparison as criticism, to the way I've catered to "work" expectations, I suddenly see I've based a lot of my life on letting the opinions of others, particularly authorities, affect me. This has led me, often, to exceedingly difficult and belated decisions.

I'm in a muddle with this because I've simply not seen it, or the enormity of its effect.

Each one just wants their jewel to shine as what it is. Surely you can see this.

Of course, I can see this. I won't even delineate it. It has been more than half my life—a great deal more than half my life—that I have bent to the expectations of others. You could take just one predominant norm, or standard: that of extroverted ways of being. I squelched all that I am, my every need—my disposition, my talents, and my devoted nature—for the communal aspects of life.

It's the same old story you've heard before. I am just getting a better take on how long it's been affecting me, and the major ways it has affected my work and my joy. When I look at my life, one of its largest burdens has been trying to find space to live quietly amidst the gatherers. And, my Mary? I have found it. I have carved out this life. It took me nearly to the age I am now, but I have done it, and nothing will make me go back. Nothing. That's the way I feel. But I do go back. If not in big ways, in small ways.

Maybe that is why I had to whine about it one last time. To see. To see that I am—done. To never again be guilted by someone saying, "What are you talking about? You don't have that much to do!" Or, "I'm living it, not writing about it!"

Because they are speaking of themselves in relation to you?

No. I don't think that's it. But maybe.

How else would it be?

The way I feel right now, and thank you so much for getting me here, is that it doesn't matter. How they "mean it" doesn't matter.

I feel a sort of liberation brewing.

M

$\mathcal{C}$APACITIES AND INCAPACITIES

Trust your incapacities as well as your capacities. You will do no harm if you remain with the caring you truly feel. If you can remember this, you will undo your "old" way of relating, a way of relating in which you have been self-protective.

This is not a disgrace. You have been self-protective for a reason. But this is the beginning of something new for you, who, like many, simply don't realize what you've been doing. After spending much of your life putting others first and working for other people, a certain pattern was given shape. Even after much time has passed, there can be a lack of realization. Remember: realization before response and response rather than responsibility. Everyone associated with your work could feel like "the boss" of you when you don't realize the pattern you are caught in.

That's a good way to put it, my Mary.

What you are feeling is being at the limit of your tolerance for responsibility—this learned way of tending to your otherwise chaotic environment. You are ready to move beyond it.

Are you fearing those who will judge you for it?

Myself most of all! But yes, I have been judged for it, and "unseated" for it. I am moved aside. Others step in. And then I feel, yes, that my incapacity has cost me quite a lot.

And then you compare, or as many call it, "go on the defensive." Your brother has spoken with you about this before, and what a deeply learned pattern it is, due to your mother's comparison, and the expectation that you measure up. Yet every parent has expecta-

tions. *There is an idea in the mind of how you should act, behave, look, comport yourself—how you should be, basically.*

And it is still there. You feel as if it is coming at you from all sides. Sometimes it is. Sometimes it is not. Sometimes it is others. Sometimes it is you. But you are ready to be done with it now, and it will be a major leap for you if you can navigate it.

I *feel* done. I am exhausted by it, and it takes me away from my heart.

You are so right. I *could* trust my "incapacity," and that it will not outweigh the gifts of my "capacity." Boy, the incapacity has been strong of late, though. I haven't even responded to several emails from Mary Love. I wish I could turn everything off right now, and not look back. Every technological thing, anyway. It's gotten almost worse than the bills. It would take over my life.

Fr. Adrian spoke, today, about how the people of your time were held captive, and how Jesus came to break down the barriers, and say, "Hey, here is something new. A new creation is happening."

Can you imagine that? How timely? How it fell right into my sense of captivity? How much I want the barriers broken down? How much I desire to be released? I feel like I won't make it to January at this rate.

My Mari, you want the barriers up, not down.

I've paused a good while. You are right. This is true. I want to be left alone.

My Mari, you owe no one. You do not owe anyone anything.

Thank you, thank you, my holy and liberating One.

M

$\mathcal{A}$ WALK INTO THE NEW

DECEMBER 18, 2019

Dearest Mary,

It's another gorgeous morning in the neighborhood. You'd have to see it to believe the feel of it. A streaky dark sky of blue and black, a little dark purple hue, a tad of peachy yellow, a swath that is light with no color. Oh my God, oh my God, oh my God, I need this so. All of it is the beauty of change, the spectacle of change—brightening, pulsing, fading, lightening . . . change.

I feel I've gotten here just as early as usual, but it hasn't been as dark. Maybe it's the cold. Stepping out the back door, it feels frigid today. There is a pulsing light I can't identify, and truthfully, every movement of light—and I've seen two planes already—causes me to feel I've been visited. Looking for signs and wonders, my Mary. Looking for signs and wonders.

Back behind the cabin it is the midnight blue that I love. She looks fine out there—the cabin. I'm a little lonely for her but I know she's not lonely for me. We're communing from here as the colors spread across the eastern sky to which I'm pointed, surrounded by the wise men and the camel and the donkey, and baby Jesus, and you, Mary. I am just in heaven as the sky retains such a glory of dark and colorful light. I'm so soothed by it. And I can use a little soothing as things lingering still haunt me. Things left undone.

Our collective language is so screwed up I don't even know what to call this. All the "virtues" of accuracy and pleasing aesthetics seem to have gotten a bad name. *You are anal. You are controlling.* That's what "they" say. And in the end, you do what you have the

time and can afford to do. You settle. And when it's public, and holy
work, that isn't good enough. That's just the way I feel. And yet—
oh Mary, I don't want to stop and clean up.

*It's not the time to stop and clean up. And the word you're
looking for is artist. Writers are artists as much as painters or
musicians. "Art" speaks more accurately of the whole of a work
and the sensibilities you bring to it. You have sensibilities that are
offended by shoddy work and work that isn't aesthetically pleasing. There is feeling, look, and tone, as well as substance, to every
art. And there is individuality.*

*You feel the same way about "your" work as "our" work be-
cause you are an artist with your writing and in your sensibilities. Compromise is not an option. Yet the current time is full of
compromise.*

*Compromise is deadening. I know you feel this. Like it is sap-
ping the life out of you.*

Yes, I do. And I feel rather helpless within it.

*That is very hard. It is too much for you. And I can say surely,
my Mari, that life has become "too much" for nearly everyone
in this time. This is why we need to speak of life from your view
within it. The view can change as does the day dawning around
you. We can take away the pressure from it. We can slow it down,
and in slowing it down, speed up the transition that is taking
place within you and without you.*

*This is true for all your sisters and brothers, but most necessary
to your sisters in this time. You aren't race cars. You weren't built
for this speed. You are not airplanes meant for a race through the
skies. You need grounding as a blessing that puts one foot in front
of the other.*

Let us call this a walk—a walk into The New. Leisurely. Taking in all the sights and feeling the earth beneath your feet. Your breath comes easily, serenely. We save the deep and powerful breath for another kind of experience.

Now, for a time, we breath the sacred in and out as naturally as we do when sleeping.

We are heading to this place where life slows down and makes sense again. We walk away from the old way and into The New because this is the real start of every journey: the movement.

This journey's movement is from "there," the old—to "here," The New. We create The New, together, by putting one foot in front of the other and feeling the earth beneath our feet. We create The New by accepting time's ability to slow alongside us.

The "quickening" of this time has nothing to do with speed. It has everything to do with new life. The babe in the womb can't be rushed, but it is growing exponentially every day, increasing, every day, it's capacity for life. Her own life. His own life.

You are held now in the womb of Mother Earth to complete this birth. When the labor has passed, you and she will exist in harmony, beloved to each other. Begin now, to be as the little children to whom time means nothing. They have no concept of it. They do not even know they are living within it. It is completely unobtrusive. Endless.

Be timeless, Mari, as we invite all to timeless living. Be oblivious to the time that once required your constant attention. You are held gently within eternal time to complete this birth.

This is the possible of this new time. The new creation whose time has come.

M

BEYOND TIMELESS: THE INFINITE

You have burdened time with your speed, asking of it what it cannot give you. Your time is the creation you have made of it. Time itself is eternal, consequent with existence itself, the measure of life rather than hours.

God is spoken of as infinite. "Infinite" conveys unlimited time and space. Have you ever given this your attention?

No. I have not thought of it in quite this way.

It is time, now, my Mari, for you and for all, especially your sisters, to see time newly. It is the moment to make this connection between God and unlimited time and space. As we consider it, also recall that God is called the everlasting. Know that no matter what happens in time and space, God will still be God. Everlasting. This can clue you in to the idea that time "in space," eternal time, is not going to go away. Infinite time and space are the pre-existent along with God, and the ageless, along with God.

This is a call to living beyond the finite . . . like unto God, life unto God. You belong to the very nature of this limitlessness and are incapable of removal from it. It is the foundation of your entire existence. Remembering this, you can live this way without testing time's limits every day.

In your fellowship with God, you possess what is of God, perpetually. And, you have an ethos which is your own, through which you are offered mutual participation, or communion. You are invited to share in and with God—always. This was Yeshua's matchless contribution to this world, love offered in communion.

You do share in the life of God. It is what being alive is. God is life. You are called to be alive in life. To be alive "with" God as well as "in" God. And to recognize, now, the nature of time in eternity . . . which is where it exists.

We have spoken of this as that which is beyond time, as the eternity of the ageless wisdom of which, and in which, Time's own awareness is dawning. With this dawning has come attentiveness to the plight of life on Mother Earth, and appreciation of God's love for Earth and all the creations of the Earth Mother. This is the time of the birth of universal consciousness: the universe becoming aware of itself. The universe that includes you. You who include the universe.

This is the time of the remaking. As you become aware of your Selves—as within, so without—you join the within and without in consciousness, one to another. The duad of the universe and her constituents is birthed of creation, the creation of the Creator in which you abide.

This has been so amazing. I feel such gratitude.

M

Dearest Mari,

With your two feet you begin this walk through the days of your time in eternity.

I didn't really think we'd be doing this walk in this nascent winter, in this new advent of 2020. I've only come to this after sitting quietly for a good while. One bunny has come out and headed over to the area of the pond. I wonder if there is still some open water there. I've put water out for the yard animals before, but they never use it. This bunny sits along the pond's edge, as if considering, then wanders off to the side.

Looking for water. On this very morning that your dream revealed that you are becoming dehydrated. Isn't that amazing?

Good Lord, yes. And I felt that, Mary, in the way of a thought that is of "us."

Is it merely the feeling of an insight?

No. Not at all. I've said "coming to know together" before, but this is now the second of two occasions when I've noticed it, and on noticing it am aware it has been happening for a while in this work, and that it has happened throughout my life.

Awareness?

I'd say, maybe—direct awareness? And now I think there may be a book called "The Direct Path," and that I likely scoffed at it. I've never desired a "direct path." Maybe shared awareness?

You've only not desired the direct path because you were unaware of what it was. Now that you are aware of what direct— let's say "direct awareness" feels like—do you see it differently?

Oh, my living God! Now I know awareness. I never understood "awareness" in this way you are revealing to me, this way I'm becoming sure of *directly*, through experience. I am basically, "being, and becoming . . . aware!"

Knowing together is the *awareness* of knowing together!

You do not even need confirmation, do you?

I'm doing that pursed lip breathing again, Holy Mary. This is incredible. I cannot even begin to count the ways images and memories are coming to me. They are not scenes or pictures. They are not thought. What I suddenly feel they are, is of all those times of awareness that I did not know as awareness! They are coming into some new sort of existence within my mind. I say "mind" because the feeling is in my head, almost like having a stuffy head.

Signaling you to open a new pathway.

Can I do that?

We can do that.

I hear my heart beating "in my head." Again, on the right side, but not at the temple this time. The feeling is just above, and to the back of, my ear.

Today's breathing is "ha . . . whoa." As I blow out with my pursed lips, there is a bit of a whistling sound again.

Good, Mari. It is good that you have noticed. Now listen to the sound of the cars. It's like a whistle isn't it? The wind of spirit is as like unto your true being as can be described. The nature of your true nature is duplicated again and again in all the whistlings of your world—all putting out the same call. The inspiration to create many of the instruments and vehicles of this world could be considered very peculiar in this byproduct of their creation.

When we spoke of the assassins and that such things were not fated, the reason was to open still another door, another portal.

When what was to come into being does not come to be, when God's desire is not met, yearning to yearning, another way opens. This is the kindness of the universe and her inspiration. The savior will be a savior in another way. What you are inspired to saves the world. Inventions, and particularly their soundings, have saved the world in an external, yet also internal way, that isn't yet realized. Creation and its unfolding have saved the world in an internal way.

I'm not feeling this so much.

Oh, my Mari, you are so right. The explanation makes you squirm. You don't need the big picture right now. You "know" what I am speaking of. Realize that it is when you know in your inter-being, in the nature of the duad, that you need no explanation and desire none. You do not understand . . . but you know.

And not knowing "what" I know is okay?

Not knowing "what" you know is the way.

The knowing is everything. The "what" is the creation in the making, creation made of the knowing. The creation of the knowing is the mode of the parents of the world, the duad of being and the life of being. The joining of the knower and the known.

The creation of the "what" is the way of the "human" being returning to all Being, via the knowing of the duad.

A nano second of knowing what you are saying just passed in and out so quickly that I cannot retrieve it.

This is what you are experiencing more and more. Could there be a reason this is happening?

That knowing and being known are becoming one?

One in being. There is no God to know without the knower.

What have you always known? That if one doesn't know A Course of Love in their own being, they will neither "know it" nor live it out. And you did and didn't know what you meant. You merely "knew this." With no "explanation."

Yes. This is true. All of this is like the knowing of a truth whose truth can't be named.

Yahweh, my Mari.

$\mathcal{A}$ LIBERATION MOVEMENT

Dear Mary,

I wonder if we can wander back from infinity, in that putting one foot in front of another way, so that you can assist me in knowing how to express what has eluded me for so long.

You spoke of saviors and I've hated when people have wanted to save me, even when I needed saving. How I've hated those humbling times of life. And they linger—like sepia images just beneath the skin—like the "age spots" that are emerging there. These spots are so very strange. They aren't there one day, and then they are the next. And they're more visible in water. I'm just rambling now, but it's better than this "problem" I bring to you, or the direction in which it is going.

Consider, rather than a savior or a saving—salvation. Salvation is simply another word for liberation. Our way is a liberation movement. Many no longer seek liberation. They believe they are already free.

And . . . maybe consider the age spots in exactly the way you just envisioned them! As sepia images of your trials seeing the light of day! Being freed of "their" confinement! Why not, my Mari? You see, "the way in which you see" is up to you now. It has always been up to you. You had this realization not so many days ago, of the tremendous liberation available to you simply from the way you see!

Hold that in your memory . . . in Memoria.

$\mathcal{M}$

ESTERING

Dear Mary,

Good morning. As I begin my day, the thought that arises is "you are my only constant." And I guess, really, it is this "way of being" that is my only constant—which of course, now includes you. But this, the coming here, is the holiest thing I do. Even when I'm eating peanut butter while I do it. Even while I'm not on my knees. I'm in my life and yours. Now. In this time that I am "with you," I am able to be with me. This I know. And the person who truly participates in two hours of meditation each morning, is doing that because it is her holy time, or his time of being in life with the beloved. Because she or he loves it! As I love this. The whole thing, this whole "morning" life, is what I am most eager for in my day, most grateful for when I arise, and look forward to most when I go to sleep.

You have told me that I pester myself, and if I quit, I get to do what I love to do.

M

The day is forming herself, revealing herself around me now. Cars traveling by out front send their lights through the living room window. Nothing is distracting. Nothing interrupts. All I see is beloved to me.

I am free to do what I love to do.

A crescent moon in a slate blue "becoming" sky, seen through the black limbs, is delicate and impeccable against the coming blue.

The below becomes light, in ways and colors that unfailingly come to be as never before. Each day is a new creation.

Simmy is even sitting quietly on the dining room table. He's learned that if he pesters me, he will have to be removed.

I love the word "pester" now because it is so descriptive. When I was little, it seemed like Mom was always saying "Don't pester. Do not pester your brother. Stop pestering your sister." I don't think that word gets used much anymore. It is a good word, and I am glad you have used it to describe the way I've pestered myself. . . so that I can stop.

M

# ONE PESTERING

Dear Mary,

It feels like a done deal now. Like I won't do it—pester myself—anymore. I don't know why, but it's how I feel this morning . . . said just as the first squirrel of the day began his run across her tree highway, leaping from there to here.

I may be . . . content.

~

And now the birds have arrived.

~

Everything is perfect. Utterly perfect.

It can be. It can be. It can be.

It is. It is. It is.

This is the greatest miracle of all. Nothing is bothering me! This is ridiculous!

I imagine myself in long dresses. And with flowing hair.

A hand strokes my hair, warm with sun.

I am seen and adored.

Adoring is the way.

Bring light clothes.

Stay.

Any request of a mother at a son's wedding, had to be granted. This is the time of the wedding.

Of the mother's requests and the granting of the requests. And it is okay if there are no requests. Requests too, can be a bother. Pestering.

Three suns shine before me. The closest, the smallest, is the brightest.

Now there are four.

Now four, and a peek at a fifth and sixth. There may be an outlying seventh.

Such is the way of the coming. Not the coming. The way.

The way is the way.

The way is the way of the presence—coming and going, blinking in and out, an idea being birthed that is the birth.

Oh, glory of glory, the Love.

M

BEING WITHIN THE SURROUNDS OF BEING

DECEMBER 23, 2019

Good morning, my Mary,

You know what this dark morning does most of all? It saves me. It, along with you, is my liberation movement. Good Lord, yes, it is. Morning is arrayed before me . . . all I see. And seeing into the blackness is what I want to do. If that is all I do, I have already done what I love. How blessed I am.

Now a pink tone is coming, and I know what I will do. I will begin to spend more time in the dark of the morning. Seven o'clock could be my noon. Most days, it would matter to no one, and if it did I could do it anyway. Praise the Lord!

I am here with peanut butter and the cat put away, and the last small light off, and the sky making awful pastel colors look as brilliant as the sun.

From here, in the dark, I will fulfill my destiny. A messenger with a revolutionized art form. Creation of The New.

And two and two and two is the first thought of The New that occurs to me. Two-by-two. Two-by-two we will go on before what passes away leaves us. Two . . . like me and my morning are two, and here it comes, something new once again . . . the triad.

Yes, you and me and the living speaking earth. Jesus, Mary and Joseph. The dark, the woman, the being beyond.

You are the woman. The woman on the ground in the dark, the cherished dark and the cherished ground of The New. Willing

to walk with equals in The New. Forget anyone else now. This is
you. Me. The day.

Oh, I see. The duad now becomes the triune of the environment
in which we join. Ours together. Does it ever stop?

What a fantastic question, come of vision. No. It does not ever
stop. It is eternal. Just as you and your friends exist in this same
eternal triune configuration: this third that makes for individu-
ality.

Here, in time, is a third that makes for individuality. Life.
Birth, growth. One's particular life and particular surroundings.
The surrounds.

Beautiful. The being within the surrounds of being.

I am beginning to feel . . . just a little . . . wise.

You are literally the wise woman sitting at the manger.

Oh, good grief! I absolutely am. I'm looking at the day past the
heads of wise men and camel, angel and shepherd. The ears of the
donkey show, and your head in its outline, flesh-toned face and
blue wrap. Like your gold and blue light. Features undefined, but
visible. The babe and Joseph are hidden in the dark, Jesus for being
too low to the ground, and Joseph for being nearest to me and so
concealed under the eaves. It is so improbable and so perfectly . . .
weird and right.

I would like to see myself as a wise woman at the manger of this
new birth. I would like that, Mary.

It will take a little getting used to, but you will see that once
you allow it, it will come to you easily. You are to be wise in the
way of The New. Does that ease your mind?

Of course. That is the only way it could be.

What if I were to share with you that you are present—right now—at the "birthing" of The New? The labor of The New. And the imminent birth.

Here? Two days before Christmas is celebrated around the world? Yes, I can imagine it. Here with the snow and the chickadees. In a place no one but me could imagine The New coming into being.

Yes. This is the realization that The New comes to each one with the dawning that The New has come. The revelation will be perfect and personal to each. Don't you love how yours has come? At the manger?

So much! It fits me so.

Exactly, my Mari. What fits you fills you with Mirari, the surest sign of The New.

Mirari and Memoria . . . The wonder and the memory of the birth.

The gestation is passing.

And oh, my Mother, the signs I've had. Especially my elongated elimination. Just like when the baby is pressing on the bladder! I was just thinking of it in the bathroom this morning. It could all make sense. The heavy womb, the way my body is hurting and moving differently. The dehydration that was announced in a dream. The babe taking "everything" from you.

And it will be like a reversal.

But right now, you are sheltered here with us, watched over for the birth, after which you will watch over the babe of The New, in the helplessness of the beginning, and absoluteness of care required, taking "everything" from you.

Created out of your own being.

This is what each will do: create The New out of her or his own being, being to being.

This is the way it has always been. It is the symbolism of the virgin birth, and of the journey to the manger, and of the attendance by the angels and the kings bearing gifts. It is homage to The New Life birthed of the mother and her God. What comes is an innocence of not knowing the future (prophecy) but knowing the imminent birth (alchemy) and that this knowing is all there is—one's entire universe, the safe passage through the birth canal.

All for the first cry of The New, and the tending one longs to do, of The New Babe. Do you see the connection? Out of one's own being The New is fed and reared as what you imagine it will be. The long awaited arrives. The savior. The Testament of the New. "Your" liberation.

You see now the great alchemy of the one who has united with the Creator. It is like unto a reverse creation. A returning to the One who is the Holy Two: being in relationship. Being . . . in relationship . . . is the creation and the Testament of the New.

M

The Treatises of Mary

fourth Heart treatise

Testament

As you began The Dialogues of A Course of Love, *your brother
spoke these words to you:*

"This is the Covenant of the New in which you honor your agreement to bring heaven to earth and to *usher in* the reign of Christ.
To *usher in* is to show the way, to cast your palms upon the path of
your brothers and sisters."*

*Now we witness to what we have begun. We testify to the
agreement that you entered and are abiding within.*
   ~Mary of Nazareth

---

* ACOL D:2.23

If we forget the way of Creation, will Creation cease to be? If we don't remember the way of the Creator, do we forget to be creators?

I am simply a writer. I am a writer like all those writers I have loved. Writing is my way of creating.

I am trustworthy in this way. By nature of what I do, this work in the dark, I can let a little light in by grace. The divine urge to accept who I am is, in turn, an urging to each to accept their gift, to accept, and then to share. As we share, we attest to the truth that we are creators.

~Mari Perron

THE MANGER AND THE
UNDISRUPTED UNITY

I have only been in the cabin five minutes. My relief is a flood. Please, Lord, I ask for nothing to make me go in before I am ready. It is Christmas Eve.

I got upset yesterday in that silly, pre-Christmas way that isn't so silly, but I'm already recovering.

This morning, I took two pictures of the scene I created in the house. Despite my irritation then, today I am a proud creator. I drank it in, quietly, by myself in the darkness before six o'clock, and I took the pictures so that I would remember. Remember what I created.

It was then that I decided I was going to get ready and come here.

M

What it means to be back is immeasurable, even though I wondered, for a minute, if it was right to leave the side of the manger where I composed during the pre-Christmas season. I had a thought, weeks back, of bringing the manger from Smith Avenue out here—the one from my childhood. If not the whole manger, the figures.

But now what's happened is that I feel the cabin is itself a manger, a refuge of my own. That's how she presents herself to me as I gaze out at "my" terrain. She is both exposed and sheltered. Quieted and full of inner . . . blowing, sounding . . . not only that of the furnace as she comes on, (her woosh like a lift off), but a category of sound that shields me from all sound other than the inaudible sound of your voice, Mary.

I am rapt. I am birthing.

Wrapped in the totality of your surrounds and the soundings of your present world, you see now that they are akin to our own. To see your "appliances" as life-giving instruments dedicated to life's lovely and lonely song, is little different than the utilization of all that was near at the time of Yeshua's birth. To hear your furnace as the sign of a roaring wind of spirit, as the breath of the divine, is also little different. For you it is that breath that allows you shelter in this time and this place.

In my day, a "manger" most often referred to a place reserved for the best of the lambs, sacrificial lambs, particularly those used for peace offerings or to be sacrificed at Passover.

I don't remember hearing of that, Mary, although now that you say it, I can almost bring forth a remembrance from scripture and the reason Jesus was called "the lamb." We say it in church: "Lamb of God who takes away the sin of the world."*

More commonly I heard, and not all that long ago, that what I called the manger was not the stable, but the place where Jesus was laid after his birth, the "trough" that held fodder for the animals. I just never wanted to use any other word. I'm attached to the word "manger" from its presence in memory and song, and my sentimentality over the manger of my youth.

Putting up the manger was the only decorating that Dad ever did, and we did it together. Each year, he and I would go down into one of the two dank, canning-type rooms in the basement,

---

* John 1:29

to retrieve the box that held "the manger." Just him and me. That room, the dark, the rarity of entering, Dad's presence, all added to the thrill of getting ready to "put up the manger." It was always the start of our Christmas preparations.

You might call this a "custom" of your youth, my daughter, and from it you can feel the pull to custom. For us, our common actions were not only following the law, but a way that lived in memory—memory that called our people to observe, according to the customs of our ancestors.

Yet we speak of the manger's greater symbolism, also as a link to Yeshua calling himself the Bread of Life. Then the imagery of the "trough" or "manger" is even more profound. Combining this with the idea of Jesus as "the sacrificial lamb," you can draw associations that testify to the unity of birth and death, and the communion that brings new life.

But the safe place of birth, surrounded by angels and animals, is also perfect, especially for children beginning to live with the story of their inheritance.

M

ONELINESS

As we are beginning again, it is the perfect time to speak of this "beginning" of the life of my son. It is one of the final essential pieces that link humanity and divinity. The coming to know of life's possibilities depends on the loneliness of beginnings . . . and of endings. These are felt in Memoria.

Loneliness is that certain discomfiting comfort of knowing within one's own . . . singularity. Loneliness is essential.

Fear of loneliness complicates the return and the departure from your near ones, the abandonment of the many for the one who is you.

You see, no one actually desires to be completely known or fulfilled. To be completed. You desire to know and be known in the presence, and, in the absence.

Being without company is not being without presence but is finding your own being in the presence of yourself. Here, you at times know the pain of being lonesome as a disconnection from a loved one, or a feeling of being unknown, or worse, unknowable. Recognizing the feeling, you realize that you have not hidden anything from yourself. You are alive in loneliness to all your feelings. You are revealed in your complexity, while stymied in your desire for relationship, which is never complete.

Rather than completion, you desire the presence of being in creation. In the coming and the going, the birthing and the dying, the creating and the letting go, you are in the presence. And so it is that—when by way of inspiration and imagination you birth that book, that babe, that craft, that love, that scientific theory, or that Christmas scene—you find the relationship in which you make something that will be complete, and that will complete you only in that moment you let it go to have life.

And then you will miss all the hours in the dark of creating, and they will be longed for again, because you are life-givers. You seek togetherness because you are, along with us, life-giving creators of The New. You are creating the scenes.

M

The Testament of the New is the voice that gives life to the Spacious One. It is the life-giving power that departs and returns. The Voice of the Void sounded your name and your destiny. To this you return and depart as you do with your creations.

"What is present 'here' is an opening in time of which you are a part, as is each one who has released themselves to what is beyond time and space as they know it. This 'knowing,' in a world of time and space, is not an easy knowing to hold or to carry. It makes your life both blessed and very nearly sacrificial."*

Where is the return? In the sacred privacy, the void of the beginning without end. The spaciousness beyond time lies within your empty spaces, in all that you leave open and undefined. It is in all that you see with the wonder of Mirari, and all that you remember in Memoria.

Your sacred privacy is the undisrupted unity, there in spaciousness. It is the wellspring of "shared" consciousness you may

---

* "Mirari," p. 105-6

draw upon, the consciousness you have accepted to receive these words. In the voice that is also the voice of the muse, you welcome inspiration, revelation, and testimony. This undisrupted unity, resting in the quiet of its own being, is filled with the presence of that which was before the before: The One.

The All Being.

In this moment, in your sacred privacy, you are Being.

Here you are refreshed in the space of the undisrupted unity—the place of no company—no accompaniment other than the Being One: You.

This is what each hope to meet in all their practices: the one that they are Being and being with.

M

$\mathcal{B}$IRTHING INTO LIFE

Remember in your early days of sex how you would call it "being with?"

"I was 'with him,' " you would say to yourself. And it meant something new and different.

Yes, that is true.

Well, my daughters, the connotation of "being with" is joining, a joining that alters you. And it is often, as it was for you, Mari, a crushing blow, beyond any reasons that you could give it, or the circumstances in which it occurred. The physical joining of the two is more than symbolic as soon as it becomes actual. In its actuality it is a trauma, the trauma of a barrier being breached. And for a woman (or a girl), there, in the breach, is the possibility of the combining of the two into a new One. The babe. This is an enormity of which she is only dimly aware.

An enormity which she, alone, must carry.

In their actual, physical reality, many women experience the elation of carrying new life. And many men, acknowledging their contribution, feel the same joy as they participate. While they cannot share the experience of the carrying, they have experienced the indwelling of being carried, and their own voyage of birthing from the womb of the mother. The voyage of birth is the experience of the womb that the sexes hold in common.

Women are called upon in this time of the "new" birth. Whether they have given birth or not, they are born with the capacity to create new life from the joining of the masculine and feminine within. To embrace a body within one's own body is to experience the two as one. To give birth is to experience the actuality of the one becoming two.

The man whose seed finds the egg in the hidden, loving shelter of the womb, and who becomes loving shelter to woman and new babe, also gains a more direct awareness of the two becoming one. Awareness is again found in the creation of a family, no matter what the means. Here, too, is a demonstration of the combining of "more than one" into a singular unity.

Birth ignites memories that are essential to creation of The New, for they give the body over to creation of The New. The body itself knows how to create new life.

M

These memories have been forgotten in time and are in need of return. It is the reason for the way of the Marys. Yeshua gave his body in death to cause life to be new. The Marys give their bodies in life to cause life to be new. We have joined and come together so that we may reflect this way again and move from death into life.

The knowing held within the life-birthing one is of the gestation and its requirement: two uniting as one. He himself is the requirement that sparks new life. Her own body is the host that delivers new life. This is an example that can be true for all in this time of birth of Self.

This is the time of hosting humankind's birth . . . her and his birth, male and female, into the full potential of being the new "one" come out of the void of the womb into The New.

And now, you and I can take this forward. The new birthing

is not a violation of one's being, but the accompaniment and completion of that within which "being" is held.

Your lives were authored, composed, painted with the brush of the Creator.

Held within.

And released.

And held.

And loved.

And given over to the possibility of forgetting.

And remembering.

And sacred privacy.

And sacred union.

Oneness of Being. And relationship. And the aloneness.

In sacred privacy, the power to create was birthed into the living expressions of Being in space and time. What was forgotten was the capacity to remain void and to create from the void.

You are held in and within the void—the spaciousness of the Creator. You are boundless.

M

And so, my holy ones, I pass on to you now this picture of creation, a scene in which you are included and of which you partake.

Do not fear loneliness or believe that your sacred privacy is merely personal. Your sacred privacy is the spaciousness within you that is like unto the void of all time. Sacred spaciousness is the womb of what was, and the womb of what will be.

Male or female, you hold the womb of all time within you.

What if you saw life and time together now? Life in time. Life beyond time.

Life in all time.

What if you saw a way to live life in time no different than life in eternity?

What if it suddenly became ridiculous to see life any other way?

What if you began to live with the true realization of the potential that you possess? The potential to live as creators of The New?

Can you believe that this could be possible? That this potential exists?

"Potential is that which exists. It exists as the power and energy, the spirit within you. It does not await. It simply is. It can remain as the untapped power of transformation, or it can be released. The choice is and is not yours. This power is a force of nature that exists, not separately from you, but not separately from nature either. It is triggered in any number of ways, only one of which is by your choice. When it was said that *A Course of Love* was a trigger, it was meant that the Course is both a trigger of choice and a trigger of nature. It was meant to convey the action of a catalyst. Now it is up to you whether you allow your true nature to be revealed.

"To struggle against your nature is what you have spent a lifetime doing. Stop. If you allow your potential to be released, your true nature in all its wholeness will be revealed." *

---

* ACOL D:Day24.3-4

Now is the time for your release . . . to the possible.

M

And "here" expands

DECEMBER 25, 2019

Accept my volunteer heart, oh Holy One. My loving heart is here for you.

In this moment of beginning, I forgot the date, its glory and auspiciousness, and it felt like a normal day . . . which I love. The beloved ordinary.

The first once again, but not the primary. The first, the one and the void, being the same. And yet there was never nothing, or one thing, or two, until there was a conscious being to speak in primal, undelivered words. Which word would be the first? Maybe "awe"? If the first being let out a first breath, might it have come with the sound of "awe"? Maybe our own deepest breathing is but a who and an awe.

A who and an awe birthed together. Babies seeing angels of light.

M

I was eight years and some months when Mom delivered Michael. She was soon to be forty.

I'd bet it was the first time she was away for more than a few hours. She didn't yet have a driver's license. She didn't spend time at the neighbors. I still have no idea how she got groceries. You'd think I'd remember more. Like what she looked like being pregnant. Like conversations about a new baby. I remember nothing, only after. And I think, now, that I know why.

My life "before" the new baby was ordinary. Maybe even a beloved ordinary. Not without its traumas, but it was the reality in which I existed in my innocence. Yes. That's it. I see it now. I lost my innocence at eight when my brother was born, and I see as clearly that Mom went into a post partem depression. What did my older siblings see that I did not?

It doesn't matter, but it's a pinpoint in time. June of 1963. When I fell from the universe of my mother's love and affection. There it was.

I am here at 5:30, in communion with that which exists beyond the self in which I am privately reflecting.

And I let out a big breath that sounds like an awe. Awe stands in, like the wonder of Mirari, for all that is unnamable.

Memories stand out too, and sometimes, the lack of them. I barely miss my parents or the holidays of old any longer, even while I am tremendously sentimental. And so, I know that the same will happen to me. My children and grandchildren will cease to remember with the poignant longing of that love lost . . . and it will be of me. Life will go on and the memory of me will fade.

M

In this reverie, a scene swings into vivid memory. It has no explanation. It is of my response to the death of "Ma," my dad's mother.

On hearing the news that she had died, I found myself in a sudden, unexpected panic of immediate grief. I try to recall how old I was, and a scene arises that delivers me to an answer. I would have been in my thirties, because I called Father Mahfoud, who had married Donny and I when I was 32. He said, "Come to Mass."

It was early morning, and I headed out quickly, and tear stained, to the church in which I was married. The scene continues to unfold in my memory, as I witness eight to ten elders—women and men—huddled together in the front few pews, an even number on each side. I sat some ways behind Sadie, Freda and Richie.

Father mentioned my grandmother's passing and prayed for her. Afterwards, each of his flock approached me. They were impossibly kind. I knew they probably loved seeing a granddaughter's tears for her grandmother.

I continue to wonder why this loss was so stunning, and why I am thinking of it. Did my father's mother, simply called "Ma"—but who was my namesake, Margaret Mary, as well as my Godmother—did her love for me finally stun me into missing her? Was I mature enough to feel it?

Next, I wonder what it has to do with . . . anything? Why did this memory arise for me this morning? And then . . . why do I now hear the words "temporal order"? I know it must have to do with sequencing and succession. I blink my eyes and turn from table to desk for the dictionary.

The temporal: pre-existent to scientific law.*

Ah! Am I called to that which stood before the naming and defining of things? I imagine that the temporal may speak of a perfectly balanced universe, birthing us (out beyond our participation) in its own tenure, holding us on its own terms, with its original intent and intensity. Is this the memory we seek? That which stands outside of the order of the type we've been speaking of?

---

* Webster's New World Dictionary, 1988

I remember that we move outside of the pattern of ordinary time in the Second Treatise of ACOL:

"Miracles *create* an out-of-pattern time interval. Thus living in a state of miracle-readiness is the creation of a new reality outside of the pattern of ordinary time. Although this state exists as the already accomplished, it is up to you to create it for yourself. You must create it for yourself only because you believe you replaced what was already accomplished with what you made. . . .You are creating the state of unity as a new reality for *your Self* even though it is actually a return to what has always been. You are changing the world you perceive by perceiving a new world. You are changing from who you have thought yourself to be to who you are."*

Exploring further I become aware of the teleological argument that seeks to prove the existence of God by way of the order of the universe itself, and how perfectly suited it is to sustaining life.

As I do this, I am amazed that I had never thought of the temporal order before. (Or I could have forgotten it if I did. My memory is not what it was. It is . . . different!) I find this amazing as I watch my own shaping of these words, this stream of my thought. It feels fully "relational." I am married to the words that come of my "stream" of consciousness. Released from its captivity, this flow of memory meanders where it will, bringing up pieces of my life to be excavated in this glorious dark unfolding.

All seems to be linked, this morning, to the desire to be loved and "remembered." And to remember love myself, as I did with Ma. What is it about the remembering? About Memoria? Is it, precise-

---

* ACOL T2:6.9

ly, remembered "knowing"? Is that what the temporal order desig-
nates? The memory of creation?

It does not matter—yet. It is only "here."

Christina just sent me a text from her dawn. We are sharing the
first light of day. And so much more.

"Here" begins to expand. Backwards and forwards it travels.
Just being with what is "here," with the meandering rather than the
matter.

Later, I remember this from Mirari:

" 'Revealed order' leaves 'ordered time' behind. The revealed is always moving to the union and relationship that is life, that is giving
and receiving as one. The life of Jesus interrupted ordinal time. You
were told that 'You and Mary' would have something to do with the
end of ordinal time." *

M

---

* "Mirari," p. 237-8

REMEMBERING

I have been imagining for a while that I will be remembered widely for *A Course of Love*—after I am gone. Yet I haven't quite grasped the why of it. Not why I'll be remembered, but why it feels so good to sense that. What is it about memory and the remembered that feels, suddenly, so essential?

Being remembered . . . here. In this journey of life. Our remembrance here on Earth. Is it like Mirari and Memoria . . . together? Not only wonder, but our remembrance of it?

Is it simply in us to feel so close to Earth and Heaven—as we do for cause of some sort? A cause within us, but denied? The end of the denial the release of something mysterious and overwhelming?

More than anything, this has all been overwhelming. I become . . . so full. Just so full. Plainly and simply, full to overflowing. And then overflowing onto the page, whether it makes sense or not.

I am overflowing from the fullness. And I realize then, that yes, after the overwhelm, the outpouring comes. The outflow. Creation of The New . . . as in a fevered dream of remembering.

I am given to know we are holding the fullness and its release. Its release into the world. This world. This time. The time of the coming of the Marys and the second coming of Christ—in us, as us. The time of passing on and passing down, the light in which we, women and men, see ourselves as who we are.

M

How much longer will Grace Zuri Love* be remembered? How long will creation be remembered?

Oh, my God. It suddenly occurs to me. Is this what we are in danger of losing? Creation itself? Creation in the remembrance of the original Creation? If we forget the way of Creation, will Creation cease to be? If we don't remember the way of the Creator, do we forget to be creators? If we don't create, do we cease to pass on that which needs to be remembered?

Is remembrance our true way of knowing?

I see, hear, and feel the undeniable appeal of knowing and being known that holds love and passes it down for an eternity.

M

And now I am tired. Too tired to pack up and return to the house. I have given and received all I can hold and still put one foot in front of the other.

There is magnitude here. *Here.*

"With your accomplishment comes the freedom and the challenge of creation. Creation becomes the new frontier, the occupation of those too young to rest, too interested in living still to welcome the peace of dying. Those who could not change the world one iota through their constant effort, in peace create the world anew."†

---

* Grace Zuri Love was the daughter of my friend, Mary Love. Grace died as an infant, and the intimacy that arose during this time between Mary, myself, and Julieanne Carver was a lifechanging experience for us all.

† ACOL C:6.17

Is our peace, as well as our freedom, connected to our willing-
ness to be creators?

M

The Preamble:
INNER GESTATION

Mine is the path of the inner. It comes to me so clearly. Here. Christmas night.

This, in my newly united voice, is the remembrance of what I am given to know that I am coming to know. I seek the personal, and this is that. This knowing comes to me personally and is of the revered revealing that is between the sacred two, one of whom is me.

Here, I birth amid the third of my surrounds. Within "the two as one," the making of the one as two is sustained. Two, of whom the second is birthed of the new intimacy.

What I imagine is that The New is always intimate—whether between galaxies, or stars, or human persons. That, I would imagine, is the Temporal Order. I imagine that it is always between and beyond at once. What happens within the psyche—the expanded consciousness—is what one draws to oneself, and what is drawing each one. The means are likely as varied as the marriage union, the babe in the womb, or the planet in the heavens. I'm given to know that nothing starts that doesn't start within the One whom we each are.

This, that I am feeling, is more of remembrance than new shores, more of recollection than exploration: Love remembered in the way of Love coming into being. Maybe love remembered *is* Love come into being.

$\mathcal{M}$

I feel that a shift has come. It feels as if the uncertainty I hold, the hesitation, is a preamble.

Then, suddenly, the very word "preamble" feels to have great meaning for me, as if I am making an overture with these words. A proposal has been accepted and I am being introduced to something new. There is no forethought or foreknowledge of what I will type, or of what will come. It, this new way, is simply and suddenly here.

I feel strangely ready for it to be here, even while I do not feel I know anything new. I am not held in a vision of The New, only in what is coming as I type the words. It feels like a composition of The New. Maybe that *is* the Testament of The New: the inner gestation put to words.

$\mathcal{M}$

COMPOSITION OF THE NEW

DECEMBER 26, 2019

The marvel of the two voices coming as one is what we have been doing all along, my Mari. As you revealed in Creation of the New,* *each one will find the two before returning to the one, united in twoness. It is a natural law. I leave you to it: within it and aware of it.*

My heart blesses you, my Holy Mary, and as I say that, I feel your holiness being shared so that I may return blessing for blessing.

M

Left to explore the natural, all I can do is look out the window, so thankful for the mildness of this winter that is allowing me to be in the cabin.

No . . . not allowing. Here I am, self-correcting in the first days of carrying the voice of the two as one . . . or is it one as two . . . or are both the same? So much self-revealing is yet to come. I can feel that too. But not in the way of old. I am left to explore what this is and to recognize those places where I ask, "What does it mean?"

And now—what is "allowing"? Who is allowing?

To discover the new question.

I am here to discover the new question. Or possibly to abandon questions.

---

* "The great birth is the birth of oneness into twoness, the explosion of a new creation where union to union, all to all, there is relation." *Creation of the New,* p. 85

And so, I must get used to this knowing becoming my own. The two in one. Relating now as one, we are each other's own. What I don't know will be revealed as I unlearn "meaning." As I unlearn "allowing," and the need to be "allowed." As I explore in my own voice.

What is revealed will guide my response, my memories, my testimony. I wonder if the change is to see my old way of knowing as *about* me, and the new way of it being *of* me, *in* me, *as* me?

M

Adoring all that comes to me, as I do what comes into view out this window, I have become the wonderer. I wonder as I wander. The amble is the way of the wanderer become wonderer.

With each word I feel more into the way in which this has always been. Our relatedness is built-in. The desire for it is not even necessary. These dialogues exist within me in the unity of relationship. Mother Mary and Jesus are in relationship with me and I with them. Their voices come to companion me, and us, into The New.

M

*T*HAT WHICH IS NOT AN IT

All that I know lies within me. All that anyone knows lies within them. It is ours to share. Ours to personalize. Ours to romanticize, praise, honor—whatever it is we do with that which is not an "it."

That which is not externalized into an *it*, instead unfolds within creation's personified power.

M

"Personification" is a device that writers can use to bring the non-human to life. Here, personification is needed for our very selves, to bring us back to life! We have depersonalized for far too long.

Depersonalization is my major critique of spiritual culture. Even some beautifully personal spiritual leaders disclaim their personhood, as if "person" is a dirty word. There are also those who depersonalize to shield themselves from responsibility as well as intimacy.

The difference in motive does not make it all that different when the refrain is the same: "This is just the way it is" . . . in business, in government, in publishing, in healthcare, in religion. These statements are absolute, and non-inclusive. They are abstract nonsense passed off as answers that do not regard persons. Reliant on depersonalized facts and decisions, they are based on make-believe.

Personification is not egoic. It is embodiment, incarnation. So, too, is imagination as it becomes "experience."

I am personifying: humanizing my own knowing. All that I am

coming to know with those who join me here becomes my own knowing.

Oh, my living God. I did not know that consciously until this moment. Until my fingers typed the words. But now I know. It is so true it is obvious. The crucial, untaken step is Holy knowing becoming our own.

M

And so, I stop and anchor myself by looking out the window, and I see again the vision of 2013: the women on their haunches around the fire, no divisions in sight. No men. The women with their swollen bellies and babes within. Humanizing and personalizing their own knowing, they know what to do.

I know, now, why we haven't known what to do, and it brings me to tears.

A calling is upon all of us who care so deeply. I am to call on myself, as well as you, to step into the one Voice that is our multiplicity of voices.

It is time to come to voice with all that has flowed through us . . . as us . . . to balance the power that has reigned and grown so lopsided it would tip the world if it could. And it could, if we don't come to voice and show the holders of power that all we have given can no longer be used.

But we must show *ourselves* first.

I think of women. One woman, and another and another. All hurt by life and translating that hurt newly into the care they provide. The creativity they extend. The great alchemists we have always been. We are ready, I can feel it, for the remaking. We are ready for the gentle yet stern care we have practiced to become a doorway to The New. Women are ready to slam the door on those who refuse to care. To refuse to care is to miscreate. To refuse to care is to surrender the manifest world.

M

Peace to all who enter here. We have come in secret, in the protection of the knowing come from the lineage of the *living* God. The knowing whose time had come in the life of Jesus, and that survived only for being protected, hidden, passed on without the sanction of the powerful. This knowing is not that which was taken up and altered by power . . . and used.

We can't hope for sanction and possess power that cannot be used. To love, to create, to care, to dream, to imagine—these are ways of knowing that can be neither surrendered nor restricted. To care for the living holy ones of whom we may be the first in this time, is to know and to share by way of recognition: the way of the holy two. For God's sake, we must witness each other and share our power for the good to predominate the power that is dominant. To, according to *natural* law, restore the celestial order from which we came. We come in secret to make the world safe for humanity, for personification of the living holy ones who've come to bring us into Being.

We are no longer heirs to those who would dominate.

I feel—so much—the rightness of this, my Mother, and all my relations. We can be the new voices of the old wisdom, there at time's beginning. We can restore time itself by restoring the temporal order in us, as us. We have been invited to rejoin the stream of life.

"This awareness of union with God is what is now within you awaiting your expression. Awareness of union with God exists in everything. It is there in every tree and every flower, in every mountain stream and every blowing wind. It is there in each and every human being. It is now time to quit acting as if it is not. It is time to be a channel for the awareness that exists in every tree and every flower, in each mountain stream and in the blowing wind. It is time to be a channel for the awareness of union with God that exists in every living being.

"This awareness is what we have been calling Christ-consciousness, but what you call it now matters not." *

This is somehow happening in me as I give up the voice of the two for the voice of the one . . . and find it to be mine as well as ours. Ours. The voice of the duad.

It is time to gather the voices of the feminine women and men—to prepare the womb of The New and to accept the seed of The New into what we have created of our own Being.

To be what is of God and not to be put asunder.

I remember that the crucifixion was not fated. We can have a do-over. We can birth that which will not be crucified in the realm of time and space . . . by altering time and space.

"If you do not accept your Self, all of yourself, you cling to suffering . . . To accept the end of suffering is to accept your true Self."†

This is not a call to turn a blind eye to the suffering. No! It is

---

* ACOL D:Day22.8-9
† ACOL D:Day2.27

so different from that! To accept ourselves is a call to end our own anguish. We can extend acceptance one to another—and that will end so much pain.

In Memoria, we remember God's disclosure to us . . . revelation. And God's discourse with us . . . creation.

We testify that revelation is not only of what is unknown. Not *only* that. Revelation comes in Memoria, in remembrance of what came before us. Revelation is right here in us—in memory, in imagination, in the intimacy of images and in our spaciousness—revealed in truth.

Scenes . . . reveal. They bring you "back."

There is something to this that I am getting and at the same time not quite getting. But I know it is significant—magnificent even!

M

A squirrel just jumped into the window box looking for food, and I had to share my peanut butter. I forgot his food this morning, so I'm happy I had something left, something to offer him in his hungry request, in his knowing that I am here, and that I feed him. Even squirrels have memory.

I must remember the ways of creation of you both, Jesus and Mary. It is what I am called to do—for you. This is so clear *so suddenly*. I don't know what to make of it, but I will. This I trust.

M

$\mathcal{T}$ IME IN ETERNITY

DECEMBER 27, 2019

Time is a question for me again, my Mother, come of something from Christmas. I still feel as if I am speaking to you and that you are listening. You are with me and within me.

I'm just wondering . . . isn't it here, after Christmas, that we head into ordinal time? Do ordinal time and the temporal order have to do with one another? The preexisting? And the existent? Was the preexisting "ordinary" before the wonder of the advent of The New which came out of your time?

And does it happen over and over again? Is this overly populated and polluted earth in a preexistence state, held in the void once again, awaiting once again the awakening of heart? In each. Where the universe is made?

The eternity of creation of The New began with the bodily resurrections of Jesus and me. Here, we enter a new time. The time of the descent. The return.

We have had the birthing, and the ascension, and now we have the coming again.

The descending. The homecoming. The continuance of the eternity of creation. I believe that is what we are speaking of. But also, it seems that we're talking of stepping out of time's chronology. That's what The New is, I believe.

It is your whirl, the cyclone of coming and going. As you foresaw almost a year ago—as you "experienced" at the start of this *year in which you continue—we are showing you the way beyond ordinal time.**

M

---

* On the day *A Course of Love* was announced, I also heard this pronouncement: "You and Mary will have something to do with the end of ordinal time." See "Mirari," p. 238

To SHARE

I am simply a writer. I am a writer like all those writers I have loved. Writing is my way. In this that I do here, back before the darkened manger, held within a beautifully dim morning of rain (of all things, and ice already), all is well. I am trustworthy in this way. By nature of what I do, this work in the dark, I can let a little light in by grace. The divine urge to accept who I am is an urging to each to accept their gift. Their way. And then to share, to attest to the truth.

LOVE IS NOT IMPERSONAL

Can anyone fail to love all children after having loved one child? After having received the love of a singularly glorious new human person, too young to care for him- or herself, but lavishing you with the purest form of love there is—love before knowing?

Such a pure love.

Such a pure love brings pure love back into being. No wonder the way of the mother is needed. Even those like myself, who had no idea what such love in its dependence would be like, had to concede to it or die of shame. It wasn't coercion—just no other choice.

It's such a non-choice that its enactment gets into your blood and bones. You wearily concede, and still feel shame when you do not do your absolute best. Then you hide the shame with feelings of obligation that make you angry. Then get all mixed up and muddled in the knowing that this love is choiceless. This care is choiceless. And it is personal. You are tending to a person.

I cannot conceive of any other way for love to be than personal. Love for one life is no different than love of all life. Like all that's been spoken of within these writings, the personal and universal are one. They are joined.

We are in an infancy of being. The fall to earth from the birth canal amid blood and water and the wind of spirit is being reenacted. Each of us is a particular human being, born with needs—one of which is to create.

Whatever name people want, or do not want to give to humanity's nature, I will tell you truly that God loves each one. It is essential to The New that each one come into Being. Being is your own. It is personal, intimate, and respective.

The whole of your brother's Courses is about identifying who you are. That Self is the knowable, relatable, loving and loved Self. Sentience itself came of that Self, to that Self, in relationship.

This is the only repeated paragraph in A Course of Love:

"Christ-consciousness is the awareness of existence through relationship. It is not God. It is not man. It is the relationship that allows the awareness that God is everything. It has been called wisdom, Sophia, spirit. It is that without which God would not know God. It is that which differentiates All from nothing. Because it is that which differentiates, it is that which has taken form as well as that from which form arose. It is the expression of oneness in relationship with Its Self." *

As you know, your readiness to hear, Mari, changed as you moved through your Course with your brother, and the same is designed to happen for each one. While a lot of early explaining was done to satisfy your desire to know, here your Jesus has walked you to the end of your need of meaning or explanation, and is stating the truth outright.

I agree, my Mary. It is the "identity" of *ourselves* that we are being led to throughout, and here, we are given the respect that proclaims that if we are willing, we are ready!

M

---

* ACOL D:Day11.7, and Day40.13

$\mathcal{S}$ OLIDARITY

Dearest Mary, I have appreciated this time of coming to hear my voice in a new way, but I doubt I can sustain it. I can't have everybody's troubles on my mind and do what I would so like to do here—or have a sabbatical.

But anyway . . .

This morning the remote is refusing to turn off the cabin's holiday lights. I know it must be purposeful. She is calling me, but I cannot answer or escape her. She is another being. But I forgot, until just the other day, that she even has a name.

It was Donny's idea that I give her a name. I wasn't too keen on doing so and gave no thought to it. Then one day, when our beloved dog Sam was still alive, she inspired him to one I couldn't resist.

Sam was always with me in the cabin then, or just outside the door. When Donny would get home from work, he'd come sit on the stoop and throw a tennis ball over and over as we talked. One day he said, "You should call the cabin Samari, for Sam and Mari." I liked it right away, and later discovered the term 'Samadhi,' with its likeness of sound, and felt even more resonance for the suggestion. Samadhi derives from the root sam-a-dha, which means 'to collect' or 'bring together,' and is associated with concentration or unification of mind. In early Buddhist texts it was also associated with the term 'samatha' (calm abiding).*

I sigh with the memories: of dog, and name, and old friend,

---

* "Samadhi." *Wikipedia*, en.wikipedia.org/wiki/Samadhi.

Steve Lehman,* who, when I told him of the name, let me know also, that the whirligigs of my beloved maple tree (the miracle tree that was cut down and regrew right outside the cabin's window) were more properly known as 'samara.' So even though I call her 'the cabin,' I am glad she was christened with her own name. I feel the sweetness of the memories even as I admit that, no matter the desire, my wonky hips make it unrealistic to reach her at present.

But I had a vision, over Christmas, of getting these mats I've heard about. They're like solar panels that take care of the snow in some new way. It's not so much a plan as a metaphor. I may need to take care of myself if I am to weave my two threads into a new tapestry.

M

The clear face of a bird feeder just flashed like a beacon as, moved by the wind, it caught the light. It stands between me and the cabin, as if between me and my freedom. Or . . . it is signaling my freedom . . . which today feels "out there somewhere," and not in here.

M

I sigh again, letting go of the holiday drama that has momentarily caught up to me. I do not feel capable of it—drama—anymore. Or maybe I am capable but no longer inclined to be. It is so unnecessary. It makes my "one life" into "two lives." While it seems less than empathetic to step aside from all the feelings and problems being

---

* Editor of *Peace: Book III of The Grace Trilogy* and of the first single volume of "The Dialogues"

shared, it is not the problems so much as the unnecessary fuss with which they are conveyed. I am close to turning that corner. And I know that when I do, I will not turn back.

I do not want this to be the time when life's dramas intrude, and I do not feel in need of reviewing former life-lessons. I desire new life.

ℳ

Your concern for your daughters, who are still struggling toward stability, is shared by mothers around the world. Young mothers, the world over, fear for their lives and their babes. Financial and socially accepted dangers are not as fierce as physical danger, but they are as present. They are nearly as debilitating.

I feel for all underachievers whose unnecessarily difficult lives support so many, as well as for the dispossessed—those forced to flee danger for new life. It does not matter if the danger comes from invisibility and individual struggle, or flight from savagery. It is all the same in the mother's heart, and the father's.

This is like unto what we are doing with our words and our new way, and another reason we began, in 2013, with the radical beginning that scared you. It is okay to be afraid, sometimes. And it is okay to be fierce in the face of the fearsome.

These ways are still watched by those who seek power. A person displaying the power of miracles might not be crucified, but obvious miracles, even of speech or writing, remain dangerously alluring, even while many such prophets are hidden in plain sight.

But this is not the reason I have come to you in this time in which you are cultivating new choices in your family, based on the ineffectiveness of your concern, and the effects of your daughters' trials. I come because they are trials amid a culture of under-achievement in a world that is based on achievement.

M

ℭHE UNDERACHIEVERS

The ways in which "underachieving lives" are given to harassment and subsequent falls from grace are common and habitual. Underachievers are counted as expendable and given to underground cultures that offer alternative ways of living—perpetually on the margin. And there are always those clever enough to watch what moves at the margin for its potential. There is something "there" that the overachievers desire. A sort of freedom and creativity that they cannot bear to see as the freedom from achievement.

This is something Yeshua came to understand only as he grew into the man he was before his death. He saw the deathliness of custom, and law, and the rule of power. He found his own power to be less than the power of human love—much to his surprise. And he began to see true power in the meek; in those on the fringe; those not so sure of themselves and their positions; those willing to "leave mother and father" for a different kind of life.

These are those whom he came to know he needed to build the new Heaven and the new Earth. The others were too blind to see, and the miracles that came from him only revealed the existent "truth" of their attraction to power.

I too, discovered this in my own way.

ℳ

$\mathscr{T}$HE DISPOSSESSED

My Mari, welcome me now, for a spell. I have waited to tell you of the dispossession of my family. This is a story of extreme upheaval, a story that has continued and is eerily present in your current time. Seventy million people are now displaced in your world.*

Today, we speak particularly of those being displaced from their homelands, as I want to speak of my solidarity with them.

Even for Joseph and me, there was no smiting the enemies of our son. There were what we might call "countermoves" given by the dispatch of the angels. Joseph was warned to take Yeshua and I to Egypt, out of Herod's reach.

I know what it is like to be hunted. To make that desperate and hasty choice to flee harm or death.

$\mathscr{M}$

Remember . . . nothing was planned, only prophesied. There is a difference. And yet in our time, faith depended on it—the prophecy. Prophets did not predict. They spoke with conviction "for" those who knew the way. Your "speaking" of what you heard from Jesus and now are hearing from me, is spoken from we who know the way. It is a measure of the potency of prophecy. Ways of prophecy never instruct. Prophecy at times commands and at times suggests, and as your brother said, at times "paints a new

---

* Since the time of the original dialogue with Holy Mary, this number has increased to over 80 million.

x

picture."* All prophets spoke words that were "given" them to speak. Then, more times than not, the words they spoke called on them to do more than speak.

$$\mathcal{M}$$

In our flight to Egypt there was a need to move quickly, with Yeshua just a babe in arms. I knew what it was to feel the heat and cold of a journey fleeing danger: the hunger, the thirst, the hostility, the inability to communicate in a new land, with a different language.

My fear for the safety of my child was palpable, and not mediated at all by faith. My blood pumped with fear. Every kindness was a miracle then. Every moment of calm without fear felt generously given.

Yeshua showed, in that time, more evidence of his divinity than he did in the next twenty years. There was no discernment in him, no fear. It was with awe and a sort of terror that I witnessed the power of God in him. He kept us alive. And what he did to keep us alive kept us in danger.

He, himself, would tell you that he was at his most powerful then—because thought and consideration had not yet come to him. These things made Yeshua more human—in a sense, less Godly, and at the same time—more Godly.

And I tell you that as Yeshua began to care for those around him, with greater draws to some than to others, there was in him, as there was in me, despite being the son of God, the wholly un-

---

* Perron, Mari. "Paint the New Picture." *The Jesus Chronicles*, www.mariperron. com/the-jesus-chronicles/2009-2/, 2009.

expected anguish of love in relationship. You might say that "love in relationship"—feeling love for each as well as all—was the first of my son's surprises.

Acknowledging the "more than one," Yeshua was also called to recognize the strength of human love—a love felt for each one in an unrepeatable way. Even today, this is an aspect of love often ignored. Just as no two are alike, no love, one to another is the same. Universal love could be seen in an egalitarian, almost neutral way, but not love in relationship.

My love for Joseph was quite different than my love for Yeshua, and it grew as he displayed love's strength. He was steadily calm, and steadfast in his love and loyalty. He reassured me so many times on our thousand-mile trek. A trek of several years. Years! Always on the move. No home. No kin.

And so, when I spoke earlier of enjoying the hard work of life in our small compound, it was in relation not only to the temple life, but to the terrors I felt on that journey. It did not matter to me that I might die. But Yeshua? I could not conceive of it, and yet I did. I held him with a mother's fierceness and became as vigilant for Joseph, and as devoted to him. I could not, on my own, have survived, even with Yeshua's miracles.

I can still remember that dread, and I do so purposefully on occasion, so as to remember with your people, the terrors of your time.

Of course, it was different to have a small child in my care than to be the mother of a grown man, a Messiah of great potency and independence, with no seeming care for his own life. He was fearless for himself, but increasingly concerned for others. No one knows the choices he made to spare those he loved. Even while he had a destiny to fulfill, my daughter, it was not up to him! This, I could tell, surprised him. He was not in control of what happened; he was but a divine "man" in a barbaric time.

Only as his life unfolded did he have the chance to partake of human life in the individuated way that each one does to this day. Only as he matured did his God nature let him see beyond what was apparent, and to reconcile his human and divine nature within himself.

The prophets had heard only what would necessarily come to be in time and place, "A savior from the house of David."

M

On our return from exile, we initially were headed to Judah, but due to the reputation of Archelaus, who had become the new king, went instead to Galilee. There, Herod Antipas was considered a more moderate ruler.

Due to this, Galilee was overflowing with fleeing refugees. And so, there we were—living at the margin of a community.

I am speaking of this because, in truth, we had much greater freedom than those who were, you might say, the overachievers of our time. Most of these were born, then as now, to the heritage of power rather than to the idea that it could be earned by brilliance, unless it was brilliant treachery.

My daughter, not one of them could trust anyone.

Trust is so important. It is why some risked everything to follow Jesus: they had finally encountered someone worthy of their trust.

The treacherous betray trust because they know it not. Dis-

trust is always there—waiting for them—rather like an attack about to happen, a calamity on the way. Danger everywhere. Safety nowhere.

So here we contrast faith and trust, for they are not the same, as you have seen. You have great faith, but not always great trust. It seems like an impossibility, as if one should breed the other naturally—and "naturally" this might be the case. But you have grown to maturity in an unnatural time, as have all of those who have hope and faith and yet do not fully trust in it.

Do you trust in me, my Mari?

Yes. But to be honest, I feel that my trust in you depends on my trust in myself, and this is not always present. I admit it.

How willingly honest you are, my Mari.

And you trust in yourself more than most—far more than those who appear to trust totally in themselves and no one else. Do you understand what I am saying? Can you see where trust in oneself has replaced trust? And where trust is also displaced by lack of trust in oneself?

Here, we will purify your trust, my daughter, and the trust of all who come to our way. Here, you are already well on your way, and the reason you are, is that you are trusting what you are "coming to know." You can only come to know, by becoming a trusting being.

Remember what you said, mere days ago? "I don't know what to make of it, but I will. This I trust." You are creating the conditions for trust, total trust, in what is revealed, even without understanding. Your understanding is what, in the past, has given you trust, while not understanding has been your impediment to trust.

But here is where you begin to see what you already know. It is a huge revelation even now: You do not have to understand to have trust. To trust that you do not need to understand, or even to be understood, is the total trust I ask of you. It is the way of The New.

Here, with a new trust in time outside of time, you develop your own revolutionary ways. These ways will fit the radical newness of this time and will reconcile life in time with life lived in time outside of time.

M

THE NEWLY DISPOSSESSED
AND THE MOVE OUT
OF THE MANGER

JANUARY 30, MA'S BIRTHDAY

Isn't it funny that I was just thinking of Ma? I love it. She always called me Marg with a hard g at the end rather than in a way that rhymes with barge.

Ha! But it's not January! Oh, my living God. Time is doing its tricks on me again. It is still December: *December* 30th. Still in the last days of the year of our Lord that has poised us for The New. Still in the last days before the "real" sabbatical, the last days before kids return to school, the last days before people return to work after leaving "the season" behind.

The return of normalcy.

And most everyone is more than ready for it. I know I am. All the different "normals." The return to the certain rhythm of life that this season disrupts . . . with intent.

Jesus, you, I know, were the great disrupter. Not only then, but now. Not only "were," but "are." Certainly, the great disrupter of my life. You came along and rewrote my life into what it was meant to be. Now I am given to our common mother and you and she are, I can feel it, preparing to leave me, or preparing me, at least, to leave some of my obsessions behind for new explorations.

With you, Jesus, there is the sense of a beloved mentor, waiting on my brilliance even as you tell me I can only shine in my way. I have always called you Lord, and thought to quit until I looked up the word.

Its earliest meaning is "one who feeds dependents." Isn't that something? And that you gave us the sacrament of communion, of bread and wine? But more than that, I like that it doesn't mean anything like "ruler." It is rather about providing nourishment.

I am thankful when Mother Mary tells us of your time. You ask me to tell you of mine and I have so little interest in doing so. I look out the window, (still at the inside window but now I've taken down the manger, a move to make it easier to set myself up for the view), and suddenly can see this time as akin to a move out of the manger. I questioned myself after I took it down early. It was as if I was doing it before I thought of doing it. It happened without intent.

M

So here I am, sitting at Grandma Ivie's table, the manger replaced by the plant and photos that more usually grace it, and with Ma's birthday coming to mind a month early. The Grandmothers. The women.

In this time, I do not know what goes on within anyone else, but my life is punctuated by wanting to do the impossible and feeling like the odds are against me! And being sort of elated by it, by not wanting life to be "normal." The "norm" has felt deadly to me since I was a kid.

M

I can remember the thought coming to me, back on Smith Avenue, maybe around Henry's age: the thought of "What's so good about life? What's the point?" I was standing in the back yard, peering up at the giant cottonwood tree that stood at its edge, asking the question in that way you do when you look around, and all you see is the norm.

What it looked like was, "You grow up, you have kids, you work hard, you die." I remember wondering if the whole purpose of life was to have children. It was all I saw around me, in small houses populated by a minimum of four kids.

It seemed like those of us my age would grow up to repeat the pattern: to have kids, who we would then have to work hard to support—the man by earning the money, and the woman by her care and chores. And I wondered, "Was that it?"

Now that way of life has nearly passed. How odd. It's odd, too, to remember that in 1966, when I was eleven years old, "That Girl," a popular television show, was the first to represent a modern working woman. *

ℳ

My questioning was furthered by literature a few years later.

At fourteen, I was reading DH Lawrence: *Lady Chatterley's Lover*. It was about shattered people whose lives had been disrupted by war and industry, who were trying to come back to life. They "knew" there was a life out there, different than the one they saw around themselves.

---

* "*That Girl* was one of the first sitcoms to focus on a single woman who was not a domestic or living with her parents. Some consider this show the forerunner of *The Mary Tyler Moore Show*, and an early indication of the changing roles of American women in feminist-era America."
"That Girl." *Wikipedia*, en.wikipedia.org/wiki/That_Girl.

I do believe I have carried that image—that exact image—with me all this time. I read and reread that book. It fed my heroic idea that you had to, at the very least, quest for a life with greater purpose, love, and beauty. Stable lives, from that early age, only appeared dull. They seemed utterly routine, and for the largest part bland—with nothing in them worth pursuing beyond a satisfaction with the norm.

I was not interested in them because they were not interesting. They contained nothing noteworthy—nothing to discover.

So, it's no wonder that I've never been interested in the "answers" to the quest. I wanted the quest itself—an unearthing of the human spirit with all its loving or tortured desire for fulfillment of that greatest mystery: ourselves.

I needed the dull life's routine only in support of that creative spark, the yearning I had in me for something else. Something more. For ideas—passionate ideas. For clues to a truth that I would long to express, and to express creatively.

I wanted enchantment, and wonder. The wonder of Mirari! I missed, maybe even as young as eleven, seeing the world with the wonder I had as a younger child, and relished the times when it came back to me, catching me unaware. Maybe that is what the cottonwood tree did on that day back at the end of the 1960's, when change was going on all around and the only evidence, and then infrequently, was my brother Ray's returns from college. The sophisticated young man and the hippie, both emerging in radically new ways. Like something I'd never seen or imagined. An "un-"ordinary life.

His was the first non-ordinary life I'd ever seen. It fascinated me. There it was: sitting in a chair in the living room.

M

I have worried about our writing getting too long, feeling like it could go on forever. Just this writing, this form of questing. My heaven being here, particularly at this time of day, before the chores of life's maintenance present themselves. Before the noise of it all. I am getting so averse to it . . . the noise.

I didn't even tell you how I couldn't sleep the night before last. The sound of the freeway, normal and nearly unobtrusive for twenty-five years, felt like it was in the room with me. Other things too: thoughts of my daughters and their sorrows. And so, I put on the audio to our Course—"The Dialogues"—and fell asleep to it, and did so again last night. I was hearing my own voice.

Oh boy. That just sunk in. "Hearing my own voice."

Is it, possibly, what we each do all this seeking to find? Our voices, our memories, our passion? I am, as the earth comes to life out the window, feeling with "Mirari" and "Memoria" both. The juncos flit. A light snow falls. The trees appear dotted with popcorn. The incredible contrast of a scene cast in black and white. All this happening in the field of time's changing seasons and the slant of the world.

I sit here with my new knowing of time, of this change she's going through along with me, and the wonder of the new possibilities. Time herself as the new exploration. The desire is for the busy, preoccupied way of life to stop, so The New can come. While I'm no longer as keen on the irregular that comes in its cyclical nature—

the celebrations I spend so much of my time honoring—I'm not yet ready to give them up. Some things that never left are coming home again in a new way. "Moments" of wonder still hold a candle in the dark, if not so much for me, for the children. It is not artificial when it leads to that. My own childhood wonder was of that pure form, of Mirari, and I likely would not be who I am without its remembrance. The memories are real and still have existence.

My mood now is so evocative . . . the evocation alongside the naturalness of it. The creation of a "mood" that evokes. A mood of the non-ordinary. Created for me, right before my eyes. And sometimes created by me.

How amazing that such celebrations still occur, really. People are given time off of work to celebrate the season of the birth at which you, the companions I speak with here, were the subjects. Its recognition is a necessity still, despite its commercialization. It is time to stop and do ridiculous, unordinary things. To embrace something beyond the norm.

Yet this is something different, more real. Here. Now. Near.

Just the thought of your life changing the world, Holy Mary. How amazing is that? How astonishing really, is the remembrance of your Yeshua's revolutionary, evolutionary, oh-so-controversial life? And this telling of the glory in the dispossessed, no matter the trials involved.

This is what we all are, isn't it? The *newly* dispossessed? We are, or are becoming, dispossessed of the *old* world.

It is about time.

M

THE SOLIDARITY OF UNION

I am wondering today about fear, my Mary. And your admittance of fear. Real fear in the cause of fear.

Fear for life.

Trust in God *and* fear for your life. Fear for Yeshua's life. Fear despite faith. Foreboding of what could come to be—and did. This whole dismissal of fear that has been encouraged in our Courses, and much of modern spirituality, is yet felt by the faithful the world over. For cause of danger.

Even if you don't want to speak of it, I feel the need for this acceptance, the acceptance of warranted fear. And maybe I need a little permission myself. I know I may have delayed this dialogue for some uneasiness of what it may bring. There are other dangers. Dangers that would block the coming of The New: the status quo that protects what "was," the type of "learning" that was, and the semblance of "order" that continues to promote inequality. I know we're speaking of discontinuation of things as they are. This isn't the same fear as I would feel if Henry was in immediate danger, but it is more globally terrifying.

As you've spoken to me of commerce, especially in the arts, I understand that good people still don't want to take the chance of change. They do things the way they have always been done and feel no need to defend what they do. "It" just "is." It is the way it is. The way it's done. The whole world seems to run by that maxim.

What I "fear" the most, is the world continuing to run in that way. Not that "the world" really has anything to do with it.

"The world" is free. It is beyond the control of its billions of residents—some of whom fear this very fact the most. There is fear of anything out of one's control, but particularly the natural law of this incomparable planet that has made herself home to us, while so many test their desire to destroy her rather than to create along with her.

You can take the word "fear" and change it to many things—like "alarm," or "dread"—but what difference does it make? If your life is threatened, there is fear. And I still will contend that it has nothing to do with faith, and thank you so much, Holy Mary, for speaking of it. You had faith in what is beyond this world—which, in a sense, is what faith has been taken to mean—*and* fear of this physical world and the actions of many of your fellow human beings. Fear of the disregard for life would seem a sane fear, a fear given by sanity.

You had so much to protect.

I had no intention of advocating for fear, but suddenly, this morning, my thought turned in this direction.

There are distinctions in these terms, though. I understand that. I "dread" administrative tasks, and the tax season, but I don't fear them. I'm "alarmed" by the state of the world without living in fear of it. But I loved your identification with those dispossessed in this time, Mary, and even if few of them ever find these words, I believe they will find help in them. They are more than words. I believe you have the power to ease their terror, if not its cause. Perhaps, before your words even get to the page, they're lifted on the wings of angels and carried to the world.

Many among the dispossessed already know you are their advocate, Mary. I hope that many more may know from the act of our sharing . . . and will truly be relieved, to not have their fears dismissed.

Dismissing it seems, now, almost cruel. And people get bitter when their fear is dismissed, whether they have lost their home-land, live in fear of crime, or are unable to pay the rent. This demonstration of dispossession is upon us all. In the solidarity of our union, you ease my fears by acknowledging them. You soothe fears that no others can, even while miracles of love do not always stop what is happening.

I know you do this, and in this moment, don't have doubt that what you do, I am doing also. This is the solidarity of our union. And the way of the feminine.

M

Feeling dispossessed from Heaven is the cause of dispossession on the Earth.

Feeling dispossessed of our union is the cause of dispossession from your birthright.

Feeling alien from your own solidarity with your life in form, is your call to be possessed of life beyond form, in form.

This was the nature of Yeshua. This is your nature.

If you were to think your Jesus was meek and mild, you would be wrong. But this you do not think.

If Jesus had adhered to the ways in which your spiritual lead-ers have categorized him, that would be different. But he was not always peaceful. Do they really think he was never conflicted?

No. He was a passionate man, a true revolutionary, and he answered to no one but God. Those who lead you to believe such a life looks only one way—never calling for passion—are talking of a different way and a different world than was our own then, or yours now. Yes, Yeshua can speak for himself, but there are times we need others to speak of us. Not for us—but of us.

He, in some ways not unlike yourself, realized and expressed his power at two ends of the range of human feeling: when calm and inspired, and when angry.

Remember that your brother spoke of it, saying, this power of being has always been yours. "The power to feel—love, hate, anger, compassion, greed, humility, and longing. . ." *

Those who would have you discount your feelings ask you to discount your power. Power is not something to be used or planned! Power, of its own, is natural. In its naturalness, power cannot be used. In its unnaturalness it is always used.

Yeshua, in "ordinary" times, with friends and family—in what you call "regular life," in the order you cherish without realizing it—was possessed of the ordinary, too. He rested in the familiar and in being a man among men in the time in which he existed. He enjoyed the companionship of women and was inspired by their way of knowing. He found adventure and Mirari in the world he traveled, and he found the wonder of possibility in the children who flocked to him, knowing what their elders knew not.

No one could live human life adequately—by which I mean, they could not continue to function—with constant expressions of their power going out from them. Your Jesus' power wearied him,

---

* ACOL D:Day36.14

much as yours does you. But you have yet to realize this as the
cause of your weariness.

$$\mathcal{M}$$

My mother, I have just heard the undisputable sound of chimes . . .
several times. Chimes and . . . flowing water.

You are hearing the flow of true power, and the sound of it.
You see? It is a soothing power.

$$\mathcal{M}$$

RESPECT FOR POWER AND PASSION

I know we must have respect for this power of God.

You have respect for your creative power, don't you?

Yes. I know it is not in my control, but I know the conditions for it. In giving those conditions room, as I do each morning, I am—and thank you for suggesting it—respecting my creative power.

True creative power is our great hope. It comes of what, you might say, is the love that birthed creation. It is a carrier of delight. An allure for the return to who you truly are. As original desires infiltrate time and space, The New will be created.

So create! And love your creations!

Love that results in creation is not the same as something you "do." Do you consider this simply something you do? In the way you "do" the dishes or make the bed? No. It takes the passion and power of love to create.

What does it matter if you must carve out time for it? Is it a sacrifice?

No. It is my passion. You are right.

As "you" realize that "I" am telling you a truth—a truth that you already know—you are realizing our union in solidarity and making real this reality. Your passion for creativity "is" your reality. Your passion is needed.

Those who know no passion in life dismiss the power of God "in them." This power is your birthright. It is the power to create change, the power to become, the power of love. Your passion to create is your testament and demonstration of The New.

Why do you imagine that Jesus' torture and death was called his "passion"?

He gave everything—everything—for the power of love to be known in this world.

And so did all of us who loved him. It's harder to describe what "we" did, but in loving him "to the end," we too, passionately created the conditions for The New. We all witnessed to his suffering in our own ways, and doing so, took upon our human forms, more than we could bear. From this depletion of the power of every bit of human might, came the beginning, in time, of humanity's overriding passion for love and love's creative power.

So many have taken all that they can bear! It causes a surrender of the human idea that you can make it on your own. Surrender makes room for the idea that you are not alone.

ℳ

We did not know this any more viscerally than do you, sitting where you are in your dark morning. We were, after Yeshua's death, so "merely" human once again, feeling so alone, so bereft. Yet we had been embraced by the power of God and emptied of the old.

You are emptied now, my daughter, of the old. And now, only now, will you begin to see what it is to live The New—not within the old—but outside of the old. Only now will you begin to see how to live outside of time—in time.

Even more importantly, here is where you are you going to begin to know what it is to live in truth with the passion of Christ.

M

On the Wake of Passion

In the wake of passion, I find utter stillness, within and without. New snow lines my trees, covers the cabin's roof, stands in hills upon the bushes. I feel a quiet enormity of love and life and a disbelief that it is only seven o'clock. It feels as if a great expanse of time has passed since we began these last passages, Mary.

Maybe it is the feeling of time passing away—in me—and the coming of a new time.

I stand aside now from what just happened, only knowing that something happened. In stillness I know that something occurred, and that something is still . . . passing through.

I am in awe and gratitude for the knowing I experienced, and yet am so quiet inside.

I suddenly realize, Mary, that you are more radical than Jesus. He more radical in his life, you more radical now.

M

Yes, he is gentler with the world now, my Mari. He spoke of fear in the way he did in A Course of Love *because you had to build on his and Helen's master work in* A Course in Miracles, *to take you, and your sisters and brothers prepared to do so, gently into a new time.*

You are "nearer" now, as you say, and I am not so gentle. Fear is no longer the issue that it was before the ego was identified and given to discovery.

We are not talking of the sort of fear that leaves one timid or in protection of ego.

We are talking of relational fear between the powerful and those who have no worldly power. Fear is what lets you do what you can to protect yourself and your loved ones in times of danger. Fear also allows you to recognize unseen dangers within intelligence and its forethought. Fear calls you to begin to correct the incorrect.

Those of this way—this way of dependence on intelligence—are still needed in this time to end all time. These, too, know a kind of fear brought to love of the intellect. They seek solutions and, knowing what they know, have fear the solutions will not be enough. Intellect is one of the approaches, one of the orientations, to love. But intellectualism based on fear can also be used. You must still have discernment there, with those inclined to love in this way.

Most orientations of love cannot be used, but some can. In this time of transition, those that can be used are still needed. Pray for those with these orientations to love, and for their love not to be separated from their response to love.

The way that is passing is as capable of facilitating a gentle passage of the old as a harsh one. In the way of time, this is the debate taking place. The debates bring accord of one form or another . . . eventually. Compromise measures, but still measures. Measures of war or peace, now or later. The issues are so complex that simplicity can't be seen . . . yet.

We pray for your faithful leaders to cease to look piecemeal at the fate of the world and to begin to see in wholeness.

We also give our prayer to imagination and creation of The New and give you our assistance by way of the imaginal realm.

You who entered, and now exit from your conception of ordinary time, will conceive imaginal time. Extraordinary time. The

Advent of a new time is here. Creation of a space for what is beyond time, is here. Now.

A space capable of holding time as what it is beyond time, is on its way into being—through you.

You and your sisters and brothers given to spaciousness, are facilitating the birth of the new time. You and your sisters and brothers, given to the imaginal, will create what the new time is to be. In its infancy, you will mother The New into being in time, with intimate care of the new babe. For here is where new life is born. Right here. In the near of your cabin, in the far of the dispossessed. Here on this planet, here in this time outside of time. . .

Time, as you imagine it, can come to be as it truly is. All is in alignment for this to be—in you and through you—which is the way of time in form.

Time is only lived—in you and through you. In your being, and through your being, time is given life in form, as is everything that exists in form, my daughter. In you and through you, what comes to be, comes to be. This is the way of creation. This is the way of God.

This was the way of Yeshua's birth into time.

This was the way that I birthed the divine into time.

Consequently, my life can now reflect the way whose time has come. I birthed the divine "into time." This is the reason that, from my being, I can address yours, and guide you to this time to end all time—by creating time anew.

Time, held in the heart of mother love, will gentle this passage to The New.

Love time. Love time as you feel it assist you in the pass-through of all time. Evoke time's memory. Feel the power of time's remembrance. *Feel this trust in remembrance as the power of time passing through you. Unrestricted time. This is the revelation of what you have been bringing into being.*

Do you see? All that is of God can exist in time, only by way of this passage into time—through each of you. Eternal time is the environment of God that, with your opening, can pass from God to you, and through you into the world.

Time "in" eternity is what you experience in the swirl. It is the whirlwind of eternal time coming into being on Earth. Now, as it passes through you, you can know. You can know in, and within, what you experience.

"If . . . you accept that these ideas that already exist were able to pass through you in order to gain expression in form; then you are beginning to see, on a small scale, the action that, on a large scale, will become the new way." *

"The Course sought to teach you to develop a relationship with all that passes through you. Now is the time when the fruit of those efforts will be reaped. For what passes through you now is a relationship without end. What passes through you now is the eternal come to replace the temporary." †

M

---

* ACOL D:Day9.14
† ACOL D:Day15.12

$\mathcal{U}$NITY IN ETERNITY

What we have just shared feels so important, so integral. I realize more than I ever have that unity, and eternity, are a unit. They are one. It stuns me, but I am not sure why. The same is true of eternity in time . . . eternity here. Could it be that the allure of eternity beyond time, the allure of it not being of this world, is a reason why I've not seen it before? Maybe . . . that humankind hasn't seen it? Would we rather imagine eternity in a separate heaven? This will be a question I feel many will have. Yet I'd guess it's a question that is not to be answered but discovered, and one that can't be discovered until we are done with looking at meaning!

Beyond meaning, is the wonder of pass through, one of those areas of *A Course of Love* that never spoke much to me. And here it is—perhaps the most important of all. I know it is true because I experience it. I know it in my being. My experience allows me to imagine it on a wider scale, and to know that the pass through causes an effect. I am in awe, in awe, in some ways, of the simplicity of it. We simply allow the pass through, as I allow *this* pass through, and probably in all kinds of other ways. Through our senses for sure. The way the beauty of the day enters and soothes us as it "passes through."

I won't invite this now. I've been at this for seven hours. And yes, the pass-through is draining. There is something extreme about it. I am very tired. Yet there is a way that it gives me—after some time to reflect—a certain peace.

Rest in that peace, my Mari. Then we will begin again.

M

THE NEW WAY

On a beautiful dark morning, darker than it's been for weeks, I went to write in my journal and realized for the first time that 2019 is as behind me as 2020 is ahead of me. But of course, I stopped, as I usually do, to read a bit of the year that has passed...

$$\mathcal{M}$$

JANUARY 1, 2019

A beautiful morning sky in slate blue and gray with coral on the rise. Two bunnies are out by the plum tree. I'm seeing them from the sunroom at 7:05 on this first day of a new year that lies open before me.

Donny is asleep. Henry is downstairs sleeping. Simmy is curled in the basket by my side. My adult children are all in various states of aloneness. I can feel Henry being ready to be ... a teen.

Tiny birds flutter by the arbor where the seed is. It's so dark I can't make them out, but suspect they are Juncos.

Starting a new journal is always a little scary and a little freeing. The old year is behind me. I think I complained in April of 2018 that I had only written 40 pages in four months, and now there are 567 pages. The first 307 are actual journaling, the remainder "slush"—letters and whatnot that I was working on. I know I'll go back occasionally to find things. I may do a review today. I may not. I may pull out the Jesus and Mary writings, I may not. The feeling is that I have much to do and do not know what to do, both at the same time. Maybe one leads to the other, and the idea of paring down stands beside the idea of going forward newly. It is the simple truth . . . the "simple" truth, I say, as pink and gold replace the silver and gray clouds, and Simmy moves to the floor beside the heater. The sunroom is not a warm place on winter mornings.

We are all one. This is something that has been in my thoughts about us, Jesus and Mary. That we are one. That the reception or inspiration, especially of your history, says something about how you live within me, as does the whole—as if we all somehow live all the lives, or they're all there in consciousness, because we are one. Which I do not want to "think" about, but simply to state. It is all within. The Kingdom of God within. The vast consciousness within. A whole world within. A vast new terrain, and yet one that is contained here—with me, in me. This yard and this horizon and these birds and bunnies. And yet it all gives me no clue how to proceed, especially when my mind drifts to taking down the Christmas tree today. The birds will like it once it reaches the yard.

I am so dull that I went back and began to look at 2018 and found Jesus assuring me that my way is to ramble (as just happened here!). That was nice to see. And a mention of Lee on New Year's Day. I may send that to him later.

I just remembered that I had a message in a waking song yesterday morning. It was the Beatles, "Don't ever leave me alone," and the beats were pulsing with crystal light. I wrote in my dream journal, "I Have New Year Message – made me happy."

Oh! Darling, please believe me, I'll never do you no harm . . . *

I thought it was Joe Cocker singing it (in the dream) because

---

* "Oh! Darling" was composed by Paul McCartney, credited to Lennon-McCartney, 1969, *Abbey Road*.
"Oh! Darling." *Wikipedia*, en.wikipedia.org/Oh!_Darling

it was so guttural. Just listened to it again, and I can see why I thought that.

It was you, wasn't it Jesus? You, telling me you'll never let me down. Or was it me telling you?

And so, Oh! Darling, will you talk to me this morning at the start of 2019?

$$\mathcal{M}$$

What if I were to tell you that you do not need me anymore?

I would hope that the emphasis was on "need."

Not to need but to desire. Not to need but to be in relationship. Not to need because I can tell you more than you can know, but to accept the need to trust in your way of knowing.

I just saw an enormous hawk swing its way from the horizon to pass by within a breath of the woods and yard trees. I thought he would alight, but he did not.

The Beatles, Joe Cocker, crystal light, a hawk. . .

My heart is beating strongly.

Because there are some things that must be spoken, written, available . . . before you can "let it be." You are tired now. Do not let it discourage you. I am with you. Mother Mary is with you.

This change is not understood, and not to be understood so much as to be lived. But without desiring the change, the very one you have struggled toward and felt resistance to, primarily from "without" but also a little "from within," the desire that others are ready to realize

RELIGION

may not be realized. Many, many are "stuck" in the old way and cannot even imagine the new. ~~Spirituality~~ has become their way of life. Knowing comes in through a back door, a "bedroom window," a dream, and this is so much more than the knowing of thoughts—but it is not realized. Being unrealized it is uninvited. You, too, have fallen to this lack of invitation—except with us.

Your split attention in this time is not ideal for this, and yet you "try." Stop trying! Your concentration will be undivided again soon. Then you and our Mother will begin again.

$$\mathcal{M}$$

I don't know whether to include this or not, but he was right, and you and I began again, Mary. I simply got caught in it, looking at the screen rather than out the window, and yet, I love getting caught in it just as much as I love being captured by each gorgeous morning coming out of the darkness into light and color. The horizon is streaming with tints, hues and blushes that shade the dawn, and the snow is sitting in that lovely way it does when no one with feet bigger than a bunny has tread on it. A coverlet of snow. Snow embracing the earth.

The circumstances are little different than last year. Donny sleeping, both Henry and Angela here after a New Year's Eve when I took to bed early after a raucous time in the kitchen with Henry's new chocolate fountain, about which this morning reveals the mess. Such is life. Sometimes the mornings reveal the mess of things.

But the kitchen door is closed on that, and there is nothing I see as mess outside the window. My view is held pristinely in the breath of snow and its light.

Listening to you again, my brother, as I read through the first and last entries of 2019, created such a strong headwind that it nearly knocked me off my feet.

Still, as so often happens, when I reread, I do not understand why, or if anyone else will feel your power. I was momentarily so convinced of its power, yesterday, that I shared it with Christina so that she would share her response with me. I was pleased that we spoke up for warranted fear, but I was more bowled over by the idea of pass-through . . . as I always am by things that "were there"* all along but that I did not fully see:

"This is the relationship you have with unity while in form—a relationship of intersection and pass-through. No longer will what enters you get stopped by layers of defenses. No longer will it meet the roadblock of your thinking, your effort, your attempts to figure out how to do it and what it all means. There is no cause for such effort."†

Eternity passes through us, as time herself changes us. Time, newly personified into a "she," a feminine accompaniment to this new movement, also passes through. Time is quickening, readying to birth the new time—not time "as usual," but still "time," even as I experience it newly. The new experience is a revelation to which I can testify.

---

* For pass through in ACOL, see C:22, T2:5.6, T4:1.27, D:9.14, D:15, also see search facility at the Center for A Course of Love: (www.centerforacourseoflove. org/discover-acol/)

† ACOL D:Day5.21-22

This morning I feel that, strangely, nothing will change all that much. The world will not collapse. People will not change so greatly as I might have imagined. Government either. But there will be a knowing that the current is moving and that a new time is swirling in nonetheless. Time—that great changer of what was—can pass through in such a way that what *was* will become the future as well as the past.

M

And a certain calm descends.

Again, my writing/our writing tells me everything. It is "pass-through"—always. Unless I am "thinking."

Oh, for the love of God!

My desire for 2020, perhaps like my desire each year, is to be devoted to you—only. And this morning it seems a little silly. I have some sort of "realistic" hat on, perhaps a "come down" from the heights of yesterday. Maybe it is all about rising and descending. And a part—just like "fear" was newly acknowledged as a part—of the reality. Like you, Holy Mother, I am a mother, and a wife, and I am in "life," which has its own requirements.

As light comes to the day, the field of physical life is coming into view too.

M

Remember how we spoke recently of your cabin's furnace, and inviting your appliances into the realm of the holy? If you were to take away your "screens" would the lack of time be so vast? The connectivity so diminished? You are not going to the stream to wash clothes or using a wringer washer. There are expanses of time that moved in, in these ways, that are always replaced by other causes of busyness. Other purposes.

And you have not liked to choose.

You are "saved" by the busyness of others that take them away from you, and you are occupied with them when they are not busy. You can live within this choiceless place with more ease than you can with choice. This is fine! Measure yourself by no one else's standards. Don't blame "them" when you are busier with their activities. Just let your rambling, wandering ways—your journey, your flight, your odyssey—lead the way, as you have. You have desired just this configuration. A dedicated and devoted life on these two fronts of family: celestial and human. As did I.

I tell you all this because I feel your self-doubt this morning. It is common in you after being greatly moved. You settle back into the ordinary.

And so, perhaps you can see the continuation of the ordinary in time, in the way of the Church. Heightened levels of being are in need of being balanced by the ordinary. And as you have seen, in this slow way, this cyclical, grounding way, your capacity for the non-ordinary has grown greatly in the balance.

You may even see why I didn't wait for your sabbatical. Here you have been in the midst of a busy and ordinary life, and also swept away by new revelations. Swept forward. Swept beyond.

In your own whirl of family, you are no longer predominant in the way that you once were. You still invite but you are "less" in-viting than before. You have established boundaries within which you decorate and clean and cook, all of it held within that choice-

less choice that works best for you. Tradition is great at providing choiceless choices, a simple way of moving through your "occupied" life. Your peopled life. Your "relationships."

Then there is the way of spirit . . . which I will contrast a little here, from being. Being is the whole of it. Spirit, matter, body, soul, even consciousness, are subordinate to Being. You are "one" in "Being." You are living out the passion of Christ, the life in which you get to know your Being "in life," and return to Oneness of Being.

But one cannot live one's entire life focused on the predestined, or there would be no creativity, no surprises, no newness. As a man, Yeshua had a greater chance to explore life, even with his shorter number of years, than did I. But given greater freedom, I would not have done much of anything different. I chose to live out my life as it came to me to live it in my Being—caring for individual people, easing fears, comforting, and soothing sorrows. I enjoyed communal life, but I became more secluded. I was deeply connected to Yeshua, much in the way you have been in terms of the Oneness of Being we are moving you toward.

I was tired too, my Mari. You might say that once one's destiny is fulfilled, you know that you can rest. There is nothing to strive for. And the miracle becomes that this time releases who you truly are too. Yeshua was released by death, to become the Christ in you. I was released in life, to be mother to all.

Here, you may see that I could only become the soother of fears by knowing fear. How else could I be in recognition of your fears? How could your Jesus become who he was to be without being brazen about fear, and by asking for the same of his companions?

In "this" time, what I am saying could be construed incorrectly. My response to life in "my time," Yeshua's response to his—these were appropriate to "that" time. Yet remnants remain. We are archetypes of The New, and these remnants offer movement, being, and expression in new forms, configurations relieved of all that would mean living life in any way other than true to who you are in your Being.

This truth is sometimes evidenced by retreat, my Mari, and sometimes evidenced by advance—by being in the world, or by being beyond the world while within the world. Together, the two ways allow for all the choiceless choices involved in being who you are. Who "You" are. Not anyone else. You. Not in any other time. You, in your time. And what moves through you in this time is vastly different than in mine. What moves through you has evolved beyond evolution, into creation of The New.

M

The beauty of our writing together, while of "this" time, is also "ahead" of time in the way of prophecy, and "changing time," in the way of alchemy. The "togetherness" is the key. Many will not be ready for it, nor want "the new wisdom" presented in this way. Others will feel a recognition of it that they can embrace. They will see their sister—you—as a human counterpart to spirit in Being. That will allow them to recognize, in themselves, the union of their person and their Being as they come to know it.

They will know, in their way, how to approach Being, with their own orientation to Being.

M

The fate of self-consciousness

It's a Wednesday night on this first day of the new year. I'm sitting at the dining room table as I was three years ago, and I've been thinking of you, Jesus, since last night. Since the memory arose of that life-altering conversation we had on New Year's Eve, 2017 when you "got real" with me and asked me to "get real" with you. You spoke to me in such a challenging way.

And I guess I need to ask you, Lord, does it matter that I am still so feeble at saying No? At stating my preferences? That I feel so ineffectual and so terribly averse to changing myself—as odd as that might sound—in practical ways? No matter how much grief certain things give me?

I like this "inner life" I am leading. I really do not want to do anything else. And I am not forcing myself as much administratively, or with these family things that are, also, my givens. I would not be able to not do them, even if I got more extreme with these feelings than I already am. I love my family. Even so, in some way I wouldn't miss these family times if they did not occur. But it is also okay that they do. At least for now.

Still, it is a strange admission, to see that I could give it all up.

It is the self-consciousness—in my own home—that I hate. It is rare now, so when it comes, it is awful.

M

You default to self-consciousness just as you grew to be

self-conscious in your first home. It is an awful feeling, and yet you get used to it. That is what you did. You got used to it. But you never liked it because you knew the difference. You grew out of your natural consciousness there, and you "had to be" self-conscious for the next half of your life.

For many it never leaves. It did for you, but then, in your un-self-conscious ways, you found reasons for guilt and shame. These sparked your self-consciousness into life again, the wondering if you should be doing something in a way other than you are, or in a time other than when it seems the "doing" should be occurring. Notice the "shoulds" in that sentence.

You moved in and out of self-consciousness in your initial and most sustained way with Mary and Julie, but you had it also, due to familiarity, during your earlier years with your friends Sally and Lou. You moved in and out of it with your birth family, and after a long trial of being deeply self-conscious around your second husband's family, it passed, as it often does. Almost everyone has an initial self-consciousness when approaching new situations, but you have felt even this leave you.

By speaking of this, you can see how self-consciousness was always piecemeal. Never a constant. This is true for most. And it is an important awareness to invite. First the realization of the onerous nature of being self-conscious, then recognizing where it does not exist, and so knowing it was never a constant. You were aware that there was always something else available when you let self-consciousness go.

This is principally important—a remarkable realization for those who associate with either side of what self-consciousness is seen to be: healthy or unhealthy. Sometimes, self-consciousness can be easily confused with what is really the blossoming of your true consciousness. People are as self-conscious about their gifts as their failings. But true consciousness can overtake your self-consciousness—completely. The closer you get to this total takeover, the more remnants of self-consciousness may compete to stake their claim.

That day, more than a decade ago, at Sundance, that day when you became aware that it was not appropriate to be self-conscious—to be focused on your own discomfort during that holy but unfamiliar event—changed the nature of the whole business of self-consciousness for you. That is what awareness does. And in this case, it was linked to power and the Great Spirit, and your respect for your friend Lou St. Clair Crain. It was a human and a divine concern. Both/and. I really got through to you on this matter in "The Dialogues," but that did not mean you were ready to live it.

"I have spoken with you throughout this time as the man Jesus so that you realize that man and Christ-consciousness can be joined. That you, as man or woman, existing in this particular time and space, can join with Christ-consciousness. You can be both/and, rather than either/or. As I speak to you now as the voice of Christ-consciousness—as your own true Self—you will not have lost Jesus as your companion and helpmate but will only know more fully the content of the man Jesus. As you join with Christ-consciousness in this dialogue, you will realize you have not lost your Self but will only know more fully the content of your Self." *

In each time of joining, your unified consciousness took hold "in the world." These "human and divine" concerns that we speak of may have affected you greatly as you received them in my words, but they are like the connecting lines in what Christina calls "the net," and may not be lived until a fitting situation arises.

I know it seems odd that this realization happened "after" your Course, but your Course made you self-conscious in a different way, especially in those early years. It has lingered due to the way your participation is seen. It is always a challenging passage out of "receiving," and into living with what you have received, and the ideas others have of it. It is not an easy life to navigate—full of assumptions, expectations, and suspicions.

But you have always had a wildness in you, and you touched into it at Sundance with your Ojibwa friend.

You struggle now, as you feel yourself losing your bodily capacity for that natural wildness. Do you know why? It is because you do not fully realize that you have it "here" and that it is a new "here," and that your most daring exploits are ahead of you in the imaginal realm.

I offer you sympathy here, for the hard road you have traveled, and the part the reception of *A Course of Love* had in it. I offer such to each who enter the arduous travels of *A Course of Love*. You each embark on the journey out of

---

* ACOL D:Day10.21

the old to the new land. We bring back sympathy for one another now, as we have a funeral for the old, sending it off with our deep regard and reflections on what it was.

We hold our sympathy in common, in mutual accord, in a correlation that reflects our mutual understanding.

I am sorry for every difficulty you have had. Yet I cherish each way your difficulties readied you for The New ... for they did. That is all you need to know. You do not need to know anything about how, what, when and where. Not about the past, and not about the future.

And I tell you that you now are in possession of what your every difficulty revealed—what they gifted you with—the time of the definitive end of self-consciousness. You have no idea, yet, how much suffering this ending will save you from, or the givens it will release you to.

Self-consciousness is "felt" as a burden and you have all burdened yourselves mightily. But whenever you "realize" such a time of self-consciousness, the door is open for you to realize the consciousness that is not natural, and thus, the consciousness that is natural.

Your unnatural self-consciousness prevents you from experiencing freedom. It leaves no opening in which to let spaciousness in. Self-consciousness is your bane and your rebellion. The end of self-consciousness is the freedom you have craved more than any relationship.

You want this quiet, uninterrupted life, so as not to be disturbed in this relationship with what is most alive in you. The desire for it is appropriate and more. It is what is calling you. It is not only this "creating" that you do with us.

You yearn for no interruptions every single time you are "in the midst of" creating.

To be "in the midst of" is like being in the imaginal realm.

For this, you only need to be "here" now, in this new "here" that our mother has revealed to you. This you know. I tell you truly not to make any "plans" for your life. One idea will lead to another as they call you "here."

By being free of plans, you will be free for all that The New will bring.

Thank you, my Jesus. This rings in me like a blessed and soothing truth.

M

RAGE AND THE THIRD WAY: PERSONIFICATION

Since I last wrote, I was visited with rage. It felt like such a fall from grace. I was feeling it most of the day. In the evening, I was speaking with my friend Kate, who was sitting in the midst of smoke from the fires raging throughout Australia. She was feeling enraged too. We have felt wonderful spiritual feelings at the same time, in accord with one another. And now this? Two women and a fire raging at the same time?

Over the next few days, each woman I spoke with was also brimming with rage. A few of us spoke of how relieved we were that anger* and rage† were given space to be.

Suddenly, I found coming out of my mouth the words, "I can't say 'Mother Mary said,' or 'Jesus said,' one more time."

A few days later I was on the phone with my friend, Lee. I said, "My miracles are so small. Seeing Holy Mary in a glowing orb! And now today, I walked in the kitchen and saw water flowing from the faucet. I thought, 'What the heck?' But by the time I walked to the sink, there was no water flowing." Then I thought, and said rather lamely, "Oh, maybe the words won't be flowing anymore."

I suspect it is true.

My question becomes, What is real? What is "here"?

I have been committed to allowing whatever flows. That is how I've come to this work. I've been "here," with openness to what comes. I never thought it would result in my inability to respond

---

* See ACOL D:Day3.1

† ACOL C:25.19 and T3:19.14

or to bring my own ideas forward to the extent that it has. Now I am given to understand the need to allow my own words and ideas to flow.

M

My Mari, this is why you are here. This is what you are doing with me. What you did with your Jesus. As I "made love" with God, and as Yeshua "made love" with this world and his companions, you are "making love" with words.

For the love of God, we make love.

Love, in "this world," is our creation of love in this world. It is all about Love. Love is the heartbeat of the world that is being restored through a way of creation known as Love.

Love in this world is never a singular creation. We all came to earth with love. We all seek to partner with each other in our humanity to create new love on Earth. Our creation is an appeal from attributeless being, to create the glory of attribute-laden being.

Being in form.

Now we restore the joy of being. The wonder. Mirari. Here we return the presence of being, the memory of it. Memoria.

We do this through personification. A person is a human "being," and has been a third way that unites the human and divine nature.

Your "personhood" remains the reference point. "Your personal identity" is your means of orientation, your way of knowing and being known in the glory of Being. This is a declaration: If you trust in who you are being, you do not "have to" do any-

thing . . . except be who you are. You will have no need to say, "Jesus said," or "Mary said." Life will flow from your trust in union "and" relationship, and in being who you are here to be.

M

 LORY

Glory can only extend through common consent. We are here, together as One, to create common consent.

Only in being who you are, who you truly are, can you experience your glory and give your consent to the full power of Love. In this you are resplendent.

Your attributes, your contribution to the world of form and the creation of the paradise that life in form can be, is your consent to Love and all the splendor it brings to attribute-laden being.

You are being you. You, surrendering to the draw of Love, and to all that you are given to love in the particular . . . from spouse and children, to friends, to the Earth herself, to justice and liberty and newly to time and to the new time rising . . . is creation.

Your creation in the field of time, is the expression into time, of the love that you—you uniquely—are here to give. Your giving is your creation, and your creation is your gift. In creation, giving and receiving are one.

To each of you beloved creators of The New, heed my words: Your creation of love is original, distinct, and particular to you. Your conception of creation is love's appearance as you and in you.

For the love of life and its origin, for God and in God's name, we create again. We create anew to create The New.

We must set things straight, my Mari, and all you daughters and sons of Love. Remember, in his Course, your Jesus told you: "Something has gone wrong."*

---

* ACOL C:12.10

"Although it is impossible for something to have gone wrong in God's creation, something has gone wrong!"*

Here, we accept that something has gone wrong. The world is off kilter. We, together, and only "together," can set the world straight again. The return to the natural balance of the feminine and the masculine is a return of humanity's balance and embrace of two realms.

That is how crucial this is.   2020 – 2050

We bring balance into being "here" to create one world . . . a fluidity of realms, rather than designations that keep one here and one there. Male here and female there.

With an ability to know complexity through a singular causative factor—the love of life and its origin—God's being flows into your being. The flow of God is the flow of creation and of time. Here, time begins to flow forth from the imaginal realm.

Life in form can become the stream of God's knowing and love. As the divine feminine flows in equal measure to the divine masculine, as the imaginal flows alongside the causative, unity returns in a dance of light, reflected in your streams. The light in flowing water will reveal that distance that is just a breath away.

"Imagine the current of the energy, or clear pools of the spacious selves, coming together." †

You will live, not only as creators, but as reflections of God's creation.

---

* ACOL C:12.10

† ACOL D:Day15.20

"Relationship is the invisible reality only expressed through form."*

M

---
* ACOL D:Day14.9

Mercy and the Winds of Change

Imagine the quietude of the void, where love first found itself to be.

Imagine the magnitude of the sounding of the winds of time assisting in this return to the way of God: knowing each other through each other's own being.

The twin polarities of time and eternity are consequent to the divergences of the masculine and feminine of time. In this time beyond evolution, in this new frontier, the convergence of time and eternity create the very winds of change and of justice . . . in you. As men accept the divine feminine in themselves, women accept the divine masculine in themselves. Christ-consciousness is "both the feminine and masculine, the 'identity' of God, or in other words, the All of All given an identity. God holds you within Himself. Christ is held within you as the center or heart of yourself—as your identity and God's identity. Christ is the 'I Am' of God, the expression of 'I Am' in form, the animator and the animated, the informer and the informed, the movement, being, and expression of creation." *

It is justice that calls upon mercy for all that has been obscured in the track of evolutionary time. Mercy from the feminine for the masculine that has been, and compassion for the masculine coming to be. Only in this way will all that can be given, come to be received. What you do not welcome, whether masculine or feminine, is what you will not receive. Welcome the divine masculine in yourselves, my daughters of light. Welcome the divine

---

* ACOL Dialogues, D:Day17.2

feminine in yourselves, my sons of fire. Embrace together the glow
of the new flame.

Justice is the way creation rights herself and becomes the new
frontier. Justice and mercy will close out the way of the past for
the eternity to come.

"With your accomplishment comes the freedom and the challenge
of creation. Creation becomes the new frontier, the occupation of
those too young to rest, too interested in living still to welcome the
peace of dying. Those who could not change the world one iota
through their constant effort, in peace create the world anew."*

And I say to all who blanche at this idea—remember me.
Remember the Mary to whom your prayers have flowed in times
of need. You are in times of need. Peace will not come without the
balancing of the masculine and feminine.

No retribution will ever come from me—only gentleness
with each true heart, even those that remain hidden. There is no
reason, here, to continue in the ways of evolution. The time has
passed when the men needed to protect and defend and provide
in ways that, quite without their original intent, made them feel
so powerful and depended upon that they could not rest, even in
the gentle arms of the women who held and provided for them
and their children.

No retribution will come to those who, weakened under the
strain, left burdens too heavy for them to carry on the shoulders
of women and mothers. No force will be exerted with pampered

---

* ACOL C:6.17

men who never had burdens to carry, and so rejected responsibility.

No force need be exerted as good men console and encourage their brothers to cease obscuring their natural right and responsibility beneath their disregard.

No love will diminish the true masculine qualities in the rise of the feminine. No love of the feminine or masculine will allow or excuse hateful acts.

All the help needed is here for the asking and for the granting. Look at where your true heart lies. This is what, as you come to me, I will show you. This is what will allow you to see newly as we bridge the space between Heaven and Earth, between evolutionary time and the revelation of time outside of time. You will see, but not always know how to act.

The change will be vast. The earth and heavens will quake.

M

$\mathcal{T}$HE TRANSITION

The cabin looks so pretty from my perch at the window. There, sometimes, I can go so inward that I can't get out. And I relish it. Our last dialogue was like that. It was incredibly intense and had a great impact on me.

You have been preparing me for the imaginal. Me and "us." That's how I feel. Is it true, Mother?

$\mathcal{M}$

You have been being held within the imaginal, my daughter. And this is now the true start of your sabbatical. "From here your life becomes imaginal." From here your life proceeds in the imaginal realm. Many will follow.

The imaginal is all that is "here" that you do not yet know is "here." Go forth to the discoveries of unknown knowing that you await. From within this realm, and within these memories of revelation, you will create The New, as well as a safe haven for every gentle heart.

And now, my Mari, I assure you that this is the transition of The New, and you can see why we write. This is where the "human" side of things is revealed, where feelings can no longer be taken as faults, or back-tracking, or "not there yet." You have nowhere to get. You are "here." Your feelings are the navigational signals of your passage into The New.

Are you with me? Do you feel what I'm saying?

Yes. I feel you, and I am with you, my Mary.

My daughter, you have made this a holy place. Accept this. We will stay together here, and if you need to, you will be given the will to protect your sacred privacy and to have no self-consciousness about doing so. You will. I will help you. And if you change your mind, I will help you with that too.

Your connection with "feelings" is the very situation that lets you become revealing of their bondage. You must "feel" the bondage before you can feel the freedom from bondage. It is the most common opportunity for the truth to be revealed.

Can you see everything in your life in this way?

Be content for now. There is another consciousness breaking through. Self-consciousness is an obstacle to it. This has been an important dialogue for you and your sisters and brothers. It goes out to the world—right now—through the imaginal realm, so that you know the difference that you seek. Remember—our way of Mary begins with a time of transition.

It begins there, and it ends in the imaginal.

The Testament of the New is your witness to the new covenant that opens the realm of creation to you. The imaginal is what is here, and forever on its way into Being. The imaginal is the fruit of our joining and the gift of all time. It is a way that the power of evolution cannot touch or halt.

And so, we begin again . . .

"This is the agreement God asks of you, your part of the shared agreement that will fulfill the promises of your inheritance." *

---

* ACOL D:2.23

"[The Covenant of the New] is the fulfillment of the agreement between you and God. The agreement is for you to *be* the *new*. As you are new, so too is God, for you are one, if not the same. As you are new, so too is the world, for you are one, if not the same. As you are new, so are your brothers and sisters, for they, too, are one, if not the same." *

M

"From here your life becomes imaginal." †

As our lives become imaginal, we will experience Metanoia, a Revolution in Consciousness.

M

7-3-23

---

* ACOL D:4.1

† ACOL C:20

END NOTE

As I was preparing "Mirari" for publication in June 2020, my husband Donny started burning the spring brush, right where the vision that began "Mirari" occurred. This year, on a crisp fall day of 2021, as I was completing my work on "Memoria," he began the fall burning. What are the chances of that?

Dressed in work pants held up by camouflage suspenders, he presents as the picture of an earthy, practical man, tending to his homestead. The rock-ringed firepit quickly comes alive with orange-red flames, grey-white smoke, and oddities of brush smoldering like skeleton bones. Donny stands with a pitchfork in one hand and his other at his hip, momentarily satisfied.

A minute later he shifts. He hasn't forgotten that I don't want my miraculous maple tree singed, and soon picks up the fork again, expertly directing the fire away from her. Satisfied, he leans the prongs into the earth and stands vigilant, his palm cupping the top of the handle.

While the time of Mirari (2019-20) was a time of hurt and protest and the fire of passionate people, this year (2021) it has been Mother Earth roaring with actual fires—with major US fires in California and Utah, in neighboring Canada, in Algeria, South Africa, Cyprus, India, Israel, Russia, Turkey, France, Greece, Italy, South America, Oceania....

In midsummer I wrote, "Usually by this time in July I've noted that full point of summer. Most years are 'normal.' This one, with the heat and the fires, and a new strain of Covid. . . is not normal. Maybe there will never be a normal again."

A little later in the month a burnt orange sun caught my eye, and my heart paused with a sort of alarm because it stood alone. This new sun (even with our mild amount of smoke) was "all" that was rising. It was causing no glistening designs. No ravishing colors. Dawn had compacted into a single focal point.

Maybe, I thought, we are slaying the dragons of the normal, the typical, the common, the usual. Maybe, what was—"the old"—will be "completeness ravished and demolished,"* as Virginia Woolf described England in 1941. Standing in the narrative fire of creation of The New, our hearts grow a new story that is never to be complete.

"Let this fire among you, and this fire going out from you, guide your way."†

M

To you, and all, I offer hope that answers to our prayers will rise out of the fire of The New; that as the flames reach skyward, they bring you the uncommon thought, the unnamed inspiration, and the self-love that allows you to find your voice, share it with a friend (or the world), and in this way, "be" the spark . . . be among the many dazzling lights that are igniting The New.

"We" are the changing form of the world.‡

M

---

* Woolf, Virginia. *A Writer's Diary.* Mariner Books, 2003.

† "Mirari," p. 67

‡ Ibid., p. 341

ABOUT THE COVER DESIGN

In the chapter entitled "Divine Memory" I shared the story of the postcard that "returned to me" when Mother Mary gave me the word "memoria." Now I can thank Terry Widner for creating another beautiful cover from this image, entitled "Passion Heart," which photographer E. Katie Holm graciously allowed me to use.

Terry and I met at the first Course of Love event I ever spoke at. It was in West Palm Beach, Florida, near where he still lives. In fact, that event ends the new memoir I'll be bringing out next. Although I say "new" it was written during the time in which I was receiving the Course and is called "Identity Crisis and *A Course of Love*." My friendship with Terry is going on twenty-years now. He's one of my "first" Course of Love friends. All who know me, know that I highly value friendship. It's where our best dialogues will always take place.

This is the fourth cover Terry has designed for me. Besides that longevity, he's always reminded me to "dedicate all thought to unity."

One of the friend's I've known even longer is Mary Love, who took the photograph of me used on the back cover. If you've read anything I've written other than *A Course of Love*, you've heard of Mary, our close friendship, and our shared experiences of "new knowing."

ANSWERS TO MY PRAYERS & GRATITUDE FOR MY PEOPLE

I am so grateful for Mother Mary and this continuation of the work we began in "Mirari." She has encouraged me to accept that the sense she gave us "of ourselves" in "Mirari" has extended beyond our reading, and found a place in our memory. With her encouragement we can accept the possibility of memory of the future and of the unknown knowing that lies within us. My sincere hope is that our words will inspire remembrance of that most cherished possibility: being who we truly are. From there, new possibilities dare us to dream of creating a new world, even in trying times.

A new and unanticipated reality has arrived in the world since "Memoria" was written. The world-wide pandemic of Covid-19 has changed us, changed the way we live. You and I have likely embraced the time of grief written of in "Mirari." It was a timely year for "Mirari" to be released. Mary not only elevated grief but offered us comfort.

In the isolation of 2020, collaborations were fewer. Big conferences feel like a thing of the past. And yet there is great warmth out there in the world. You and I can tap into it more and more as we return the "personal" to a higher station than it has had. In this new time, many more of us aspire to be true to the Selves we are.

Shortly after "Mirari" was published, and I returned to the already written "Memoria," the disheartening end days of Donald Trump occurred and found their way into Mary's words. I pray that the wild dogs will soon disperse, and anticipate that if they don't, women, and men too, will unite the feminine and masculine to protect the babes of The New.

M

My gratitude in this time extends to many.

First, Michael Mark, often referred to as "my writer friend." He found *A Course of Love* (and me) in 2009 and we've been friends ever since. I was overjoyed when he agreed to edit with me. His patience could be described as legendary and his skills precise. He has been my eyes as well as my hands as he guided me through this 500-page book. It's been no small undertaking and I feel like we've been together through a long and significant voyage.

Lee Flynn's faithful friendship must also be noted. Lee holds his "friends" in the same high regard as do I, and his faithfulness includes the ordinary as well as the extraordinary. He's awed me with his profound understanding of ACIM, and of ACOL's relationship to it. Few have the eyes to see, as yet, what he has found.

Christie Lord, who has not stopped reading "Mirari" since she first held it in her hands, has continued to be a faithful companion as the way of Mary continues, as have Christina Strutt, Kate Macnamara, Helen Burke, Susan Lister-Bernardini, and Paula Hardin, each in their own distinct ways. Helen, and Paula, as well as Fredi Alesso, Steve Gilbert, Miguel Carvalho and many more have given generously. Each gift is so appreciated.

I am *grateful to all* Course of Love readers who have embraced this way of love and shared with me their anticipation for *A Course of Love*'s way of Mary. ("Memoria" is the second book of three that will comprise this way of Mary series.) You have given me much to be thankful for.

Donations have increased since "Mirari" was published, likely because Holy Mary, in the way of one women looking out for another, sounded the call that your support would be a blessing to me! Among them were two directed donations, one from Christina and Colin Strutt and the other from Danny Neese, that have made this publication possible. I am so thankful. It is all a wonder to me! With each donation, I feel that a great kindness has been extended.

I also am once again delighted and appreciative to be working with the local talent at Wise Ink. The gifts here include Victoria Petelin's coordination, Patrick Maloney's interior design, and final production details by Abbie Phelps.

Each of them also worked with me on Mirari.

M

Being moved and being able to "move" even one other person with words, is a privilege. It is a joy and a power many of us can call upon in creation of The New.

I invite you to embrace the memory of who you are that exists in "Memoria," to combine it with the wonder of "Mirari," and to find your very own way of coming into The New, and creating anew.

Mary of Nazareth's ability to give shape and vision to the dawning of this new age, and our union with it and within it, feels, in this book, even more stunning. We are *uniting*: feminine and masculine, time and time outside of time, the earthly and heavenly realms . . . and doing so with wonder, and memory, and imagination. We are, as well, continuing to be the women around the fire with our fertile presence, courage, and protection of the life of The New.

I am beyond thankful for Mother Mary's way of being and relating, and for her support as we anchor this teetering world even as we dream new dreams. Our next book explores the revolution in consciousness that is occurring as we are embraced by the imaginal realm.

I invite you to accept our gift of memory,
to become radical creatives for The New,
and to create only Love.
Mari Perron, September 22, 2021

REFERENCE GUIDE AND RELATED WORKS

References to quotes from *A Course of Love:*

The Course (C)

The Treatises (T) (as there are four Treatises, they are related as: T1, T2, T3, and T4)

The Dialogues (D) (as there are both Chapters and Days, you will see: D:1 as well as D:Day1)

The references follow book, chapter, and verse. Example: C:2.1 signifies The Course, chapter 2, verse 1

You will find this same order in regard to the other books of *A Course of Love*'s Combined Volume:

T1:2.1, T2:2.1, T3:2.1, T4:2.1

References to paragraphs within the Epilogue or the Addendum may be referenced simply as, for example, E.6 or A.4.

RELATED WORKS BY MARI PERRON

Mirari: The Way of the Marys (2020):

Mary of Nazareth reveals herself as a powerful advocate for the living. Beginning with a potent, archetypal scene, she calls women to both creation and protection of the "new babe" who is . . . "us." It is through union: union of the feminine and masculine and union of the earthly and celestial realms that The New will be created. In this first of a three-book series, Mary of Nazareth gives expression to the fullness and the power of the divine feminine, and the innate ways of being and knowing that women and men can bring to a wounded world. She invites a time of grief even while "Mirari" means "wonder," a wonder that is to be found in the call to create "The New."

A Course of Love

Three books: The Course, The Treatises, and The Dialogues, first published in single volumes beginning in 2001. Republished in a Combined Volume in 2014 by Take Heart Publications.

Received from Jesus, The Course, the Treatises and The Dialogues are arranged in such a way that they guide us from who we thought we were to who we truly are. In this movement, learning is left behind as we enter new ways of knowing and being. This way of the heart dwells within us. The heart's memories are called upon for creation of The New. Dialogue is revealed as a new means of coming to know and being known, the way of Mary is introduced for the first time.

The Given Self: Recovering Your True Nature (2009):

In this most personal of Mari Perron's work, she shares from her ordinary life as the event of her dad's death and the birth of her first grandson occur within weeks of each other. With grief and joy intermingled, her exploration ranges from the ordinary to the sublime to the practical. As she comes to embrace her authentic self, she draws from her humanity, her memories, her loneliness, and from mystical experiences, revealing that they are all of one piece and that none remain neat or orderly.

Creation of the New (2007):

This mystical experience has relevance to this new work, especially due to its vision, language, and imagery. It came from what Perron feels is her "own" mystical voice, to announce The New.

The Grace Trilogy (1997):

The Trilogy includes

"Love: A Story of Connection," by Mari Perron, Julieanne Carver, and Mary Kathryn Love

"Grace: Finding the Light" by Mary Kathryn Love, and

"Peace: Meeting at the Threshold," by Mari Perron

"Love" shares the story of the experiences of three close friends and work mates who, together, "felt into" new ways of knowing, being, and sharing. Their profound experiences occurred with each other and with angels.

Mary Love's "Grace" is a personal, profound, and tender experience of grief and new life.

In "Peace," Mari connects with an angel and experiences her initial encounter with other worldly realms. She discovers their enduring wisdom, shared in companionship.

Mari shares:

In rereading the Trilogy recently, I was so grateful for that miraculous time being captured when it was. It is always a wonder when a book transcends the time in which it was written. While "Love" is available as an e-book, the three paperback editions, ("Love," "Grace," and "Peace") are out of print. I do, however, have a limited number of the original editions available. You can order them by writing Course of Love Publications or sending your request to perron.mari@gmail.com.

ONLINE RESOURCES

The Way of Mary: www.wayofmary.com

The Way of Mary extends the reach of Mary's words into today's world.

A search facility enables further exploration, as do selected quotes and reviews.

Mari Perron: www.mariperron.com
On this website, Mari's focus is on exploring the breadth and depth of the "new way" that we experience after we live into the message of *A Course of Love*. She also offers Musings (a blog) and The Jesus Chronicles, never-before published conversations with Jesus.

A Course of Love: http://www.acourseoflove.org
A Course of Love is the major theme here. Many resources and possibilities for connection are noted. You can find more on Mari Perron's experiences and vision from the 'Mari Perron' tab on the drop-down menu at the home page.

You may also see Mari's videos about the Course of Love and Life on YouTube at www.youtube.com/c/MariPerron/videos.

THE CENTER FOR A COURSE OF LOVE

The Center for A Course of Love
https://www.centerforacourseoflove.org/

The Center's focus comes from the model given in The Dialogues: Attending to "the dawning of the consciousness of unity . . . a state that cannot be learned . . . only revealed to you through unity and relationship." (ACOL T4:12.25)

Mari hopes that you let *A Course of Love* (ACOL) embrace you in a way that invites you to be and to create The New. ACOL, read in love and wholeheartedness, can propel you into a future different than the past.

The "Center for A Course of Love" holds the copyright and Trademark for *A Course of Love* for the hopeful reason of embracing a new way of knowing, being and creating . . . with love and wholeheartedness. Part of this is going forward newly and part letting go of the past.

The Center offers two search facilities. One, "Discover ACOL," will be helpful for those who would like to easily find the context of any of the quotes from *A Course of Love* that are referenced in "Memoria." Another is "COCREATE ACIM OE/ACOL," a combined tool for searching ACOL and the wonderful ACIM OE (Original Edition) simultaneously. https://www.centerforacourseoflove.org/discover-acol/

Dialogue videos with readers and friends:
http://www.centerforacourseoflove.org/dialogue/

The Center for A Course of Love is a 501 (c) 3 nonprofit. The Center, and Mari Perron, gratefully accept your gifts.
https://www.centerforacourseoflove.org/ways-to-give/

SPREAD THE WORD
Amazon Reviews
A great gift you can give to an author as a grateful reader is to rate and review their work on Amazon. This makes a lasting contribution to sales, the ability of the work to reach those who are looking for it . . . and supports the author too. Please consider commenting on "Mirari" as well as "Memoria." Thank you!

CPSIA information can be obtained
at www.ICGtesting.com
Printed in the USA
LVHW031924180522
719074LV00007B/824

9 780972 866811